EDDIE TURNBULL

EDDIE TURNBULL

Having a Ball

Eddie Turnbull

with **Martin Hannan**

MAINSTREAM
PUBLISHING

EDINBURGH AND LONDON

First published in Great Britain in 2006 by
MAINSTREAM PUBLISHING COMPANY
(EDINBURGH) LTD
7 Albany Street
Edinburgh EH1 3UG

ISBN 978 1 84596 187 9 (from January 2007)
ISBN 1 84596 187 0

A catalogue record for this book is available
from the British Library

The author has tried to clear all copyright permissions,
but where this has not been possible and amendments
are required, the publisher will be pleased to make any
necessary arrangements at the earliest opportunity

Typeset in Janson and Formata

Printed in Great Britain by
William Clowes Ltd, Beccles, Suffolk

For Carol, Valerie and all my family

Acknowledgements

I wish to thank the many people who have helped me to produce this book. My grateful thanks go first of all to Martin Hannan for his hard work in helping me to write my story. Thank you to Martin Buchan for his foreword, and for his friendship and support through the years. Thanks also to Bill Campbell and everyone at Mainstream Publishing, and especially Graeme Blaikie and Claire Rose.

My gratitude goes to those who contributed pictures and to Frances Anderson for her advice and help; to Gary Imlach for permission to quote from his excellent book *My Father and Other Working-Class Football Heroes*; and to the staff at Edinburgh and Aberdeen central libraries for their assistance with the research. I want to thank the press and broadcast media for their interest, especially during the time prior to my finally being 'capped'.

I had a heart attack and pneumonia while writing this book, so I wish to place on record my appreciation of all the excellent doctors and staff at the Western Infirmary who assisted me in my recovery. Thanks go to all who wished me well during my recuperation, especially Lord Provost Lesley Hinds of Edinburgh and former players such as Robert Clark, John Blackley, Eric Stevenson and Alan Gordon.

My thanks go to Rod Petrie and all at Hibernian FC for making me so welcome in recent years. That applies also to those at Aberdeen FC. I particularly want to thank my colleague from the Famous Five Lawrie Reilly for his support and friendship through the decades. To my friend Gordon Milligan, I extend my thanks, especially for his encouragement in the early stages of writing. I am grateful to all the fans of Hibs, Aberdeen, Queen's Park and Scotland, but I particularly want to state my sincere appreciation of the many Hibs supporters clubs that have honoured me, especially those of London and Northern Ireland.

Last but definitely not least, my eternal gratitude goes to my wife, Carol, and all my family.

Eddie Turnbull

Contents

Foreword by Martin Buchan   11

1   Having a Ball – Capped at 82!   13

2   Starting the Ball   26

3   A Very Cold War   42

4   The Accidental Footballer   55

5   Early Days   69

6   Becoming Famous   85

7   Champions   99

8   Europe, Scotland and Beyond   123

9   A New Career   138

10   The Northern Light   156

11   How to Build a Football Club in Several
Uneasy Lessons   171

12   Winners at Last   194

13   Turnbull's Tornadoes   221

14   Glory Days   242

15   Oh, by George – Bestie and his Part in my Downfall   268

16   In the End is my Beginning   283

Foreword

As a football coach, Eddie Turnbull was light years ahead of anyone else I worked with at club or international level in my career, which spanned 19 years, including the World Cup finals of 1974 and 1978.

After he joined Aberdeen in 1965, he released or sold 17 players at the end of his first season and embarked upon a youth policy whereby he took young hopefuls, many of them local lads like me, and worked us hard. He gave us the most wonderful education in the game, and, in the process, he made men of us. He realised, of course, that he needed experienced players to help bring on the youngsters, and even these hand-picked seasoned pros that he brought in, men who thought they'd seen it all, were to learn more about the game and become better players under his guidance.

When I left Aberdeen to join Manchester United in 1972, after Eddie had returned to Edinburgh to manage his first love, Hibs, I felt I could have gone anywhere in the world and played in any system known to football thanks to the things he taught me about the game.

It's a measure of the man that after all these years, his players from his days at Pittodrie and Easter Road still call him 'Boss'. He's been guest of honour in recent years at a company golf day arranged by my old teammate Ian Taylor, always on the same day as the European Cup final, and he's in his element seeing his 'boys' and presenting the prizes, then giving his verdict on the match in the evening. We almost feel guilty if the occasional 'Eddie' slips into the conversation, because to anyone who played for him, he'll always be 'Boss'.

Martin Buchan,
former captain of Aberdeen,
Manchester United and Scotland

1

Having a Ball – Capped at 82!

Have you heard the one about the footballer who was awarded his first cap for his country at the age of 82? Well, it's a true story, and I should know, because that footballer was me.

I first played for Scotland on 28 April 1948. I remember that time very well because just four days previously my club, Hibernian FC, had won the championship of the Scottish Football League for only the second time in its history. I was 25 years old and had been a professional footballer for only 20 months. Prior to that, I had served king and country in the Royal Navy during the Second World War. Although I was relatively inexperienced, I knew I had enjoyed a good season as a member of a very fine team and I was aware that I had been watched by the selectors. (There was no national-team manager in those days and selection, like most things in the Scottish Football Association, was decided by committee.)

The news came via a telephone call to Hibs manager Hugh Shaw and was confirmed by letter. I had been selected to play for Scotland and I was told to report to the national stadium, Hampden Park in Glasgow, to play against Belgium. I can remember as if it were yesterday the thrill of finding out that I was going to play for my country. I was fit to burst with pride, and my family and friends – most of them back in my home village of Carronshore, near Falkirk – were delighted for me. I would like to report that I recall every minute of those heady days, but the truth is that the events all happened so quickly that I only have vague memories of the time.

I went through to Glasgow on the morning of the match in plenty of time to meet the other players. I was among friends in the dressing-room, as there were five of us Hibs players in the team. I knew most of the rest of the side too, from having played against them. There were no special coaching sessions and there was no great deliberation over tactics because there was no management to speak of. Instead, we players were allowed to get on with things ourselves. I cannot recall any big team talk beforehand, just a quiet word from the captain, George Young of Rangers, whom I knew well – we had played in the same school team as boys. There was the usual laughing and joking, as there is in every pre-match dressing-room, but there was also a serious side to things. Everyone there saw playing for Scotland as a great honour and responsibility, and, for someone like myself who was making his international debut, it was even more of an onerous task.

As I pulled on the dark-blue jersey of Scotland for the first time, I swear I felt my chest just about explode. It was an extraordinary feeling, a mix of pride and apprehension and, above all, a determination to do my very best for my country. I had been picked at inside-left – younger readers had better prepare to ask their elders about the antique terms in this book – which was my preferred position for Hibs. But I would have played at left-back, outside-right or even in goal for the privilege of turning out for Scotland.

The match passed in a blur. I can barely remember any details except that the Belgians were better than we thought but we still won, with goals from my fellow Hibs player Bobby Combe and East Fife winger David Duncan. The crowd of 70,000 or so went home well pleased to see Scotland the winners, but, personally, I had not done as well as I had hoped to do. I wanted to be the best player in the world, but perhaps the occasion got to me; I was not entirely happy with my performance.

Having been selected for Scotland and having played for my country, you would expect that I would then be presented with my cap, football's traditional gesture of recognition to a player who has worn the national jersey. But that did not happen for 58 years, and here's why. Back in 1948, and indeed right up until 1976, the SFA had a rule that you could only get a cap if you had played in the Home International Championship against England, Wales or Northern Ireland, and, being stingy tightwads, they granted each player only one cap per season rather than one per match.

The championship was the oldest in international football, but it is long since gone, having died a death of indifference in 1984 as international matches multiplied and the more important World Cup and European Championship qualifying tournaments became marathons. Back in the '40s and '50s, however, the Home International Championship matches were the biggest games of the season and, in a blinkered fashion which I would come to learn was typical of Scottish football, caps were awarded only for these games, not for matches against 'foreigners'. Apparently, we Britons were superior to teams from outside the UK; within a few years, we would see how wrong that thinking was.

I will describe my international career in full later, but suffice to say I kept my place in the team for the next match against Switzerland and then played against France and Austria, the latter match taking place in 1950. I did not play again for Scotland for eight years, and then I played five matches in a row, including three in the 1958 World Cup finals in Sweden, the last of which was my international swansong, at the age of 35. At no time did I play in a Home International match, so I never earned a cap. I would have liked one, not least because they are attractive items, with gold thread and a gold tassel over blue brocade embroidered with the initial letters of the countries that you played against. Some players

I know have had to pawn or sell their caps after their careers, so they are valuable assets, too.

But we all knew the rules back then, and I accepted them and just got on with playing. I very nearly did get that elusive cap near the start of my Scotland career, as I was selected to play against Wales but got injured the day before the match and had to miss out. That was just bad luck, but what robbed me of many more caps was an act of sheer malice. For, until very recently, there was within me a deep sense of injustice about the way I had been treated by the SFA and it was nothing to do with the cap issue. That was merely an irritant; the real damage done to me is something that infuriates me to this day, some five decades later. Some friends and family know what happened to me, but I have never revealed in detail how my Scotland career went down the toilet – make that 'down *in* the toilet' – in December 1950.

In the last match of the first of my spells with Scotland, Austria came to Hampden and beat us 1–0, and again I did not play as well as I wanted to and certainly not to the level of my own expectations. There were reasons for my below-par display, not the least of which was that I was playing with unfamiliar teammates, some of whom were good enough players but not fit to play for their country. I was still annoyed with myself when, after a post-match drink, I went into the toilets deep within the stadium. The man who came in to do his business next to me was none other than a member of an SFA committee, Walter Johnston, who later became chairman of selectors.

Now, Johnston was one of those 'blazers' who thought he knew it all about football. He was a potato merchant from the Dumfries area who rose through the SFA's ranks of committeemen to gain his exalted position. I've no doubt he gave many hours of service to football, but, as far as I was concerned, he was just a blazer-wearer, a time-server on a committee that was full of its own importance.

The chairman of selectors in effect picked the Scottish team at that time, after hearing the arguments of the various representatives on the committee, who all had their own agendas. Many players were selected or dropped on a whim or because a committeeman wanted to push a vested interest. In the '40s and '50s, for instance, Rangers and Celtic were often outplayed in domestic competition by clubs like Hibs and Hearts, but it was an unwritten rule that players from the Old Firm would be selected so as to guarantee the interest of their vast support.

It also irked me that players were treated like serfs by the SFA. The committeemen always went first class and stayed in the best hotel rooms, while the players were lucky if they didn't have to sleep in bunk beds.

So here was I in the toilet with a member of this amateur organisation that I already knew was full of bunglers and bores. I should have kept my mouth shut, finished my business and left, but Johnston decided to make a cutting remark out of the side of his mouth to the effect that I had let the side down.

As you will come to learn, I am one of those people who never backs down and always stands up for himself. I did not give a damn who Johnston was or even that he might have been to some extent entitled to make his criticism. Still urinating, I gave Johnston a verbal volley right back. I am apparently known for the saltiness of my language on occasion, a legacy perhaps of my naval days. I'll try and keep it to a minimum in this book, not least to keep the asterisk count down, but you will be able to guess that some exchanges have been censored. I will certainly give you the 'expletives deleted' version of what I said to Johnston. Suffice to say I queried his knowledge of football, his motivation for being on the committee and also his parentage, if you catch my drift. Basically, I accused him of being a self-serving ignorant bastard. Only my language was not so diplomatic. I was spoiling for a fight with this blazer, and if he was stupid, he would give me one.

Shaking with anger, or was it fear, he did up his flies and uttered these words, which have remained lodged in my mind ever since: 'As long as I have anything to do with picking the team, you'll never play for Scotland again.' He stomped out of the toilet, leaving me to seethe at his arrogance and ignorance. I wanted to run after him and thump him, but I controlled myself in time.

Walter Johnston duly became a selector and was as good as his word. Even though I played for Hibs at their peak, scored an average of more than 15 goals a season and became the first British player to score a goal in European competition, I never played for Scotland while he was a selector. Yes, there were other fine players in my position at that time. The great Billy Steel of Dundee – you will read more about him later – often occupied the Scottish inside-left berth, and I could have no complaints about that. Over the following seasons, however, many pundits and fans questioned my exclusion from the Scottish team, especially as I was a member of the 'Famous Five' forward line of Hibs and the other four were selected more often than me; Willie Ormond played fewer full internationals but gained several more Scottish League 'caps' than I did. They did not know what I knew – that I had an enemy at court, so to speak, who would always block my selection. I did not immediately regret my remarks to Johnston, but, when I was left out of the squad for almost all of the next eight years, I did occasionally wonder if my life would have been different had I said nothing in that Hampden toilet.

When Matt Busby of Manchester United brought some managerial professionalism to the Scotland set-up, and the manager began dictating things to the selection committee rather than the other way around, I was re-called to play for the Scottish League representative team prior to returning to the full Scotland team in time for the 1958 World Cup. Indeed, Busby made me captain when we played the English League. I played in two preparatory internationals against Hungary and Poland, and in all three World Cup matches in Sweden.

That long exile from playing for Scotland at Johnston's behest hurt me a great deal, bothering me much more than the mere absence of a cap. Even though I captained my country's League team, I long ago resigned myself to never owning an actual international cap, and indeed it was a matter of some indifference to me. I had the memories of those games I did play, and I still have the crystal vase presented by the Swedes to every player who took part in that World Cup. Apart from an SFA blazer and flannel trousers, that was the only souvenir we got in 1958. I don't have a Scotland shirt – the SFA insisted we return them after every match – but I do have pride in knowing that I pulled on that sweet dark-blue jersey nine times.

Even that number – nine – was denied to me for a long time. For some bizarre reason, the official records showed that I had played for Scotland only eight times, but I was certain I had played nine matches – I should know, I was there!

What happened was that my appearance against France in 1948 was not listed in the newspaper reports of the team for that match, which in turn led to the various records being distorted. The events of that day in the Stade de Colombes in Paris are crystal-clear in my mind: Billy Campbell of Morton damaged a boot before the match, and in those days there were no spare pairs lying around, so Billy had to sit it out while Sammy Cox of Rangers took his place at left-back. But, somehow, it was reported that Charlie Cox of Hearts was the late replacement, and, as he played in my position for Hearts, it was assumed that I had dropped out to make way for him. But that was simply wrong. I definitely did play, and I remember the game well, because I hit the bar – the closest I ever came to scoring for Scotland.

The confusion over the two Coxes thus led to it being reported for years that I had only eight international appearances. Indeed, some records still show that to be the case, so anyone reading this who is in charge of websites or whatever, could you please adjust the figures beside 'E. Turnbull, Scotland' to show 'nine' instead of 'eight'? But I never did get nine blue cloth caps, as all my matches were against those pesky 'foreigners', and had it not been for a remarkable book, I might still possess none at all.

Gary Imlach is a very fine journalist and broadcaster whose father Stewart I had known way back in the 1950s. Imlach senior had played alongside me in the Scotland team at the 1958 World Cup, and I remember him as an affable, laid-back laddie, a product of the north-east fishing community of Lossiemouth who had gone south to make his name at Nottingham Forest. Stewart was a pacey left-winger and a valuable player in that Scotland side which so nearly achieved something in Sweden.

But we never did make the second stage, and, like me, Stewart Imlach played in the group games against Yugoslavia, Paraguay and France but never played for Scotland again. Stewart went on to coach at Everton but sadly died of cancer in 2001 at the age of 69.

Not too long ago, Gary Imlach called me with an amazing story. He was preparing a book called *My Father and Other Working-Class Football Heroes* (it's a remarkable read for anyone who loves football) and had realised that myself, the late Archie Robertson of Clyde and his father, Stewart, had all been denied caps even though we three had played for Scotland in the World Cup. It turned out that his father had written to the SFA in 1994 asking for the rule to be relaxed, but then chief executive Jim Farry had written back to say the rule had to stand, as if an exception was made, it might invite demands from a lot of former Scotland internationalists. To my amazement, it turned out that there were around 90 of us in the same position – we had played for Scotland but not against home countries, so we did not have caps. Among the names were some very famous footballers, such as George Connelly of Celtic, Alfie Conn of Rangers and Celtic, Alex Cropley of Hibs, and many more.

I told Gary that it had all happened a long time ago and that

I had accepted the rules at the time and didn't think they would be changed. I kept my resentment towards Walter Johnston to myself.

The story then took a real twist. Since it is his book, he is best to tell it himself, and Gary has given me permission to quote his own words about what happened next:

> I was inclined to agree with Eddie's stoic acceptance of the rules as the rules, and the players simply victims of the period in which they'd played.
>
> Then I spoke to Tommy Docherty, who had gone on to manage the national team in the early '70s, and heard the story of how he'd intervened to help get a cap for Bob Wilson. Bob, he told me, had played for Scotland but never against the home countries.
>
> What? The Scottish Football Association, with its fear of floodgates and its respect for tradition, had been dishing out retrospective caps on a selective basis? It was only Tommy Docherty's famous assertion that the best football managers are liars that kept me from calling Hampden Park there and then. Instead, I contacted Bob Wilson. He cautiously declared himself unaware of any intervention by Docherty on his behalf, but otherwise confirmed the story, which apart from the outcome sounded exactly like my father's. He'd written periodically to the SFA over the course of two decades with no success. It was only after Craig Brown took over as national manager that he'd got his cap. Jim Farry had also been helpful.
>
> I mentioned this discovery to Eddie Turnbull. 'The English keeper? He got a cap? You're kidding.' He was scarcely less incredulous by the time I'd outlined the sequence of events to him. 'That's ridiculous. That takes some believing, that Wilson got a cap.'
>
> To many people, Bob Wilson – born in Chesterfield and a key member of Arsenal's Double-winning side of 1970–71 – was an English keeper and a very good one. In fact, he was perfectly well qualified to play for Scotland through his parents and turned out

twice for the national team: in a European Championship qualifier against Portugal and a friendly against Holland, both in late 1971. His cap, inscribed with the initials P and H, finally arrived in 1996. That made it two years after Jim Farry had first written to my father, all sympathy and tied-hands, to say that it simply wasn't possible.

The implication was clear: a well-known, well-connected television presenter who could call on the Scotland manager to lobby on his behalf was worth an international cap in the eyes of the SFA; an older name could be safely fobbed off with the official line. I wondered how many others had received the same treatment as my father. And how many exceptions had been made. According to Craig Brown, Bob Wilson's wasn't the only one.

Hearing this from Gary and then reading it in print when his book came out convinced me that an injustice had been done to dozens of us. I did not begrudge Bob Wilson or any other player a cap, but it began to rile me that the SFA had favoured some people and not others. And all the time, I knew within myself that a much greater injustice had been done to me by the SFA in the person of Walter Johnston.

I wasn't the only one who was upset at this apparent double-dealing by the SFA. Newspapers picked up on the story, and, though I prefer to live quietly nowadays, I was prepared to be quoted about the slight done to those 'uncapped' footballers. The first paper to carry the cap story by Gary Imlach was *Scotland on Sunday*, and its sister papers, the *Edinburgh Evening News* and *The Scotsman*, did a remarkable job in unearthing the facts.

Other papers joined in, and soon there was a clamour for us to be capped. Rod Petrie, chairman of Hibs, has been a great friend to me in recent years. He is an office-bearer with the SFA, and he took up the cudgels within the organisation. My old colleague Lawrie Reilly, a man who had played alongside me in the Famous Five and who had been capped for Scotland, also weighed in on my behalf, and I quickly became the most high-profile 'victim' of the SFA's intransigence.

For, at first, the SFA stuck to their guns and trotted out the old argument that they could not change the rules retrospectively. But chief executive David Taylor is a lawyer by trade – surely he could see that the Wilson case had set a precedent? A friend of mine who knows Taylor also thinks he was well aware of the damage the issue was doing to the SFA's often-battered image.

As more stories appeared, that same friend met Taylor at a Scottish Cup match, which is how I got the first, off-the-record hint that something was about to happen. In early February of 2006, the SFA board discussed the issue and, though there were some who wanted to stick by the original decision, the majority voted to award a commemorative cap to those players who had played for Scotland but never received one. In the case of deceased players, their families would be asked if they wished to be given one.

Most remarkable of all, the SFA decided that I would be asked to attend the next international at Hampden and receive my cap in a symbolic ceremony at half-time during the friendly match against Switzerland on 1 March.

Now, as you will learn, I occasionally do not do things the easy way. During the period in which I was writing this book and just before the SFA's announcement, I was out for my normal walk on a Sunday morning when I felt very unwell and keeled over. Shortly afterwards, I was in Edinburgh's Western Infirmary being treated for a heart attack. At the age of 82, no heart attack is mild, but the damage was apparently quite minor, and I was soon up and about.

I was absolutely determined to make my date at Hampden. Having beaten cancer not once but twice – lung and bowel – I certainly wasn't going to let a little thing like a heart attack bother me. I was able to do the exercises given to me by the physiotherapist, and each day I felt stronger. Eventually, I confirmed to the SFA that I would attend, and when the big day came, I was feeling pretty good. Hibs' PR man David Forsyth and Rod Petrie took me through to Glasgow, and, as the SFA had said I could bring two guests, I took my daughter Valerie and grandson Graeme Low with me.

It was a chilly evening, but I got a very warm reception at Hampden from the SFA officials, and a lovely lady called Sandra was assigned to look after me. In the SFA's hospitality suite, I finally met David Taylor, who was a quite charming fellow. I was also delighted to meet Ernie Walker, the former secretary of the SFA and an old acquaintance who for many years has been a major player in European football's administrative body, UEFA (the Union of European Football Associations).

After a good chinwag, we made our way to the VIP seats in the stadium. All around me in the stand were well-wishers who congratulated me and also some familiar faces from my career. At one point, I heard a shout of 'Hey, gaffer' and turned to see Tommy Craig, the brilliant player I had once made the most expensive teenager in British football. That was 37 years ago, and I'll tell you about it later in the book. I said to him, 'Where are you now?', and he told me he was coaching at Newcastle United and 'still using things you taught us'. There's a lot of players and coaches say that!

At half-time, I made my way slowly onto the pitch with Graeme and Sandra in attendance. It was an emotional moment for my family, but, I have to tell you, I was absolutely loving every second of it. As SFA president John McBeth presented me with my cap, I think I said something like 'Better late than never', but we could hardly hear each other for the noise of the crowd. The ovation was long and loud, and certainly the Tartan Army seemed to approve of the gesture the SFA had made. Someone suggested later that perhaps I milked the applause. Well, of course I did! I enjoyed every minute of the occasion, and it was great to be back centre stage. That's the one thing retired entertainers always miss – the appreciation of the crowd.

The only disappointment on the evening was that Scotland lost to Switzerland. I will have some advice for Scotland manager Walter Smith later.

The cap is now under lock and key, and, though I'm not the sort of sentimental person who gets worked up about a mere hat, I do like to look at it now and again. I suppose the really wonderful thing about getting the cap after all these years is that I have something tangible from my playing career to leave to my family, and it is destined for my grandson Graeme. I know he will look after it, and, after reading this book, he will know how hard-earned it was.

Above all, I have a sense that, 50-odd years on, an injustice has been corrected and it's time to let bygones be bygones. No one in today's SFA could possibly have known about my clash with Walter Johnston, but, by giving me this cap, they have gone some way towards making me feel that a wrong has been righted.

And that is the story of how I am now in the record books for gaining my first cap at the age of 82. It seems an appropriate time to look back on things, as I have had a long and mostly wonderful life in football. In fact, I have had a ball, as you are about to find out.

2

Starting the Ball

This is my story, the life of a football man. Some parts of it will be familiar to those who know their footballing history or who shared the experiences that were common to so many of us down the decades. Many other things that I will tell you have never been revealed before, and I trust you will find them interesting.

In one way or another, I have been involved with football for nearly 80 years, either as a player, trainer, coach, manager or spectator. Apart from my family, the game of football has been the most important thing in my life. At the outset, I want to say how grateful I am for the 34 years during which I was gainfully employed in football and for the many other joys the sport brought me. I had plenty downs but many more ups, and I love to think back on those special days and nights – memories I hope I'll never lose.

Football became my life, but it did not make me who I am. That happened in a family and a community of which I remain proud to this day. Later, I would be moulded in the larger family and community that was the Royal Navy in wartime, but my roots were deep in the surroundings of my childhood.

I was born in Carronshore, a little village on the banks of the River Carron in what is now Falkirk district, on 12 April 1923. I was the youngest of five children of James and Agnes Turnbull. I was born at home – there were no NHS maternity hospitals back then.

It is important that you know that my father was a miner all his days. They were a unique breed, those who toiled down the pits, and the influence of my father and the greater mining family has stayed with me into my ninth decade. The 1920s were a time when central Scotland still had heavy industries, and Carronshore was at the heart of an area dominated by coal mining and iron foundries, with the population roughly split between miners and ironworkers. In those pre-war days, Carronshore was home to around 1,000 souls and it really was a close-knit community where everybody knew each other. The village had grown up at the time of the Industrial Revolution, when the great Carron Iron Works, just a mile away from our home, was the largest foundry in Britain. Among other things that they had manufactured was the carronade, the cannon that secured the British Empire.

The nearby coal pits, which supplied the foundries with their raw power, were numerous and very deep, and employed many thousands of men, one of whom was my father, James. Like so many of his fellows, he died at a comparatively young age. I have no doubt that the harsh life down the pit was the cause of his early death. He smoked a pipe, but that was a trivial danger compared to the constant menace of the coal dust which invaded his lungs day in and day out. I always remember that, though he would shower at the pit and bath at home, he never considered himself to be entirely free of the grime that came with his job. And, as happened with so many miners, the damp conditions down the pit combined with his dust-affected lungs to weaken his heart, which is what eventually killed him.

Although he was no academic, like so many miners my father had a life away from the pits which was full of culture. He had finished his formal education early, but he was a clever man and taught himself many things, including music. He played the trumpet and was a member of the local brass band, the Kinnaird and District Silver Band. As a child of a band member, I would share in the terrific excitement in the village when the band marched through Carronshore each Christmas-tide. All his life, he was devoted to the works of Scotland's national bard, Robert Burns. He could recite passages of Burns' poems and songs from memory and was a member of the Burns Club at Kincardine, whose premises he frequently visited. He also delighted in taking part in many of the Burns Suppers held annually around the date of the poet's birthday, 25 January.

But the truth is I never actually saw a lot of my father when I was growing up. He worked nights and came home at about 6.30 a.m., or 7 a.m. at the latest, and would go off to sleep. When I got home from school in the afternoon, he would be getting ready to go off to work again. It was his pattern of life and we were used to it, but an ordinary working man nowadays would have much more time with his family. I don't think the present generation would understand how anyone could live like that, but it was a common way of life back then.

He was a tall man, around 6 ft, with broad shoulders, which he needed to wield his tools down the pit. I did not inherit his height, but I think he passed to me some of the strength and stamina which would become important elements in my footballing ability. I cannot say that I got my love of football from him, as my father did not take much interest in active sport. Gardening was his hobby, and he spent much of his spare time tending his plot, where he grew vegetables which were an important part of our family diet.

One of the proudest days of my life was when I was able, as a player with Hibernian FC, to get him a ticket for the Scottish Cup final of 1947. It was played on 19 April at Hampden Park in Glasgow and was the first post-war final, the competition having been suspended from 1940 to 1946. Some 82,140 people attended the final, and my father was proud as punch to be there to see me play for Hibs against Aberdeen, even if the score went against us.

I'll tell you more about the game later, but I remember my father came with us to the hotel at Queen Street Station in Glasgow where the Hibs players and official party met before heading off to Hampden. He was able to get a lift on the team bus to Hampden and just sat there saying very little as we made our way through the busy streets of Glasgow. Afterwards, on the journey home, he was as down as the rest of us, but I could see that he was quite proud that his youngest son had taken part in a Scottish Cup final, though he would not boast about it – that was not our way in Carronshore.

With my father working long hours, our home life centred around my mother, Agnes. My father and my mother both hailed from a small village called Kinnaird, a few miles from Carronshore. Just as he was tall, so she was petite and lovely. She was very kind-hearted and a great mother to us all, dedicating herself to the care of her family as a housewife. My mother, too, died at what would now be considered a young age. It was cancer which took her, though she never smoked.

My mother had one hobby, and even that was useful for keeping house. In those days, there was no money in our household for buying carpets, so she would collect scraps of material and make them into rugs, carefully stitching the patches together with great patience. Old clothes would be cut up and after she had sewed them all together, there would be a lovely rug for the house.

We needed her skills, because a miner's wage was not much. My father was a contractor miner, which meant he had men working under his management. Wages were earned on piecework – you were paid by the amount of coal you had hewn each week. Even though he was a contractor, however, he did not have a very much greater income than the average pit worker, and there were five of us Turnbull children to look after. The eldest was my sister Nancy, then my brothers, James and Alec, with my other sister, Mary, the nearest in age to me. Only Mary still survives, and she now lives in Bonnybridge, not too far from Carronshore.

Ours was a typical small house in the kind of 'miners' row' that you can still see around the former coalfields of Britain. It was a lot of people to squeeze into a house with just two rooms. We children would sleep in one room, where there were two beds. The boys would sleep in one bed on one side of the room and the girls had the bed on the other side. My mother and father would sleep in the main living room of the house. That main room also contained the kitchen area, where there was a sink and the fire. Though we had a small gas cooker, most of the cooking was done on the fire, in pots suspended over the flames. There was no washing machine or anything like it. To the rear of our house was a communal washhouse, where the mothers who lived in our row would take their turns to do the family washing in a great steaming tub.

I suppose, by modern standards, we were probably living on the breadline, but we did not consider ourselves to be poor or deprived. I know it is a cliché, but we were too busy getting on with life and being happy as a family to be envious of people who were better off than us. Nevertheless, there were no luxuries in our house. Nothing was wasted and my mother and father were always careful with money. We may have had no double cream in our porridge, but we were always properly clothed and we always had food on the table, including my favourite – mince and tatties. For those not aware of this delicacy, it is simply minced beef and potatoes, and a healthy meal it is, too. In those days, a 'miner's steak' was a block of cheese, and many's the miner who was grateful for his 'steak'. We had one regular luxury on the table: just a wee pat of butter to do us over the weekend.

As I say, we didn't really know we were impoverished, and we were all happy together, but we did know there could be a brighter future. Ours was not a particularly religious or political household, but my father's love of Burns and that poet's form of socialism was one reason why ours was a Labour-voting household. Back then, they were the party of the working class, and we respected our local Labour MPs and councillors for the work they did on our behalf.

We also respected our parents, and there was never any need for them to discipline us physically. If I was a naughty boy, as I frequently was, my mother would simply say, 'I'll tell your father when he gets in,' and that was enough to keep me quiet for a while. My father did not believe in belting us. He knew how to command respect without using his hands – as you will discover, I wasn't always able to follow his example with recalcitrant footballers.

We were not the sort of people to make a great play of birthdays and other anniversaries, and I suppose the only regular ritual was my father's weekly night off. Every Saturday night, he would go off to Kincardine to the Burns Club. While he was there, my mother would go to visit her family, who lived about a mile and a half from our house. As the youngest, I would have to go with her to visit her sister, my lovely Auntie Jenny. She had three daughters, my cousins, and usually there were one or two of them around and we could play together. Every Saturday night, without fail, I would ask my mother, 'Can we catch the bus to Auntie Jenny's?' and she would always reply, 'Aye, but it's a Walker's Bus,' meaning we would have to walk to their house at Long Dyke, which, again, was a miners' row.

All of my brothers and sisters were clever people – a lot more clever than me! They all got good jobs and were industrious people all their working lives. And looking back on it, because I was the youngest, I suppose they did spoil me a bit, especially my sisters.

I imagine I was like every other wee boy and could be a bit mischievous. My eldest brother, James, had a bicycle and sometimes he would cycle home for lunch from his job as a fitter – he would rise to be foreman in his department – at the Carron Iron Company foundry. It would only take him a few minutes to cycle there and back, and he would leave the bike outside. It was too much of a temptation for me . . .

James's bike had a bar on it, and if you ever tried to ride such a contraption when you were only a wee lad, well you'll know that sure as God made little green apples, an accident is inevitable. Sure enough, when I was ten and had had my fair share of devilment, the inevitable happened and I took a hefty tumble. I got a fair old row, but fortunately I wasn't too badly hurt and the bike wasn't too badly damaged.

My other brother, Alec, was particularly smart and he got an office job in a foundry at Larbert. To be a white-collar worker was quite something in those days when most young men could only look forward to going down the pit or into the heat and mess of the foundry.

Not far from where we lived were two confectionery manufacturers, McCowan's and McNichol's. McCowan's was the more famous of the two and its Highland Toffee is still popular today. My elder sister, Nancy, was a senior worker in the quality-testing department of the latter, and that proved to be very good news for me. Every Friday, I would wait for her to come home because she would have a big bag of boilings and I would get my share, which was a real treat for me. She married a man called Arthur Ewing, and later, when I was playing with Hibs, he would come to the games.

My other sister, Mary, was also a clever person, and she ended up doing her bit for the war effort after 1940 by working at the giant Rolls-Royce plant at Hillington, near Glasgow.

All four of my siblings ended up in promoted posts in their various jobs and that stemmed from their dignity and capability for hard work, which in turn came from their upbringing in that miners' row in Carronshore. Come to think of it, I suppose I was no different, except that my trade was football and my work took place in a rather more public forum.

Football was very important to me in my childhood. It was literally the only game in town – we didn't have access to rugby or cricket and wouldn't have thanked you for it, while golf came much later, when I could afford it. Modern children have so many more opportunities, with access to all sorts of sport, plus computers and PlayStations and the like, but back then we only had football. That's the main reason why Scotland doesn't produce as many professional footballers as it once did; in our day, we had no choice but to play football, while nowadays kids often seem to think of football as just another sport among many they're able to choose from.

I had a few good friends in the village back then, and we all played football almost incessantly. I gradually lost touch with them over the years as they and I moved on. My best pal was called David Kemp, and, sadly, I know only too well what happened to him. David joined the Royal Marines and was killed aboard HMS *Charybdis*, a cruiser which was sunk in 1943.

Another of my close friends was Alex McLaren, who played centre-half for the school team and who would later join Falkirk FC. Though he never made the highest grade as a professional, he was still a fine player, and the fact that two of us out of a handful of chums did sign for senior clubs shows how Carronshore produced more than its fair share of footballers over the years.

Philip Campbell was another of my mates and, like my father, he was a great lover of Robert Burns. At school he would recite the bard's poems and he really knew his stuff about the ploughman poet. He passed on some years ago, but I still remember how he could speak of Burns.

Football was the game we all played and our main 'pitch' was the street, although there was a fine football field near by. Our house was at the end of the row and adjoining it was the Vennel, a Scots word meaning 'alley'. It was an alleyway of a fair width which had a brick wall down one side and on the other a fence made of railway sleepers. There was just one entrance or exit, at the bottom of the Vennel, and it led onto the village football pitch. When the local juvenile team played there, the club's officials would set up a table almost blocking the Vennel and collect the entrance money. Who needs turnstiles when you only have one way in or out?

It was there I started playing football. Of course, in those days, you rarely saw a real leather football, except when playing for the school team. If you got a ball as a Christmas or birthday present, you were really lucky. I once was fortunate enough to get a small ball and I would go off and play with it for hours, all by myself, kicking the ball against the wall and learning how to trap and control it.

But mostly we boys would take a whole pile of used newspapers, crush them into a rough ball shape and then wrap it in string to make a rough-and-ready 'football', which would last a short while before it came apart. It was always us boys who played football. There were girls in the village, of course, and we would play games with them such as tig – life was a lot more innocent in those days – until their mothers came to call them in, presumably to remove them from the bad male influence. Actually, they just got in the road of the football!

There was also no traffic in those days. Hardly anybody in Carronshore owned a car; the street lighting was very poor, but there was no need for it. In summer we would play football in the street until bedtime, and in the darker days of winter we would have a game of 'kick the can' under the lamps, safe in the knowledge that a motor car was a rare beast in Carronshore.

Across the road from where we lived was a quite large house owned by people who were considerably better off financially than the rest of us. We knew they were 'rich' because they had a garden with fruit trees in it and if the ball went over the fence and into their garden, it caused a real crisis, for they had dogs who looked after the property only too well. You had to be very quick and very wary to go in and get the ball and escape with your backside unbitten. The worst thing was to get trapped inside the garden by the dogs, though the man of the house would usually come out and let us go, contenting himself with giving us a good bawling out.

My father once did something with a ball which I'm sure helped me to develop into the footballer I became. We used to be able to get hold of a small, solid rubber ball, and my father would put a poker in the fire and then force a hole clean through it. He would then tie a piece of string through the hole. On my way to and from school each day, I would dangle the ball in front of me and kick it, first with my left foot and then with my right, back and forward, to and fro, all the way to the schoolhouse, and the same again on the way home. It was a terrific way to learn coordinated, two-footed ball control, and that one trick stood me in good stead all my playing days. Also, there was a piece of waste ground with a wooden fence near our house, and I would spend ages each day just learning to shoot the ball hard and fast against the fence. Some people reading this may recall that I was renowned for my thunderbolt shooting – I developed that skill on the wasteland at Carronshore.

Football was a hugely important part of my life throughout my schooldays. Our local team was Falkirk FC, and in our family we always followed them, but we also had a keen interest in the fortunes of other clubs, especially the big Glasgow clubs, Celtic and Rangers. It was Celtic, Rangers and Motherwell who were the top teams in the '30s, and Celtic had a local man, Charlie 'Happy Feet' Napier from Falkirk, in their ranks. We would follow their activities in the newspapers, as we couldn't afford to go to games. This will undoubtedly surprise you, but I can honestly say I never saw a First Division match in my life until I signed for Hibs. I can't recall the first time I saw Hibs play, but by then I was already on their books as a professional. I do not know if I'm unique, but there surely can't be too many people who went to their first-ever top-level match to support the team for which they were already playing.

Apart from the school of hard knocks and the university of life, I only attended one educational establishment in my life, and that was Carronshore Primary School, where I received a basic education in the 'three Rs', reading, writing and 'rithmetic. To be honest, my lessons were not my priority, as from the age of about seven or eight I was only interested in football. I used to be told by all the teachers that I should be working harder – I was the original 'could do better' boy – but football just seemed more important to me. Often, my father would look at my report card and I would know that he was reading that dreaded 'could do better' verdict because he was usually none too pleased. Sometimes I have regretted not paying more attention in class, but I did get a good grounding in the basics, and I have taught myself a lot since then. I have always enjoyed reading, and most people who know me think I'm a good talker!

It was at Carronshore Primary that I first played in organised 11-a-side matches. It quickly became clear that I was better than average, and I came to the attention of Mr Johnny Brown, the teacher who doubled as manager of the school team. He was a good teacher of the normal subjects such as reading and writing, but I suspect he was really just as interested in the fortunes of the school team, which was his pride and joy. He was a huge influence on me and encouraged me to really stick in and learn the basics about football – how to control the ball, how to pass, tackle and shoot. Each day after school finished, just before 4 p.m., he would watch as we played five- or six-a-side games on the football pitch, and plenty of advice was given to us. But there was no real practical coaching as we would know it nowadays and certainly no tactical stuff on the blackboard.

Every Tuesday was football match day, and he would take charge of us for games. There was no messing around with Mr Brown, who was a strict disciplinarian. He was a real enthusiast who taught us to enjoy the game, yes, but also that winning was important. I suppose Mr Brown's legacy to me has been those qualities –

enthusiasm, discipline and the love of winning. Any teacher who can impart those qualities to a pupil has done a good job.

From about the age of ten or so, I was training hard to get into the school team, and from eleven onwards I was a regular in the side, until I left at the age of fourteen. There was one trophy which Johnny Brown wanted to win above all, and that was the Henderson Cup. The Cup was the Blue Riband for schools football in our district and was competed for fiercely by every primary school for miles around. There was none of that 'no competitive football for youngsters' nonsense back then – we played every game to win, and our opponents did so as well.

Every Saturday morning, we would play in the schools league, and every week we would be handed our strips in advance of the game. Woe betide you if your mother had not washed and ironed the strip by the time Saturday came. We always had to look our best for Mr Brown. We were also nearly always watched by Miss Hutchinson, one of those teachers who would mark 'could do better' on my report card. She was a very nice lady and a good teacher, but, perhaps unusually for those days, she was always desperate to see 'her boys' doing well on the football field as well as in the classroom.

The Henderson Cup games were particularly competitive, though that prize seemed out of our reach, as we were one of the smallest schools in the Falkirk area. But I am proud to say that when I was 13, tiny little Carronshore Primary managed to win the Henderson Cup. It might have been the proudest day of Johnny Brown's life, for all I know, and it was certainly one of the proudest of mine.

Also at that time, I was selected to play for Falkirk and District Schools, which was quite an honour in those days. It meant that you were the best of the schoolboy talent, and it almost guaranteed that a scout from a professional club would make a note of your name. In those days, there was a clear split between the Scottish

Schools Football Association (the SSFA) and the SFA proper, and the professional teams were kept well away – a scout could not even approach a schoolboy's family. It was a crazy system that lasted for decades, and I wonder how many young footballers missed the chance of being taken on and developed by professional coaches because of bureaucracy. I suspect I was one myself.

That Falkirk and District team was not bad, even if I say so myself. In our ranks were Bobby Brown and George Young, who would both later play for Scotland, the latter as captain of Rangers. There was also Davie Lapsley, who would play in the senior ranks for St Mirren and other sides. I was inside-left in the team, and one of the people I played against was Billy Steel, who was then a schoolboy in Denny and District and who would later sign for Greenock Morton and become one of the biggest names in Scottish football with Derby County, Dundee and Scotland. Maybe some scout saw me playing against him that day (to tell the truth, I had kept him in my pocket for the whole game), because that is the only explanation I can think of for some of the events which led to my senior career and which I will recount later.

But, all too soon, my schooldays came to an end and with them my fledgling career in football. In all honesty, it never occurred to me to try and make a career in football at that time, as the priority for me as a 14 year old in 1937 was to find a job. I was not approached by any scout, and no one mentioned trying to join an amateur or junior (i.e. semi-professional) side, probably because I was too young to be playing against grown men. So I dropped out of education and football simultaneously.

The fact is that I was delighted to be finished with school. I couldn't get away quickly enough, even if it did mean the end of organised football matches. I suspect a lot of people of younger generations will find it difficult to believe that I was so anxious to end my formal education, and I do not begrudge any youngster nowadays the chance to go on studying for as long as they need to, but it was a different culture in Scotland in the 1930s, as the necessity to make ends meet was the overriding priority. With my elder siblings moving on and marrying, there was a pressing need for me to go out and earn my keep and bring cash into the Turnbull household. I never thought of doing otherwise, and I was happy to hand over my wages and get my few shillings a week pocket money. I thought that one day I would have a trade and my own house and family, but until then I would make my contribution.

By the time I was 16, we had moved house to 56 Webster Avenue, and what a transformation it brought to our lives. It became fashionable when Margaret Thatcher was in power to knock council housing, but it was a godsend for tens of thousands of Scottish families before and after the war. That council house gave us things we had never had before, like a kitchen, two bedrooms upstairs, one downstairs, a bathroom, hot and cold running water, and all sorts of other amenities we did not have in our miner's cottage.

I remember that at the bottom of the street there lived a locally famous man called Tully Craig, who had played for Celtic and Rangers (in those bygone days, you could do that and not be a media sensation like Maurice Johnston). Tully was then the manager of Falkirk FC, a club that would play a tangential but vital role in my life.

As for just about every lad with my background, there were two choices: the mines or the foundries. Since I did not fancy going down the pit, I elected to go to the Carron Iron Works. I was able to get an apprenticeship as a gas-fitter, and I felt that would be a good trade in the long run. I settled down to the life of a young apprentice, and it was certainly a way of growing up quickly, for it was hot and heavy work, even for a fit youngster like myself.

But, a little way into my apprenticeship, a certain Herr Adolf Hitler intervened in my life, and those of tens of millions of people around the world.

Even before the formal declaration of war in September 1939, the foundry was gearing up to supply iron and steel for rearmament and eventually the war effort. I was working at a forge which made star cutters for the mines, huge tools which carved the coal out of the face. There were also many steel plates, presumably for the ships of the Royal and merchant navies on which Britain depended. One tool I used on these was a giant steel buff, which we would use on the rough edges of a cast piece to file them down to near-perfect smoothness.

It was hard graft, especially for a boy of 16, and, though they gave you a mask, like everybody else, I suffered from the dust which permeated the atmosphere. Again, it was piecework, meaning your department or section was paid by the amount of finished goods it produced, and, as war grew ever nearer, we were working twelve or more hours per day, six days a week. It meant that we earned an extra few shillings a week, which was very welcome, since my pay by then was only averaging two pounds per week – I had started by earning seven shillings and sixpence, or thirty-seven and a half new pence, per week.

The fact was that there was simply no time for me to play any kind of football apart from the odd kickabout in the street or at work. There were plenty of good juvenile and junior teams around, and I'm sure that if I had been able to get sufficient time away from work, then I could have got a game for one of them, perhaps the likes of Carron Juveniles or Airth Castle Rovers, who were run by the local baker, Gavin Fraser, and were a very good team. Nor had I any time to bother with such luxuries as a girlfriend. We worked all the hours we were sent – day shift, back shift, even night shift when the demand grew.

By the time I was 16, Hitler had already conquered large parts of Europe, and we were preparing day and night for his Luftwaffe to come and bomb Britain. Like everyone else, I would read the newspapers and listen to the radio and knew that war was approaching. I vividly remember the picture of Prime Minister Neville Chamberlain on the steps of his aircraft in 1938 saying 'peace in our time', and then I remember his sad voice when war was declared on 3 September 1939. None of us knew what it really meant, but the older generation who had lived through the Great War were very sad indeed.

We soon got to know what the war would mean. The first bombing raid on a target on the UK mainland took place only a few miles down the River Forth from Carronshore just a few weeks after war was declared. German bombers attacked the naval base at Rosyth and other targets around the Forth, only to be driven off by RAF fighters. One of the Spitfires from City of Edinburgh 603 Squadron managed to shoot down a Junkers 88 bomber, the first German plane to be shot down over mainland Britain.

The so-called phoney war meant no let-up at the ironworks, and by the end of 1940 I had seen quite enough of the forge. Though, as an apprentice engaged in war work, I could have been exempted from the services, I felt it was time to get myself out of a job that had long since lost any attraction for me.

The main reason I left, however, was a genuine feeling that I wanted to do my duty for my country in the fight against dictators who we knew, we just knew, would do everything in their power to destroy Britain.

3

A Very Cold War

This may seem strange to a modern generation, but back then we were brought up to believe that we had a duty to defend our country and our allies. There were posters everywhere exhorting us to do our bit, and the newspapers reported daily on the numbers that volunteered or were called up.

There was also Winston Churchill. He had taken over as Prime Minister in 1940 when all looked lost, and, at first, he did not seem to be that much of an improvement on Neville Chamberlain as Hitler's forces pushed us back. But from Dunkirk and the Battle of Britain onwards, he led us by his never-say-die example and his stirring speeches which we listened to on the radio – I can still hear his voice growling 'we shall never surrender'. He was an incredible motivator, a dynamic man who made modern politicians look like whimpering babies.

Some of the lads in Carronshore who were a bit older than me had already seen active service. There was a barracks for the Argyll and Sutherland Highlanders just along the road at Stirling, and a few local men had joined them. When they got their leave, we would meet them in the village and listen spellbound as they told us of their experiences. Of course, they may have exaggerated their exploits, but it certainly sounded exciting. I wanted to do my bit, and I couldn't wait to join up, but I didn't want to be a soldier.

No, in a completely life-changing decision, I opted for the Royal Navy.

I ended up in the senior service by a process of elimination. Despite the soldiers' tales in Carronshore, or maybe because of them, I did not fancy joining the Army one bit. The Royal Air Force was seen as a service which was not really for working men like myself, who tended to end up doing the rough stuff in ground crew instead of actually fighting, so that left the Royal Navy.

Knowing full well that this war was going to go on for a while, I stayed in the ironworks until just before my 18th birthday and then went along to the recruitment office and indicated that I wanted to join the Royal Navy. It took a short while for my papers to come through, but I had taken the crucial step. It was only then that I informed my parents. They both knew that my joining up had been inevitable, but they were obviously saddened at the prospect of a son going off to war.

At that time, I had never actually been to sea; the closest I had come was paddling at the shore of the Firth of Forth. But after years of toiling in the forge, with the air full of dust and dirt, I fancied working in the fresh air and sunshine. However, I was to see precious little sunshine at times during my service career and often experienced nights that lasted as long as 18 hours a day. For I was destined to serve in one of the most dangerous long-running operations of the war: the Arctic convoys.

I did not know that when I joined up and went off by train to Weston-super-Mare in Somerset, where we were to do our initial training. That first trip was by far the furthest I had ever gone away from home, and, though she tried hard to hide it, my mother was quite emotional when I left. To me, having just turned 18, it was all a big adventure. Once I got my billet, I never looked back and came to love the naval life. There was a lot of marching and drill at first, under the command of the chief petty officers. It was all about getting you used to discipline, and frankly I had no real problems with the discipline in the Navy. From the outset, I was clever enough to realise that if you misbehaved in the wartime forces, then you suffered the consequences, and I did not want to experience loss of pay, loss of leave, or being confined to ship or locked up in the glasshouse.

Having completed initial training, from Weston-super-Mare I went up to the great naval base at Portsmouth. There I learned about looking after torpedoes and depth-charges, as well as the basics of seamanship. I was proud to be an able seaman and could hardly wait for the Navy to find me a ship, which they duly did. I was assigned to the crew of HMS *Bulldog*, a destroyer. She was a beautiful old ship, like most destroyers, and had a sister ship HMS *Boadicea*. Although we did not know it at the time, because it was classified information, before I served on her *Bulldog* had played a vital part in the war, capturing U-110 and its Enigma code machine in May 1941. The captain was an eccentric gentleman by the name of Thumby Lee. His hobby was carving wood, and he would sit for many hours, surrounded by the second lieutenant, the helmsman and others, just happily whittling away at a piece of wood. I suppose it was his way of staying awake during the long hours on watch. He was a brilliant skipper, and it was mainly due to his seamanship, particularly when we were under attack, that the whole ship was kept safe.

My very first trip was on a convoy to Russia, and it meant a brief visit back to Scotland as HMS *Bulldog* was then based on the River Clyde at Greenock, having undergone some repairs at the shipyards in Govan. All the escort ships for the Russian convoys gathered in the Firth of Clyde or in Loch Long and picked up the merchant ships as we headed out into the Atlantic. Plenty of records and statistics show how dangerous the convoys were, and we sailors were only too aware of the casualty rate. I would soon get accustomed to the feeling in the pit of my stomach that every sailor got: when you left Greenock, you wondered if you would make it to Murmansk, and when you left Murmansk, you wondered it you would make it to Greenock.

I would describe that first trip as a baptism of fire, except that it was too cold for words. In the space of a few months, I went from the sweltering heat of the Carron forge to the icy blast of the Arctic winds as our ship sailed north round the west coast of Iceland and up round the north of Norway into the Barents Sea.

There have been numerous books about the Arctic convoys, and I suppose my fellow Scot Alistair MacLean made as good a fist of it as any writer in his novel *HMS Ulysses*, probably because he served in the convoys; but it really is virtually impossible to adequately portray in words the hardship we went through as we escorted ships carrying vital supplies for the Russian war effort. We may not have been on their side in the Cold War, and plenty of people already had their suspicions about Marshal Stalin, but the Russians were our allies in what they called the Great Patriotic War, and we sailors were determined to get the munitions and other supplies through to them. But the price that was paid in terms of lives and suffering was enormous. People often mention the disastrous convoy PQ17 as the worst of the Russian voyages (four-fifths of the 35 ships were sunk on that run), but believe me, every journey was fraught with danger. You lived with the constant knowledge that underneath you could be men in submarines trying to kill you and that every sight of an aeroplane might be your last. But there was another killer: the cold.

My first experience of the sheer cold we would experience on the convoys is something I will never forget, and it would be repeated all too often. It hit home to me just how cold life aboard ship would be when I found I was unable to get warm even deep within the ship. We would be wearing sheepskins, duffel coats, sou'westers, gloves and sea boots on deck and be chilled; but even in a supposedly warm hammock below decks, we would still be freezing, our teeth chattering with the chill as we tried to sleep. On top of all that clothing you had to wear your life jacket, and it was compulsory to do so; you were pretty stupid if you left it off, as you never knew when 'action stations' would come. That's why you would only take your sea boots off when you went to your mess for a sleep alongside similarly clad mates. It might amaze you, but after a while you get used to the smell of bodies and clothes that haven't been washed for days.

There were some advantages to life on board ship. Everyone got a daily tot of rum, or sixpence a day extra on your pay if you didn't take it. Most people took their tot. The food could also be surprisingly good, especially after leaving Greenock, when we had just taken on a full load of supplies. It also helped us that we had a couple of men on board who had been in the Royal Naval Reserve and knew the ropes about making life more bearable on the crowded ship, where you were living quite literally on top of each other in bunked hammocks.

Norway was filled with the occupying German forces, and their air force seemed determined to attack us on a regular basis. They had dive-bombers and torpedo bombers, and even when the Luftwaffe let up, there was the constant threat of the U-boats lurking silently below us. The convoys were often battered by mountainous seas, and since the escort vessels had to match the speed of the slowest merchant ship, progress was often slow. Things would get even slower in rough weather, which was a regular occurrence even in the short summer up there, when it is daylight practically 24 hours a day.

And we really were under the cosh round the clock. Every single person on the ship had to be alert to the dangers that were all around us. Each individual member of the crew had his part to play when the ship went into action or came under fire, and you knew that not only might your life depend on the man next to you, his might equally depend on you. It was a tough lesson in the real meaning of community and comradeship, in how mutual dependence is so important in many walks of life. Certainly, that was one of the many things I took from the Navy into my later life: the knowledge that you can't do things yourself all the time and that teamwork is essential for success.

I also learned that practice makes perfect. We never could see the point of the endless drills and dummy runs the captain put us through – until the day came when we had to do things for real and everything went like clockwork, just as the drills had taught us. When action stations sounded, you knew exactly what your specific task was, and woe betide you if you failed to carry out that task or get to your post on time. Not only did you feel the officers' wrath but you also felt you had let down your fellow crew members.

There were several times on *Bulldog* and later on other ships when I thought that we were done for. The worst were the occasions when we were attacked by torpedo bombers coming out from Norway. You could see them approaching and dropping their weapons, and sometimes you would see the track of the torpedo heading for the ship. All you could do was watch and wait and hope that the captain was taking the correct evasive action. Thankfully, he always did. One direct hit and we would have been killed outright or thrown into the sea, and I'm sure none of us would have survived.

As a torpedo loader, I got the chance to fire a few 'tin fish' on trials over the years, and I can still recall the 'whoosh' that they made as they left the tube and headed into the distance. I don't think any of my torpedoes hit anything, but at least we fired them! My task on *Bulldog*, and on later ships, was to prepare, load and operate our torpedo tubes or depth-charge launchers. I knew the weapons I was firing could kill men, but I never gave it a second thought, as they were the enemy and were trying to kill us.

If the conditions were tough, so was the discipline. Before the last convoy on which I served, I went for a wee drink in Glasgow with a fellow crew member who was from that city. We had been told that our convoy would be leaving that night, so obviously we wanted to have some final fun before the long voyage to Russia.

We were to make our way back to Greenock to catch the liberty boat that would take us out to our ship, which was lying at anchor in the Clyde. We had a couple of jars or so, and by the time we got to Greenock, we had just missed the boat and the naval police were waiting for us. They got us out to the ship, where we knew we were in trouble. But the officers let us stew. It was Christmas Day when we were summoned before the captain to answer for our offence. By that time, we were off the Norwegian coast in the depths of winter. I can remember us going in, taking off our caps and hearing the sentence: two weeks' loss of pay. We didn't earn a lot of money, but it was still a hefty penalty to pay for being a few minutes late.

More than anything, though, I remember the cold. Later in life, when I worked at Aberdeen FC, visiting teams and their supporters would moan about the cold wind blasting off the North Sea into Pittodrie Stadium. I would just shake my head – they had no idea what cold really was. For instance, when we were north of Norway, we would often have to break the ice off our guns before we could use them. It was also very difficult to see anything in the driving rain and snow that we often encountered.

On the side of the ship were scrambling nets. These were to be used whenever a ship in the convoy was torpedoed or bombed and the crew had to abandon ship. Even with a full set of winter clothing and a life jacket on, a man could survive just a few minutes in that water, which was only slightly above freezing level. The Admiralty's orders were that we were not to stop to pick up survivors, as the ship might be endangered, but if there were men in the water, we would run alongside them and try to encourage them to grab hold of the nets and haul themselves aboard to safety.

Up in the Barents Sea, I saw ships being torpedoed and going down, the telltale plume of smoke the only clue to the disaster which had confronted the vessel. We diverted to try to give the survivors the slim chance of boarding our ship, but the men who grabbed the scrambling nets were doomed in any case, as their fingers froze to the nets and they became trapped on the side of the ship until it was too late. This happened more than once, and the sight of a ship going down and men dying in the pitiless sea made us very bitter towards the Germans.

In fact, I lost only a few close shipmates during my time in the Navy, though you heard of plenty of former crew members who had moved to other ships and been killed in action. I do remember a man called Tug Wilson (everybody called Wilson got the nickname 'Tug') aboard HMS *Bulldog*. He had been on board the battleship *Royal Oak* when it was sunk in Scapa Flow in Orkney by the U-47, which got through the submarine nets and torpedoed the great ship, which went down with the loss of 833 lives. Tug had escaped from the sinking *Royal Oak* and served alongside me on *Bulldog*. He was great company and a terrific guy to be on board with.

The convoys did have their lighter moments. I recall a merchant seaman talking in a television documentary recently about how he stayed in Murmansk for seven or eight weeks after his ship docked there, and it appeared to have been one long party for him. In the Royal Navy at the time, we thought we too would get the chance to experience the hospitality of the Russians – so we were led to believe, anyway. And sure enough, on my first trip, when we had passed through the Kola Inlet and tied up in Murmansk, there to greet us on the jetty were plenty of important-looking Russian officials. Did they give us vodka or cigarettes? No. They pinned on our chests a cheapish-looking metal badge with a hammer-and-sickle emblem. Being Royal rather than merchant navy, we were not allowed onshore. So later on, we all had a game of bingo on the cruiser that was leading our convoy – so much for larking around in the Navy.

Sometimes, there was an even dafter activity. On board the cruiser, the chefs would get busy with all the food that had not been consumed on a voyage, and there would be a grand eating competition involving one rating from each ship to find out who could eat the most. Well, we couldn't let the food go to waste . . .

Later in my service aboard the destroyer, we got a welcome change of scenery and temperature when we were sent to patrol off Africa. We had the traditional 'crossing the line' ceremony (an initiation for sailors who have never before crossed the Equator, with 'King Neptune' in attendance in all his splendour), and it was a pleasure to be in the warm sunshine after so long in the Arctic. We moved between Gibraltar and Freetown, and it was all such a contrast to our other convoys.

It was not all work and no play aboard *Bulldog*, as whenever we were back in Greenock, we would challenge any nearby ships to a bounce game of football on the nearest available pitch. We didn't do too badly, and Able Seaman Turnbull acquitted himself quite well, I thought. While *Bulldog* was being refitted, I was sent to Havant Naval Camp, near Portsmouth, and it was there that I became reacquainted with organised football, which, if you'll remember, I had not played since leaving school. As I was then twenty, I had not played 'proper' football for nearly seven years. A notice was posted asking for anyone interested to join the camp team, so I popped round to the guardroom to hand in my name. A short while later, we were matched against other camp teams, and I was down to play inside-left, while Johnny Malarkey was the name at outside-left. Johnny was a typical Glaswegian, and he and I hit it off right away. He could play a bit, too; he had pace and skill, and was useful with right and left foot. I don't think he made it into the senior ranks and often wonder what happened to this terrific footballer.

One day, we were playing the team from the local Royal Marines barracks, and we were certainly impressed by the size of these big tough guys. Their centre-half was a marine called Reg Flewin, and I remembered the name, as he was obviously a class apart. He would later sign for Portsmouth FC and play for England. But we ran rings round them that day, and both Johnny Malarkey and myself were invited to try out for Pompey, as Portsmouth are known. It shows you how little interest I had in professional football at the time that I never even bothered going along for the trial.

I did acquire one legacy of Portsmouth. The details are a bit hazy, as drink was involved, but, like so many sailors, I got myself a tattoo, which adorns my left forearm. And like those of so many tough seamen, the tattoo says 'True Love, Mother'. It was just a bit of fun at the time, and only later did I reflect that, if I had ever been captured by the enemy, I could hardly have passed myself off as a Frenchman or other foreigner!

After *Bulldog*, I served as an able seaman responsible for depth-charges aboard a brand-new ship, HMS *Alnwick Castle*, a corvette which had been built on the Clyde. She was a fine ship, and I enjoyed my time aboard her; it was while I was serving on *Alnwick Castle* that I saw the enemy up close and personal for the only time in the war. It was something I am unlikely ever to forget.

We were back on Russian convoy duty, and early in the morning of 17 February 1945, *Alnwick Castle* and HMS *Lark*, a sloop of the modified Black Swan class, picked up the unmistakable Asdic trace (Asdic being a powerful sonar apparatus) of a U-boat while we were patrolling in the Barents Sea near Murmansk. The word 'contact' reverberated through the ship, and the Asdic operators began to track the U-boat, following its course through their earphones. The German submarine was nearing the Kola Inlet – they must have been very brave or very foolish to attack such a heavily defended shipping area.

We zeroed in on the target, fired our depth-charges from the stern and unleashed a newish weapon called a 'hedgehog' from the bow. The hedgehog discharged a number of mortars which exploded on contact and thus had a greater chance than the more precise depth-charge of hitting its target.

With the adrenalin coursing through you as you realise it is kill or be killed, you soon forget all about the cold. When something like that is happening, all you think about is destroying the enemy submarine.

We were soon gratified to see the conning-tower breaking the surface near our ship. The submarine was clearly not far from sinking, and the crew scrambled out onto the deck, screaming what sounded like cries for help as they clung to the guard rail. The sailors manning our Oerlikon cannons were already in action and promptly let them have it with volleys of accurate fire which cut the Germans to ribbons and completely riddled the U-boat, the number of which we could clearly see was U-425.

I heard our captain shouting 'cease fire', but the noise of their weapons was so loud that our gunners did not hear his command and kept on firing. I saw the German crewmen scythed down before our guns fell silent as the U-boat sank beneath the waves. Of the fifty-three men aboard U-425, only one survived. I would later learn that her captain was called Heinz Bentzien and that in almost two years of service his submarine had not actually sunk any Allied ships.

It was the one and only time I saw the enemy in person, alive and then dead, and the only time I helped bring a U-boat to the surface. I suppose, if it hadn't been accidental, the shooting of the German crew might have been considered contrary to the rules of war, as they were probably trying to surrender. We hated the enemy, though, and no one complained about what happened. After all, the U-boats in general had no compunction about sinking unarmed merchant ships in the middle of a freezing ocean.

In any case, within a few hours of our sinking U-425, we were given a terrible reminder of the kill or be killed nature of our war with the U-boats. Having shared in our victory over U-425, HMS *Lark* was herself torpedoed by a German submarine, later identified as U-968. *Lark* had been built at Greenock, but not even the strongest Clyde-built ship could survive having her stern blown off. She floated long enough for the crew to manage to beach her on the Russian coast, though she was declared a total loss by the Royal Navy.

After service on HMS *Alnwick Castle*, I moved on to HMS *Plover* which was a coastal minelayer in the English Channel. Having worried about U-boats on *Bulldog* and *Alnwick Castle*, on *Plover* it was E-boats we had to worry about. These fast patrol vessels were the enemy boats which we really feared, and we were on constant lookout for them. It was dangerous work, especially when we were clearing mines rather than laying them. We found out the war in Europe was about to end when we came in to tie up one morning in early May 1945, and though for a brief while it seemed that we might be sent to the Pacific to help finish off the Japanese, that was in fact the end of our active service.

I had survived the Second World War, both physically and mentally, though there had been times when it was very tough going indeed. But I emerged from active service a stronger, better person, as I knew nothing I would face in life could ever be worse than the dangers I had experienced, on the Arctic convoys in particular. We lived under the constant pressure of knowing that we might not survive another hour or day, but it all made me tougher.

The discipline I learned in the Navy has been a key element in my approach to football management in particular. If the services had not had tough discipline during the war, I'm pretty certain this book would be written in German, and I have felt strongly all my days since then that a disciplined approach to any task is a successful one. I also learned the benefits of a communal approach to survival, and the experiences I gained of life in such tough conditions have served me well throughout my life. I still feel that if I put my mind to something I can achieve it; at the very least, I will endeavour to do my best, no matter the circumstances, and that stems from my time in the Royal Navy.

There was another legacy from my Navy days. I know many people in football reckon my language is a bit salty at times (though never in polite company). Like the Navy of my day, football is a man's game, and sailor-type language is commonplace. I learned plenty of curses in the Navy – I still haven't used them all!

Perhaps you might think it strange, given the bad experiences I have detailed of my life in the Navy, but I had grown to love the sea. As with so many sailors before me and since, the sea had got into my blood, and I could happily envisage spending the rest of my life on the oceans. Yes, there were times when I thought my last moment had come as a mountainous wave headed towards our relatively tiny ship, but there were also days and nights under the midnight sun of the far north when the sea was as calm as a millpond and you could see for miles and miles. The sea could be a beautiful mistress, but you never for one second relaxed in her company. Even deep inside the ship, you would listen to the rhythm of the engines and you could tell by the rolling of the vessel and the variation in the 'thump-thump' noise that we had just encountered a deep trough in the waves.

That familiarity with the sea and ships deeply affected me. Late in my service, as we realised the war was coming to an end, I began to think of what I would do afterwards and decided that if I could not get a decent job back home, I would go to sea again, either in the Royal Navy or on a merchant ship.

Aboard HMS *Plover* we still had some 'tidying up', i.e. mine clearing, to do, so it was early in 1946 before it came my time to be demobbed. I had absolutely no idea what I was going to do in civilian life. I had started my trade as a gas-fitter at the Carron Iron Works, but, shortly before I had signed up, I had been moved to what was known as the dressing shop, where they finished the steel, sanding it down, and I did not enjoy working in that dust-filled place. So though I had a job waiting for me, I knew that I didn't want to go back to the ironworks, and I had a hankering after a life in the open air. But even then, I certainly never gave even a single thought to playing professional football.

4

The Accidental Footballer

In many ways, I suppose, I am the accidental footballer. Having left the Navy and picked up my standard demob suit and allowance of £75, I returned to Carronshore for a reunion with my family, with precious little in the way of prospects for a life on land.

I met a local man, Jock Henderson, who worked with the district council in nearby Larbert. He was a stonemason, and, after a quick chat, he offered me a job working with him. It was not very well paid, but it was an outdoor life, and so I thought I would give it a go for a few months. If it didn't work out, I could always go back to sea again.

I enjoyed the masonry work but had been there only a few weeks when the event that changed the course of my life took place. You will remember that I had played only a few games of organised football since leaving school and had still never seen a First Division football match. However, I was fit from my naval service – I would say a very fit 23-year-old man – and the fact that I continued to walk miles every day and often went running just to keep my fitness levels up ensured that my strength and stamina had not wavered.

Word got around Carronshore that I was home, and perhaps one or two people remembered that I had been a useful schoolboy player and passed on the word to clubs which were looking for players; or maybe the fact that my brother Alec was playing for Blairhall Colliery Juniors over in Fife counted for something. That side was known to be a nursery team for Celtic, and, who knows, if Alec had perhaps had a bit more determination, he might have become the professional footballer in the family. Whether I was approached because of that family connection or because someone remembered me from my schooldays, I simply don't know. The fact is that the local juvenile and junior teams were short of players in those days, as many men were still in the forces, and soon I had a local club secretary calling at the door to ask if I was interested in playing. This gentleman was David Lapsley, who was secretary of Forth Rangers, a decent junior club. It helped me to make up my mind that this David Lapsley had been a hero of mine when I was a schoolboy. He had a nephew, Davie Lapsley, who was a big strapping centre-half who had played with the local Gairdoch Juveniles before going senior with St Mirren. As a kid, I was so in awe of David Lapsley that I used to go and volunteer to clean his boots, and now here he was asking me if I wanted to play what would effectively be a trial for Forth Rangers. To this day, I still do not know who or what made David Lapsley approach me, but of course I said yes right away. If it had been anybody other than a Lapsley, I might well have said no, and my life would have been entirely different.

My brother James was not too pleased, as he had connections with Forth's great rivals Bo'ness Juniors, but I had given my word and the date was set. We went up to Brockville, and I played in borrowed boots at inside-left for Forth Rangers against Bo'ness. It was a good game, and I didn't think I had done too badly for someone who hadn't played serious football before. Plus I scored a goal.

In the bath afterwards, I was talking about the game with my fellow players, none of whom I had ever met until a couple of hours earlier. Some of them were well-known youngsters in the junior ranks and had reputations as good players who might one day make the senior grade. But I was about to beat them all to it, even though I just thought I had played a good wee game of football and that was that.

My brother James came dashing into the bathroom, came straight up to me, grabbed my wrist and pulled me away, before hissing, 'Don't sign for anybody! Don't sign for anybody!'

My first reaction was to say, 'What the hell are you talking about?' and I meant it. I did not know that in the crowd there were scouts from various senior clubs. Then in came Ernie Godfrey, who was the trainer at Falkirk FC. He was a lovely man, who had a habit of talking very quickly.

'Don'tsignforanybody! DON'T SIGN FOR ANYBODY!'

The words came pouring out in one go, and he chattered on. 'You belong to Falkirk and you'll sign for us!' he said.

By now, I was wondering what was going on, because this was a completely new experience for me. I realised I had played quite well, and, more importantly, I had thoroughly enjoyed myself. Now here were people telling me not to sign for anybody . . . what did they mean? After all, it wasn't as if anybody could have followed my footballing career since I'd left school, because there hadn't been one! A few games in the Navy did not make an apprenticeship in football, and though I knew I had been a good schoolboy footballer, surely no one could have remembered me after nine or ten years, even if I did best the great Billy Steel in one game.

When I got home, I was met by my other brother, Alec, who was still staying in the family home at that time (James had married and moved away to nearby Bainsford, between Carronshore and Falkirk). Tired from my exertions, I went to lie down, and the next thing I knew, Alec was shaking me awake. 'Lukie Reid is picking you up at five o'clock tomorrow night to take you to Easter Road.'

You can picture the scene. There was my brother telling me this momentous news and me looking at him as if he was daft, because I simply couldn't take in what he was saying. Lukie Reid was the local taxi driver from Bainsford, the same village where my brother James now lived. A well-known local character, he was reputedly a man with his finger in a lot of pies. It turned out that he had been sent by Willie McCartney, the manager of Hibernian FC. Apparently, Mr McCartney had been at Brockville and had seen me play, but what could he want with me at Easter Road, the Edinburgh home of the mighty Hibs? Surely they could not be interested in signing me? I knew I had done well at Brockville, but this was ridiculous.

The following morning as he was leaving for his work, Alec repeated his message: 'Remember that Lukie Reid is coming for you at five.' Sure enough, at five on the dot, Lukie Reid was at our door in Webster Avenue. The last thing my father said to me as I went out was: 'Don't you be signing any forms tonight.' I assured him I would not. As soon as I got into the taxi, Lukie said we would be diverting to pick up my brother James, and by the time we collected him at Bainsford, I had plenty of questions for him. 'Hibs? What's going on, James?' He assured me it was just talks, with a view to me possibly – only possibly – signing for them. I was flabbergasted, but resolved to stay cool and calm and keep my word to my father that I wouldn't sign any forms.

We made our way to Easter Road in Edinburgh, and I had my first sight of the stadium. I had never seen anything like it and was hugely impressed by the scale of it all. I knew roughly what Easter Road looked like from pictures in the newspapers, but in the flesh, so to speak, it was a truly wonderful thing to see, though I did not get a full stadium tour until much later. We made our way through the imposing entrance and were shown to the main stairway. At the top was an office in which stood a massive gentleman, immaculately dressed and wearing a bow tie. You couldn't help but be impressed by his demeanour.

This was the legendary Willie McCartney, manager of Hibs,

and he ushered James and me into the magnificent boardroom while Lukie went off in the company of a man I would later come to know very well, Hibs' trainer Hugh Shaw.

Mr McCartney – I called him 'Mr' then, and I still do so out of respect for the man who did so much to guide my life – had an unmistakable aura about him, a charisma that wasn't just about his powerful physical presence. I would come to know that he nearly always wore a Homburg hat and a red carnation in his buttonhole and was always neatly dressed. He sat between us, and we made conversation for about ten minutes or so, talking about the game at Brockville, before he rose and went to a cupboard, bringing out a bottle of whisky and two glasses, which he set on the table. He offered James a dram and then poured one for himself, saying, 'You don't drink, do you, Eddie?' As it happened, I did enjoy the odd refreshment, but I was no great drinker of whisky and this didn't seem like the time or the place for one. After all, who takes even a small drink in front of a prospective employer?

He then began to talk about the Hibernian side he was in the process of creating. He explained how, during the war, Hibs had enjoyed the services of professional players who were in the forces and had ended up in Scotland. Among these players was Matt Busby, the man who would go on to create the modern Manchester United. Other famous names were Bob Hardesty, Alex Hall, and wee Jimmy Caskie, who had played for Rangers. The manager's hope had been that they would carry on playing for Hibs and provide the sort of entertaining football which had given the wartime crowds such pleasure. I knew that Hibs had indeed had a terrific team during the war, because I had read all about it in various newspapers; I also knew, however, that they had not been able to keep those famous names at Easter Road. Now here was Mr McCartney telling me that he was determined to carry on with his vision and that he wanted me to be a part of it. It was very flattering, and I couldn't help wondering if he knew about my lack of experience.

As he spoke, he continued to pour James dram after dram. And as anyone who has been subjected to that kind of 'flattery' will tell you, the more drams you get, the rosier the picture becomes. Eventually, we all got down to talking about the terms of my signing for Hibs. I could hardly believe it . . . here was myself and my almost inebriated brother hammering out the contract for my start as a professional footballer – a contract for me, who had played precisely one match of any consequence since leaving school nine years previously. Honestly, you couldn't have made it up.

The offer was £5 per week to start, plus bonuses. I would get £7 per week if I made it into the first team, again plus bonuses. These were the days of the maximum wage in football, which I think was then set at £10 per week in Scotland. Players did not earn that much more than, say, a foreman in a dockyard or a shop manager and earned much less than lawyers or accountants. In some ways, that made them seem all the more admirable, because we knew they were mostly men from working-class backgrounds who were not flash with their cash, as they didn't have the sort of riches players enjoy nowadays. Still, a fiver a week was excellent money to a man then earning less than half that sum as a stonemason's labourer.

In the space of one short conversation, I had at least doubled my weekly income, and I was going to be paid for playing football. Sure, I had dreamed about it as a schoolboy – which kid doesn't? – but here was I now a signature away from achieving that aim, even though I swear I had not even thought about such a career since my days kicking a string-and-paper ball around the streets of Carronshore.

Mr McCartney also held out the possibility of going on a summer tour with Hibs, perhaps to the Continent, and that prospect excited me, as my Navy days had given me the travel bug. But the deal-clincher was the signing-on fee, which Mr McCartney produced with a flourish. It was a giant white Bank of England £20 note, the largest denomination I had ever seen in my life and certainly the biggest note I had ever had in my possession. I signed on the dotted line and thus became a professional footballer with Hibernian FC.

I felt I was living in a fairy tale – one match for Forth Rangers and bingo. Incidentally, if you look in the official records of Hibs, you will see that I am listed as having signed from Forth Rangers. I never did find out if they got a fee for me, and I don't suppose anyone will remember now, 60 years on.

There was still the problem of telling my father I had signed the forms despite saying I wouldn't, but I had a ready-made excuse in the shape of James, who had enjoyed his drams well but not wisely.

We went home in Lukie's taxi, all three of us in high spirits, and James in particular feeling no pain. In fact, he slept most of the way. I asked Lukie to drop me at Bainsford as well, as I didn't want us to roll up in his taxi at the front door of our house where everybody in the village could see us. My intention was to walk home by a different route and sneak into Carronshore, because I didn't want to meet my neighbours and friends and have to tell them what I had done. I knew it would be big news in the village, and I really wasn't used to being the centre of attention – frankly, I didn't like it. My main fear was that people would think I had become a big shot, a celebrity, and that they would think that I didn't want to talk to them, which was just not the case. They would also think that I had gone off to sign for the Hibs and had kept it secret. Again, nothing could be further from the truth, as I had no idea that I would sign for them that evening.

The fact is that I had no concept of what being a professional footballer would mean for me and my family, but, as I made my way home that early-summer night, I was determined that I would give it my best shot.

My father took the news calmly, though I think he gave James an earful later. By the time I got up the next day, the word was out

– 'Eddie Turnbull has signed for the Hibs' – and my initial fears about the reception of this news soon evaporated. Everybody in my village wanted to congratulate me and wish me good luck. They wanted to see one of their own doing well in senior football, and they were pleased as punch for me. I soon got a rude awakening about the realities of football, though. Hibs did indeed go on a Continental tour that summer, but they went without E. Turnbull, who was back in Carronshore training and running incessantly in preparation for season 1946–47.

There were still plenty mornings when I would awake at our home in Carronshore and pinch myself to ensure I wasn't dreaming. After all, footballers were normally recruited through the scouting networks of clubs, who would often spot a schoolboy and track him through the juvenile and junior ranks until he was ready for senior football. Or else they would watch a junior player during several games and work out whether he could be improved to make the grade. But here was I, after just one game as a juvenile and not having played any kind of serious football since school, ready to go along to Easter Road each day for training as a fully fledged full-time professional with a major club – indeed one of the biggest in Scotland.

Hibs, at that time, were the third-best-supported side in Scotland, after Celtic and Rangers. The club had been formally founded in 1875 in the Irish Catholic immigrant community in Edinburgh. The aim of the new club was to provide sport for young men and to raise funds for charity. The founder was an Irish priest, Canon Edward Hannan, and the name 'Hibernian' was adopted from the Roman name for Ireland. From the outset, Hibs had no religious or race barriers, though it took some time before they were officially accepted by the Scottish Football Association as a 'Scotch not Irish' club. Hibs soon became one of the most successful sides in the country, becoming the first team from the east of Scotland to win the Scottish Cup, in 1887.

When Glasgow Celtic were founded in similar circumstances among the Irish community in Glasgow in 1888, Hibs lost several of their best players to the new club, and for a time Hibernian FC looked as if it might not survive. But Hibs recovered to win the Cup again in 1902, and had been runners-up on four more occasions by the time I joined them. They had won the Scottish League only once, and that was back in 1903. But they retained a large and loyal support, and there was plenty of optimism around Easter Road in those early post-war days.

Now I was to play for this great club, and, greatly to my own surprise, I would soon be featuring in the first team. First of all, however, there was the ritual of pre-season training. I had been told to report to Easter Road at 10.30 a.m., so on the first morning I made sure I was up bright and early, and caught the bus from Carronshore to Falkirk, where I waited on the 9 a.m. bus to Edinburgh. As I stood waiting to catch the bus, a big athletic-looking chap joined the queue. In Edinburgh, we got off at St Andrew's Square bus station, from where I had been told to catch a tram which would drop me not far from the stadium. Having enjoyed my ride on the 'caur', as tramcars were known, I made my way into Easter Road to start my real working life.

I was shown to the dressing-room, and the first person I saw as I walked in was the guy from the bus. The trainer, Hugh Shaw, introduced me to the squad, and, though I was not overawed, I was certainly impressed to meet people whose names I knew only from newspaper accounts of their feats on the pitch. I knew that in a certain sense I was very lucky to be there, but I steeled myself to thinking that I would give it a real go and see if I could emulate the success of these men I could now call teammates. I would have to – I had nowhere else to go except back to sea.

The man on the bus turned out to be Jimmy Cairns. He was a left-half who then lived in Grangemouth but hailed from Bonnybridge, where he had played for the local junior side until he was recruited for Hibs. He and I had a lot in common apart from being relatively near neighbours. Jimmy had also been in the Royal Navy during the war, and he had also signed for Hibs only a few weeks previously. He and I were soon chatting away merrily, and it was clear to me even at that early stage that there was a great camaraderie in the dressing-room. Most of the men in the room were established players such as Sammy Kean, big Jock Govan, Davie Shaw, Bobby Combe, Peter Aird, Hugh Howie and Gordon Smith. But in those days, everyone pitched in to training together, reserves and first-team players alike both doing the same basic routines.

The reason for that was simple. At Hibs, the players who were classed as reserves were expected to match their first-team colleagues in commitment. You never knew when the call would come to step up to replace an injured or out-of-form player, and in any case the reserve league and other competitions had considerable prestige in their own right and were certainly much more the focus of attention than they are nowadays.

At the end of that first session, which was tiring but not backbreaking, I went for a bath and then I got ready to go home, thinking I had done well on my first day. Jimmy Cairns asked me where I was going and I said 'home'. But Jimmy had other ideas. The club chairman, Harry Swan, had a restaurant in Leith Street, and Jimmy suggested we should go there for a bite of lunch, which was provided at a discount. After lunch, we went to a nearby cinema before returning to the chairman's restaurant for a 'high tea', as the late afternoon meal was called. This was my introduction to the life of a professional footballer, and I remember thinking that I might get to like it.

Each morning, I would meet up with Jimmy and we would catch the bus to Edinburgh together. We soon became friends with another player, Willie Clark, who was the captain of the reserves. Like us, he had been in the forces during the war, only he had been in the RAF, so you can guess there was a lot of inter-service banter between us sailors and the 'fly boy'.

Those early days at Hibs have stayed in my memory throughout my career, as well as making a tremendous impression on me at the time. It was as if chairman Swan and manager McCartney were creating one big family, and time and again in my managerial career I tried to encourage players to develop the sense of comradeship that we shared at Easter Road in the late 1940s and early 1950s. You may think I am looking back through rose-tinted spectacles, but there really was a unique sense of belonging to a small community at the club. The beneficial effects for Hibs as a football team were tangible. Players just couldn't get to training quickly enough. Hugh Shaw was a hard, tough man on the training pitch, but he would enjoy a laugh with us afterwards, and we did laugh a lot in those early days.

One of the regular haunts of the players was a snooker hall which was close to Jackson's the Tailor. They were known as 'the fifty-bob tailors' because they could outfit you in a suit for the princely sum of £2 and 10 shillings, which is £2.50 in today's money. Hugh Jenkins was the manager of the Jackson's shop in Edinburgh in those days. He was a Glaswegian and a 'bluenose', a fan of Rangers, and he sorted me out with my first suit, other than my demob suit. But when it came to tailoring for Jimmy Cairns, Hugh had a problem, because Jimmy was insistent on getting more cloth for his money. He told Hugh he wanted his trousers done naval style, as wide at the ankle as possible. As he also wore winklepickers, sharp pointed shoes, long before they were the height of fashion, you can imagine Jimmy had a somewhat unique look to him.

He loved his winklepickers. 'I could kick the eyes out of a potato with these,' he would say. He was a good player, too, and though he started at left-half, he soon switched to left-back, as Mr McCartney couldn't find anyone good enough to fill that position and encouraged Jimmy to have a go. He also had considerable power in that left foot of his. This was the era of the laced-up leather ball, long before the synthetic products which are in use today. In rainy conditions, the ball would become progressively heavier, and even in the dry it took a fair bit of effort to move it any distance. But Jimmy could ping a pass 40 or 50 yards without any difficulty, and that was a great weapon to have in your side when you were going forward.

One day, we were having a practice match in training and Hugh Shaw was refereeing. The boss knew Jimmy's ability with the long ball and wanted him to switch play to the right wing, where Gordon Smith was already making his mark. You'll learn more about Gordon, so let's just say at this point that even early in his career, we could all see he was a bit special. Jimmy did as he was told by the boss, and, when the opportunity came, he let fly with a real hoof from one side of the pitch diagonally to the right wing. But Shaw could not get out of the road quickly enough and took the ball full in the chest, knocking him flat out.

I had so much respect for the chairman, manager and trainer at that time. But they had earned it. Hugh Shaw's training methods were basic – we did a lot of running – but they got us fitter than, or at least as fit as, any side in Scotland. There was precious little talk about tactics from him or the manager. Harry Swan was genuine in his desire to make Hibs a family club which operated as a family. And as for Willie McCartney . . . well, what can I say about the man who gave me my start in professional football and who was my mentor in those very early days?

It was he who spotted that I could run all day, that I had the engine to do the hard work required on the left side of midfield, providing the link between defence and attack but also roving forward to go for goal. It was he who encouraged me to express myself and enjoy my football, and to shoot with either foot when I got the chance. It was he who laid the foundations for my career and who started the glory years for Hibs. But, sadly, Mr McCartney did not live to see the outcome of his efforts, because he died shortly before the Hibs side he did so much to create finally won the Scottish League. And, in a twist of fate, I, who owed him so much, was the last player to see him alive.

It was 24 January 1948, and I was injured and out of the team when we were drawn to play Albion Rovers in the Scottish Cup at their Cliftonhill ground in Coatbridge. The conditions were terrible, and the game should never have been played, but the home side had somehow neglected to inform the referee that the pitch was frostbound. By the time he turned up, the pitch looked as though it might be playable. Even though I didn't take part, I walked out onto the pitch, and it was not playable in the slightest. Not surprisingly we were soon toiling, as hard ground is a great leveller and did not suit our style of play. Albion Rovers were a Division Two team, but they had us under pressure from time to time, though we won 2–0.

In the middle of the match, Mr McCartney collapsed, clutching his chest, and the immediate fear was that he had suffered a heart attack. There were no ambulances with defibrillators in those days, and Mr McCartney insisted that we weren't to make a fuss, that he just wanted to go home. Chairman Swan grabbed me and said that he had arranged for a chauffeur and limousine to take the manager home, and that I was to go with him and ensure that he was delivered safely.

He was very quiet in the limo, and I did not feel much like talking either. He was clearly ill, and I wondered about the wisdom of taking him home instead of to hospital. But that was what he wanted, and his condition did not seem to get any worse as we made our way from Coatbridge along the old A8 to his home, a big house in Queensferry Road in Edinburgh.

The family doctor had been called and was waiting when we arrived. I helped Mr McCartney out of the limo and into the house, and then took my leave of him with no fuss. He was such a big man, I felt sure he would recover quickly and would soon be back at training giving us all a hard time.

I was so sure he would be all right that I was unwilling to break what had become our standard Saturday-night routine. The team had come back to Edinburgh from Cliftonhill, and the usual crew of myself, Jimmy Cairns, Willie Clark and Sam Waldie had our normal few bottles of stout and then went off to a dance-hall. When we emerged near midnight, the early editions of the Sunday newspapers were already out on the streets, and on the corner there was a news vendor shouting, 'Sudden death of Hibs manager! Willie McCartney dies of heart attack!'

It was a dreadful, terrible way to find out that the boss had died. I just couldn't take it in, but the newspaper reports confirmed that Mr McCartney had passed away not long after I had helped him into the house.

Perhaps it was the first heart attack which killed him, or maybe another came along when he was in the house. It might be that he felt the pain at Cliftonhill, knew he didn't have long and just wanted to die in his own home surrounded by his family. I don't know what really happened, but his death was a real shock to me and everyone connected with Hibs. It was as if the head of the family had died.

But I am getting ahead of myself. For, by the time of Willie McCartney's death, I was an established first-team player and had taken part in my first cup final and my first foreign tour, and we were on our way to glory in the Scottish League.

5

Early Days

After the summer tour and pre-season training, the real stuff began for season 1946–47. My very first match for Hibs was for the reserves against Queen of the South down at Palmerston Park in Dumfries. It was a fine August day, and indeed it became uncomfortably hot during the match; there were no lightweight Lycra strips in those days. I was playing at inside-left (by the end of my career, I would have played in six different positions for Hibs), and ahead of me at outside-left against Queen of the South that day was a guy called Bobby Nuttley. He had been a first-team player until being called up for war duty and had served as an officer in the RAF. He was a typical Scottish winger, small and tricky, but he could handle himself.

In the first half, I hadn't done too badly, I thought, and had got forward a lot, but I had taken some stick from Nuttley. During the interval, big Jimmy Cairns went up to Nuttley and growled at him, 'That young lad who's been running himself ragged all day [gesturing at me]? You just let him get on with his job and you stick to yours, or else.' It seemed I had a minder, and Nuttley did not give me any further problems at Hibs.

We won well, as did the first team at home at Easter Road – they thrashed Queens 9–1 – so the 1946–47 season was off to a flying start. I was pleased with my performance in my first game but knew

I still had a lot to learn, and Jimmy's 'lesson' in how to take care of troublemakers was certainly an eye-opener, and one I did not forget – I soon learned to look after myself on the field of play.

Being in the reserves at Hibs was a great education because you were surrounded by very good players. Indeed Hibs reserves dominated their league and cup for several years after the war, thanks to the talent they possessed and the management's insistence that first team and reserves all trained together. But I was not to spend too much time in the reserves; in fact, I was a reserve-team player for all of three more weeks. I knew I had been doing well, but what happened in September 1946 still came as a bit of a surprise.

Jimmy McColl was one of the greatest names in the history of Hibs. A very fine player and one of the first people to take training and coaching seriously, Jimmy was an influential figure for more than 50 years at Easter Road. At that time, he was helping with the training and the reserves, and he told Willie McCartney about my progress.

The chairman and manager had arranged a challenge match against visitors from Czechoslovakia, as the country was then called. Sparta Prague was one of several clubs from Eastern Europe to visit Britain after the war, of which Moscow Dynamo were probably the most famous. These clubs came to Scotland on what were ostensibly goodwill visits by our former wartime allies, but the matches also raised cash to help football get going again in those war-ravaged countries.

In those days, the manager would come down to the dressing-room on the day before the match with a piece of paper on which he had written the names of the chosen 11 – there were no substitutes to worry about at that time. He would pin the list to the wall and then make his exit. As soon as the door shut, we would all hustle over to see who had been selected. On the team sheet for the Sparta Prague match was the name of Turnbull. 'Crikey, what's my name doing there?' I remember thinking. After only a few games in the reserves, I was to make my senior debut for Hibs, and there was my name alongside the fans' heroes.

It may have been only a friendly match, but it meant everything to me to see my name on the team sheet, though I was determined not to show it. I am not generally a particularly laid-back character, and never have been, but I was determined to display a businesslike attitude, and so I tried to act coolly when my friends and colleagues congratulated me. I hadn't let the German navy and air force bother me, so I wasn't going to be fazed now!

I had been selected at inside-left, my favoured position, and I was lucky to have behind me Sammy Kean at left-half. Sammy and Billy (sometimes known as Willie) Finnegan were the great wing-half partnership in those days, and both players were hugely encouraging to me.

My debut went well, and we won comfortably. There was a banquet after the match, as there always was when a foreign team visited Easter Road. The meal was held in the prestigious North British Hotel, now the Balmoral, and was as sumptuous as was allowed in those days of rationing. After the banquet, the coach of Sparta Prague paid me a big compliment. Speaking through a translator to Billy Finnegan, he said, 'The number 10, he will make a very good player.' What a good judge of footballers he was . . .

I kept my place for the next match, and I must have been doing something right, because I became a recognised first-team player – and my wages went up to £7 per week plus bonuses. Maybe it was because of my sheer determination to succeed or maybe it was because I would fight for everything on the field – and fight others' battles, too – that Willie McCartney took a chance on me and gave me a run in the side. Apart from injury, and fortunately I did not have many of those, I would stay in the first team at Hibs for most of the rest of my playing career.

The team in the early part of that season was usually: Jimmy Kerr; Govan and Shaw; Finnegan, Aird and Kean; Smith, Combe, Jock Weir (or sometimes Johnny Cuthbertson), myself and Johnny Aitkenhead. The latter was very talented, a great ball-player, but he was not the fastest winger in the world – his way of beating opponents was to trick them with his ball control and then keep the ball off them. Sadly, Johnny suffered a very bad knee injury, the infamous torn cruciate ligaments, and was never the same player again. That injury let a young fellow called William Ormond into the team at outside-left. I was to see a lot of him over the next few years. Also coming into the team was Willie Peat, a Glasgow man and a very fine player.

Jock Weir was our centre-forward and, like many of the breed, he was a colourful character. He was not the most skilful player, but he was very fast and good with his head, and he scored a lot of goals. He was a strapping, handsome man, and he loved the attention of the ladies. 'Weiry' was a charmer all right, always smiling, and was never short of female company. After training, he would often be found in Edinburgh in the afternoon dancing sessions at the various dance-halls, so he must have had stamina as well.

One day, before training, Weiry was called upstairs to see Mr McCartney, and after he went, Hugh Shaw began to parcel up Jock's boots in brown paper and string. We all went out to training, and when Jock came downstairs, he was handed his parcel of boots and a single ticket to Blackburn. He had been transferred to Blackburn Rovers, the deal done over the telephone by the two clubs' chairmen and managers. There had been rumours in Edinburgh that bookmakers had persuaded Jock to take part in the annual Powderhall Sprint, one of the world's most famous races for professional runners. These days, it is run at Musselburgh Racecourse, but back then the sprint took place at Powderhall greyhound track in Edinburgh, and the bookies often made a killing by preparing their own runners for the race. I don't know whether that rumoured involvement offended our chairman and manager, and nothing was ever proved, but there was no doubt that Jock Weir's transfer happened so fast he did not even get the chance to say goodbye to his colleagues. Think of it – he went into work and within an hour or so he was on a train to England and a new club. But that was often the way it happened in those days. A player could be bought and sold in a phone call and that was you, on your way, with no say in the matter.

No doubt there was a decent fee for Jock, but his going left us some problems in filling the vital role of centre-forward. Arthur Milne was playing in the reserves, but his best years were already behind him and Johnny Cuthbertson was a more regular choice. I didn't take to 'Cubby' at first, largely because he was a bit of a 'clever clogs' and had been an officer in the RAF, while the likes of Jimmy Cairns and myself had been 'other ranks' and somewhat further down in the social order. He was really the only one I didn't get on with, and by the time he left later to sign for Third Lanark we had reached a working arrangement – we had a job to do together and we got on with it. Cubby did have one annoying habit: put him ten yards out, straight in front of that eight yards by eight feet space called a goal, and he would regularly miss. But Cubby would then confound you by scoring from out on the wing and from the most acute angles – must have been all those brains in his head!

We were starting to play some very good football and making progress in the First Division of the Scottish League. Above all, we were trying to entertain the fans. The chairman was an astute man, who had seen how good players playing attacking football could bring in the crowds even during wartime. He had decided that would be the blueprint for the post-war Hibs and was not afraid to spend money to achieve his aim. It was Harry Swan who bankrolled Willie McCartney and encouraged him to sign the kind of players that would excite supporters. As for Mr McCartney, his philosophy was simple: don't worry if they score, because we will score more.

The chairman did not interfere with the day-to-day running of the team, but he did know the importance of team spirit, and long before the phrase 'team-building exercise' was coined, Harry Swan was encouraging us to gel as a group and helping to keep our morale high. Every so often, he would appear in the dressing-room and say,

'Get the golf clubs, we're off to North Berwick for the weekend.' While we were down there, he knew, we would want to go out and have a beer or two. None of us drank to excess, but we all enjoyed a bottle of stout or beer, and big Jimmy Cairns liked a pint. The chairman was canny, too. While we were down at North Berwick, he would put a dozen crates of lager and stout in a room and tell us to go and help ourselves. It was amazing how few we actually took.

But one of his finest innovations was the club dance – again, another exercise in building team spirit. It was held annually at the North British Hotel, and he made it a big social occasion, with the Lord Provost and Chief Constable in attendance. Everyone looked splendid in best bib and tucker, the players – except for Gordon Smith who didn't like such events – all there with their wives or girlfriends, and the Grand March led by the chairman starting the occasion. It was always a marvellous evening, especially over the next few, successful years. All the camaraderie that developed off the pitch carried over into matches, and in that season, I believe, the foundations were firmly laid for the success we would enjoy over the next few years.

It also helped that Hibs had one of the best scouting systems in the country. All over Scotland, Mr McCartney had his spies on the lookout for the type of player that could learn to play the Hibernian way. At one time in that post-war era, Hibs had more than 50 players on their books, and while many did not make the grade or moved on to other clubs, quite a few proved to be inspired choices, as the majority of players in the side that would later win League titles were like myself: bought cheaply and reared at Easter Road.

The Scottish League First Division was then the premier competition in the land and the one tournament every team wanted to win. And in Scotland in those days, it was not a question of which of the two big Glasgow teams would win it, as has been the case during the last two decades. On the contrary, the standard of football was high throughout the League. There were lots of good teams in the First Division, and very few matches, if any, were seen as easy street for Hibs, Rangers or any of the top teams. Celtic, for instance, were in a fallow period, but they were still mighty tough opponents. Raith Rovers may be languishing in the lower leagues now, but back then they were a force to be reckoned with. Even Third Lanark, who would go out of business in the 1960s, could put up a stuffy performance, especially at their home ground, Cathkin Park. Their tin hut dressing-rooms, with a stove for heating, were not particularly welcoming.

At Easter Road, we were rewarded for our play with a magnificent sight: game after game, the crowds flocked to the old stadium, and we regularly played in front of between 30,000 and 40,000 people. The old Hill 60 terracing was nearly always full. The appetite of the fans for the Hibs brand of football was insatiable. I recall one match against Hearts when the crowd figure was 28,000 – and that was for the *reserves*.

It was a travesty that we did not win the League that season. We beat Rangers at Ibrox and drew with them at Easter Road, and as we neared the wire in the chase for the title we won our last five matches. Yet a series of draws, particularly at home in December and January, meant that we had given ourselves too much to do to catch Rangers. Eventually, we finished runners-up to the Ibrox club by just two points.

To lose the League to Rangers by such a narrow margin was heartbreaking. The post-war years saw ourselves and the Ibrox club dominate the Scottish League, and our matches against them were often seen as League deciders. But other teams held sway in the Scottish Cup, and I often felt that we had players who did the business in the League but sometimes were not up to the special demands of a cup tie. Hibs did not have a good record in the Scottish Cup, it is fair to say. The club had not won the Cup since 1902 and had experienced only a few near things since then. In season 1946–47, however, we swept all before us as we advanced to the final.

We thumped Alloa Athletic 8–0 and were then drawn against Rangers. A 0–0 draw at Ibrox gained us a replay at Easter Road, and, in one of our best performances of the season, we beat them 2–0. Rangers got their revenge by putting us out of the new Scottish League Cup shortly afterwards.

Dumbarton from the Second Division were seen off 2–0 in the quarter-final before the semi-final against Motherwell at Hampden Park. I remember that game well, as it featured a new centre-forward for Hibs, one E. Turnbull Esq. At this point, the club still hadn't solved the centre-forward 'problem', and I presumed the manager was looking to me as a stopgap, because I certainly didn't see myself in that position permanently. The stopgap didn't do too badly – I scored the first goal. Motherwell equalised in the second half and there was no further scoring before the final whistle. The format in those days was that the first team to score in extra time would win. No doubt younger readers will be surprised to learn that the 'golden goal' was being used in Scotland many years before FIFA and UEFA tried it as a way to end drawn matches. The Motherwell goalkeeper was another lad from my area of central Scotland, Johnny Johnstone. He kicked the ball downfield, and waiting for it was our centre-half Hugh Howie. He just hit the ball on the drop and it sailed right back over Johnstone's head and into the Motherwell goal. What a way to win a semi-final!

I have to say that I did not really relish the build-up to the final on 19 April 1947. It was all happening so quickly and so early in my career that I wasn't able to take on board everything that was going on around us. As I recounted earlier, I was able to get my father a ticket, and I don't know if the feeling that he was in the stand watching had some kind of effect on me. In any case, I don't think I did myself justice in the final.

We had been going well in the weeks leading up to the final, but we knew Aberdeen had a very good side. They had two South Africans, Stan Williams and Billy Strauss, in the team and a number of fine Scots such as Joe McLauchlan, Geordie Hamilton, Archie Baird, and Joe Johnston in goal. We lost 2–1, and, needless to say, it was a crushing disappointment. In retrospect, I would never get a better chance to win the Cup as a player, and Hibs have not since won the trophy, at least not at the time of writing. Nevertheless, we had finished the season as runners-up in the League and Cup, and that was arguably the best performance by Hibs since 1903. We were upset at not having won either tournament, but we also had huge confidence that we could go one better the following year.

Our close-season tour was to Sweden, and this time E. Turnbull did get to travel. Going abroad to experience Continental ways and see how they played the game in Europe was part of the innovative culture which existed at Easter Road at that time. Indeed, the club were Scotland's trail-blazers in Europe, a fact which was appreciated by the new powers running European football, and something that would stand the club in good stead and lead to me establishing a record that can never be beaten, as I will explain later.

On each tour, we would take our own stock of footballs, the old 'T' leather style, and the agreement with the Continentals, who manufactured their balls to a different and supposedly lighter design, was that we would play one half with their football and the other half with ours. Imagine FIFA or UEFA agreeing to that nowadays!

In Sweden, we came up against Norrköping. Included in their ranks was Gunnar Nordahl, a great centre-forward who would later make his name in Italy. It was early in 'our' half of the game, playing with the good Scottish leather dumpling, when somebody cleared the ball high into the jam-packed terraces. We waited and waited, but that ball did not come back. Of course, the rest of our stock of balls was back in the team hotel, so we then had to play the rest of the match with their lightweight ball. The thought that 'they nicked our ball' inspired us, but we were playing 12 men. In all my born days I have never seen such a biased referee, a Swede who literally got in the road of play. We were going forward when he 'intercepted' one of our passes, which went straight to one of Norrköping's players, who ran up the pitch and scored. That was their third goal. The ref also awarded three penalties to his countrymen for tackles that would have been considered perfectly fair, even innocuous, in Scotland. It made me think, 'Maybe that's why Sweden remained neutral in the war – they couldn't take a tackle.' The name of Norrköping was filed away in the Hibs memory bank and we got our revenge over the Swedish side many years later in European competition.

We had a tough start to the 1947–48 season, losing 1–2 away to Hearts in the League Cup, but the League began with a bang: a repeat of the Scottish Cup final with Hibs going to Pittodrie to take on Aberdeen. It was a match that captured the public imagination. Even though it was played on a Wednesday afternoon, some 40,000-plus people turned up and the gates had to be closed. Fans could be seen perched high on the stand and were stood ten deep right round the track.

We were desperate to get revenge for that Cup loss, and all the way up to Pittodrie in the bus we spoke about the game and what we would do to Aberdeen. As play wore on, we were attacking the Beach End when we got a throw-in on their 18-yard line from our left wing. I drew a defender and secretly motioned to Willie Ormond to take the throw-in, pointing to the space where I wanted the ball. The Aberdeen player was fooled by my movement and Willie threw the ball perfectly for me. I turned and hit the ball full on the meat, and it whizzed straight past the goalkeeper, who had been caught completely unawares. It was one of the most memorable goals in my career and set us up for a 2–0 victory.

The next away match was our local derby against Hearts, and again we lost 1–2. Our side featured Kerr in goal, Govan and Shaw the full-backs, Howie, Aird and Kean at half-back and Smith, Leslie Johnston, Alex Linwood, myself and Willie Ormond up front. We would lose only three more matches in the League that season, to Rangers, Falkirk and Dundee, and the last-named match was a meaningless encounter on the last day of a tumultuous season.

We started the home season by beating Airdrieonians 7–1. It was a portent of things to come at Easter Road, where we remained unbeaten in the League all season. Perhaps more importantly, the football we had begun to play was hugely exciting for the fans. The supporters wanted to see the ball slamming into the net, they wanted to see crosses being pinged across the penalty area and people having a shot from distance; that's what fans still want from their football. Well, we gave it to them in that post-war age.

Everything about Hibs in those days was class. The players might not have been highly paid by modern standards, but we were well looked after, and management and the backroom staff paid great attention to even the tiniest details, so that all we had to do was turn up and train or play.

We also had our fair share of fun and games, as you might expect from young men in good jobs with time on our hands. In 1950, we were on a tour in Germany – we would finish it unbeaten – and had played Borussia Mönchengladbach in a couple of matches. After the second game, we were told we would have a few days off in the Black Forest at a place called Bad Herrenalb. It was a beautiful village, and the solitude was ideal for us to mix together and prepare ourselves for the season ahead. We played games against local sides, and almost every night there was a banquet at which the entire Hibs contingent were either hosts or hosted.

The football writer R.E. Kingsley, better known as 'Rex', of the *Sunday Mail*, was then the biggest name in sports journalism in Scotland. Everybody read Rex on a Sunday at that time, but our chairman had a bone to pick with Rex: he did not think that the Glasgow-based newspapers gave enough coverage to Hibs and their achievements. I dare say there are plenty Hibs fans who think that is still the case today. Harry Swan decided to try and interest Kingsley more directly in Hibs, so he invited the journalist along on the fortnight-long tour. This was an unusual move in those days, and it proved a very successful trip for both Hibs and Rex, who gave his readers a real insight into the club at that time.

He was also a bit of a practical joker, and had found out from the staff of the hotel that, even though it was still summer, chairman Swan liked to have a stone hot-water bottle in his bed each night, just to take the chill off the sheets. Kingsley approached Willie Ormond and myself and asked us if we would like to join him in playing a wee prank on the chairman. We asked him what he intended to do.

'You know how the chairman always gives a wee speech after the post-match banquets?' said Kingsley. 'He's always talking about "cementing friendships" in these post-war times, and that always goes down well with the Germans. So why don't we take him at his word and put some cement into the friendship?'

Willie and I were up for it, and off we went to find some cement. There was a lot of rebuilding going on in Germany at that time, and, sure enough, not far from the hotel there was a building site. We approached the workers and, with some broken English and a lot of hand gestures, a bag of cement was exchanged for a packet of cigarettes, which were a useful currency in those days. Then we brought the hotel manager in on the scheme, and he agreed to turn a blind eye and instructed his staff accordingly.

That night, the lovely maid turned down the bedclothes on the chairman's bed, and we were on hand to insert instead of a stone hot-water bottle a large and very cold bag of wet cement.

We were all straight-faced as we wished the chairman good night, and could only imagine his face as he got into bed with the cement. He soon emerged from his room shouting the odds, and then realised he was the butt of the joke. 'That will be the friendship cement,' cracked Rex. Being the kind of man he was, Harry Swan took the joke in good heart and joined in the laughter. From then on, our hosts and guests could never understand why the phrase 'cementing friendships' had the players creased in laughter.

One of the other attractions of playing for Hibs at that time was the fact that we were not dragooned into playing a rigid formation. We were no slaves to tactics or a particular way of playing. Mr McCartney (and later Hugh Shaw) put us in position, told the defenders who to look out for and then encouraged us to do our own thing. That approach paid off as we developed a fluid passing style, which, any football purist will tell you, is the way the beautiful game should be played.

Personally, I liked nothing better than to get as far forward as I could or have a shot from far out. If I got a sight of goal and there was no better option available, I just used to let rip. My attitude was, 'If it goes in, it goes in,' and while many of my shots missed or were saved, quite a lot of them did go in over the years. It also helped that I could shoot with either foot, the legacy of all those days when I would go to and from school juggling the rubber ball from left to right and back again. My right foot was the stronger of the two, but I scored plenty with my left.

Quite quickly, the Scottish football-loving public, if not all of the media, latched on to what we were doing. The crowds began to grow at Easter Road, and, wherever we went, people came out to see us, which was hugely rewarding for a bunch of players who saw themselves as entertainers more than anything. The selectors of the Scottish international side also recognised our strong performances. I deal with my international career elsewhere in this book, so let me just say that one of the high points of a season that was memorable for so many reasons was being picked for Scotland against Belgium in April 1948.

One of the best matches of that season was in the League Cup against Clyde in August 1947, when Gordon Smith ran riot and scored a hat-trick. But Hearts beat us twice in our section, and we exited the League Cup. The Scottish Cup was much better but again ended in disappointment when we lost 1–0 to Rangers in the semi-final.

In the League, however, our goals went flying in from all angles, and I'm glad to say I got my fair share. Indeed in 14 seasons at Easter Road, I averaged nearly 15 goals a season in competitive matches. In all, I scored 199 goals for Hibs, which is not a bad record for someone classed as a midfielder, a toiler in the engine room. I had a football brain as well, though, and that enabled me to get into positions from which I could score.

In November 1947, I got my name on the score sheet against Dundee in very unusual fashion. Playing down the slope at Easter Road, there was a bit of a mêlée in front of goal, and I found myself lying on my backside. But, suddenly, the ball popped up in front of me, and, even though I was prone, I lashed out, and the ball flew into the Dundee net. It didn't bother me how I scored them, and it certainly made a memorable picture in the newspapers that weekend. We won that match 2–1, and that victory put us top of the First Division for the first time that season. We were not to relinquish that position.

During the early part of the season, something happened which was at once very worrying and very flattering. Bury were then a top First Division side in England's Football League, and, in common with many of the bigger English clubs, they were always on the lookout for Scottish players. Scottish football had been seen for decades as a conveyor belt of talent, providing the backbone of many an English team. In that post-war era, the English clubs paid bigger wages, although only marginally so in those days of the maximum wage. They could pay larger bonuses and signing-on fees, however, the latter usually being a percentage of what they paid your club. Even 10 per cent of a £10,000 fee was equivalent to two or three years' income for a Scottish player, so a transfer was often good news.

At that time, there was no freedom of contract and certainly no agents. Players had their contracts and registrations renewed annually, and no player could move anywhere if a club held on to his registration. Players were bought and sold like cattle, so when I heard Bury were looking to sign me, I was a bit apprehensive, not least because I had only just settled in Edinburgh and I didn't want to go south. Bury's chief Scottish scout George Gallagher came to see me play several times and then approached Willie McCartney. I don't know what they offered for me, but I was very pleased with the manager's reaction. He said in no uncertain terms that 'Turnbull is not for sale.' And then, to emphasise his verdict, he told the newspapers, 'Turnbull is not moving at any price.'

Mr McCartney told me privately that he meant every word and that I would be at Easter Road for the foreseeable future. It was another reason for me to be grateful to him, but within a few months he was dead. I have already recounted my involvement in this sad event, and all I will add is that every player at Hibs was as devastated as I was. The manager's funeral took place on 27 January 1948, and we were all in attendance.

We had a massive game just four days later – Rangers at Easter Road in what was already being touted as a League decider. Though it was never shouted loudly, there was a sense among us players that we wanted to win the League for the 'old boss'. We knew he had fashioned us into a team, and, though any professional wants to win for himself first and foremost, we had the additional spur of wanting to show that the team Willie McCartney had built was indeed the best in the land. In a very tough match, we gave everything we had, and undoubtedly we won the game for the old boss. That 1–0 victory made us believe our time had come.

Even though we missed Mr McCartney, the club had to continue to function as normal. Hugh Shaw had stepped up from trainer to manager, and he carried on with the job, getting us all to do the same things we had been doing under Willie McCartney. Shaw had actually been the first trainer appointed by the SFA to coach the Scottish national team, and he enjoyed the respect of all the players at Easter Road.

By this stage, our momentum was unstoppable. We had always had faith in our own abilities, but now we began to believe that not only could we win the title, we could do it in style. As events would show, we were actually some way short of our peak as a side, but it was vital that, unlike in the previous season, we went on to fulfil our destiny and win the championship. Had we finished runners-up for a second year running, it might well have broken our spirits, especially with Willie McCartney gone.

A 1–1 draw with Celtic at Easter Road in a match that we should have won had annoyed us back in November, but in April we went to Parkhead and gassed them 4–2. The league flag was in our hands, and after a narrow 1–0 squeak over Partick Thistle, we thumped Motherwell 5–0 at Easter Road to make sure of the championship.

That season, we won the Scottish League, the Scottish Reserve League and the East of Scotland League. We won almost everything except the Cup, and chairman Swan said that 'having learned to win the premier glory of the League championship, further honours will come our way'.

For myself, I was still trying to take things coolly, just as I had done on the day when I saw my name on the first-team list. I did not see myself as a different person just because I had played for my country and was now the owner of a league-winner's medal. When I signed for Hibs, all I wanted to do was my best, but I never realised that I could reach such heights, and, looking back, I don't think I really appreciated the enormity of going from the Royal Navy to becoming a professional footballer and winning a league title in the space of two years. I was proud, yes, but I hope I was not seen as arrogant, and I certainly tried not to be so, for never, ever in my wildest dreams could I have predicted what happened to me.

And, in many ways, the best was yet to come.

6

Becoming Famous

Following our championship win, season 1948–49 was a bit of an anticlimax for Hibs. But something happened in 1949 that was to bring great joy to all the Hibernian supporters, transform the fortunes of the club and make five of its players rather 'famous'.

Willie Ormond had come to Hibs from Stenhousemuir FC, a club based on the other side of Falkirk from Carronshore. Willie lived near Falkirk, and he joined Jimmy Cairns and myself on the bus each morning to Edinburgh. Can you imagine three modern professional footballers catching the bus to work?

The three of us travelled back and forward every day and became firm friends. But soon the daily travelling became a bind, and it came time for me to leave the family home in Carronshore. It is always a wrench to leave home permanently, but I had been in the Navy for five years and was used to being away from my family, so it was not too much of an ordeal, especially as I was going to be well looked after. I moved into digs in Edinburgh at 5 Cambusnethan Street with Simon Waldie, the centre-half in the reserves, as my fellow lodger. Our landlady was a wonderful woman, Nina McEachran, who cared for us as if we were her own family. She had a son, Neil, two step-daughters and her husband, Charlie, to care for as well as us, but nothing was ever too much trouble for her. It was a warm, caring household in which there was a lot of laughter. She would call us 'my boys', and, really, you could not have asked for a better home away from home.

Nina would always wait up for us when we came in late from the dancing which was our main recreation in those days. Mostly we would visit the Excel Ballroom or the Cavendish, and when things wound down, unless we 'got a lumber', i.e. met a girl, we would be home before midnight. There would be Nina waiting for us with a late sandwich, anxious to hear our chat about the events of the day and evening. In her own way, Nina was part of the extended Hibs family, and she also taught me a lesson I would keep for my managerial days: that a good landlady can often make the difference between having a good disciplined player or a toerag on your hands.

It was while I was staying at Nina's that I became one of a handful of people entitled to count themselves a member of one of the best forward lines ever to play football. As long as they play the game in Scotland or anywhere else they appreciate fine attacking football, people will remember the Famous Five. It was then, and remains now, a privilege to be counted one-fifth of that number.

Our aims back then can be summed up in a few words – score goals for Hibernian and give the public a treat. That people remember us 50 years and more later is proof that we achieved our ambition. And Hibs did score a lot of goals at that time; look at the statistics and you will see that in our four or five seasons together, Hibs were usually the best-scoring team in the Scottish League.

We were not known as the Famous Five until some time after we started playing together. In fact, the first nickname for the Hibs post-war attack was 'the £50,000 forward line'. That was a colossal sum in those days, equivalent to many millions in modern money. The name was given to an earlier incarnation of the forward line by a newspaper after Leslie Johnston was signed from Clyde for £10,000. Going by that valuation, the papers had calculated that the whole front five must be worth £50,000, and nobody disagreed – except us, as we thought we were worth much more.

The Famous Five nickname was really given to us by another newspaperman, the same R.E. Kingsley or Rex of the *Sunday Mail* who had cajoled us into playing the cement prank on chairman Swan. It was quickly adopted by all the fans, and the name stuck. In fact, the nickname didn't actually please us, as the original Famous Five were a gang in a series of children's books by Enid Blyton. We also thought the whole team deserved the praise, but we did kid each other about it, and I suppose we were secretly pleased to be 'famous'.

Getting the Famous Five together took a lot of trial and error on the part of Hugh Shaw. When you consider that Hibs had as many as 80 players on their books after the war, it's a miracle we played together at all! It did not happen overnight, and there were a few permutations in the forward line before the final line-up emerged. For instance, Hibs bought three centre-forwards before the boss finally gave the job to Lawrie Reilly.

Gordon Smith, Bobby Johnstone, Willie Ormond and myself were pretty much guaranteed our places, but that vital centre-forward position was to take some filling, especially as Jock Weir and Cubby Cuthbertson had been tried and moved on. I had played there too, but I was clearly better in other positions. The three 'external candidates' for the job were Alex Linwood, who was a good player, and then Leslie Johnston, another fine player, before they bought a big fellow from Dumbarton, Bob Stirling, who was 6 ft 5 in. but was not the most accomplished of players. None of them made the grade, and then it dawned on the boss that Hibs might already have the answer on their books. He gave Lawrie the number 9 shirt, which he made his own in short order.

The first game ever played by the Famous Five was a friendly at Nithsdale Wanderers down at Sanquhar in April 1949. We won 8–1, surely a sign of things to come. The first time that we played together in the League was on 15 October 1949, against Queen of the South, and we won 2–0, with yours truly scoring from 25 yards. I have to say that my long-distance efforts were a regular feature in those days. The funny thing was that the newspapers concentrated on the half-back line, but then it was a very good one, consisting of Archie Buchanan, Hugh Howie and Bobby Combe. Hugh Howie would later contract tuberculosis, which in those days was almost a death sentence. He never recovered from the disease and retired in 1954. He was killed in a car crash four years later.

The whole point about the Famous Five was that we were a particularly well-balanced line. When I stopped playing and started managing sides, I was always looking to create a balance between the strengths of one player and another, and that largely stemmed from my experience with the Five, where our various individual skills and strengths complemented each other.

So, with the Five, on the outside-right you had the silky Smith; on the outside-left was the direct Ormond; inside-right you had the subtle skills of Bobby Johnstone; at centre-forward there was Reilly, never giving a defence a moment's peace, always harassing his opponents; and at inside-left there was me, the grafter who would never stop – and could play a wee bit, too. We all had different facets to our game; but that was the strength of the Five – that we were so different as players but nonetheless gelled as a team. We also looked after each other, and I certainly made it my business to ensure that any illegal attempt to thwart the skills of Smith or Ormond was dealt with accordingly. When you took the sum of all the parts, it was a marvellous machine that worked so well.

It helped that we all got on pretty well off the field. We all had different natures, of course, but once again we complemented each other. Gordon was a wee bit of a loner and was not really a mixer in social company; Bobby was as genuine as you could find, a Borders man through and through; Lawrie was also a man who tended to go his own way, while Willie was gregarious and good fun to be with. Bobby, Willie and I tended to socialise together, but Gordon and Lawrie and ourselves always got on fine at training and on match days.

The funny thing was that we were not all the same age, as is often thought. In October 1949, I was the oldest at 26, Gordon was 25, Willie was 22, Lawrie was not yet 21 and Bobby was still 20. Gordon had been with Hibs the longest, having signed in 1941, while the rest of us all joined up after the war. Even with six years between youngest and eldest, we all respected each other's views. We talked to each other incessantly about the game, either reflecting on the previous match or looking forward to the next one. We were honest with each other and listened to each other's opinions but weren't afraid to offer positive criticism.

It may surprise modern football fans to learn that not once were the Famous Five ever subjected to formal coaching about how to play together. In these days of coaching theorists, that will no doubt come as a shock to the philosophers in tracksuits – they won't want to be out of a job. We were never, ever coached by anyone about how we should take up a position or make a pass or find space or any of that. It just seemed to happen naturally, though of course we did practise things, either together or individually. After training with the squad, for instance, Smith would get a ball and go right round the pitch keeping the ball up with his left and right feet so that it never hit the ground. That was how he worked on his ball control, and it was the practice that suited him, so the rest of us would just watch and let him get on with it. And with lots of good humour about, training was also fun as well as hard work – very hard work.

All of that contributed to the football we created. There was no great secret to our game plan: get the ball into the opposition half as quickly as possible, then score. Simple, eh?

I like to think that most of the time we did make it look simple and straightforward, and, after all, football should be like that. It helped that we seemed to have a communal sixth sense about where the others were on the pitch.

Our attitude was that if the opposition scored three, we would score four, and often that had to be the case, as our defence was occasionally capable of leaking a few goals. And we did like our defence to stay at the back and do their job and leave the rest to us. The idea of an attacking wing-back would have given us an attack of the vapours. If, for instance, right-back Jock Govan ever crossed the halfway line, we would go mad at him. 'What are you doing here? Get back and leave the attacking to us!' we would scream at him.

Our aim was to score quickly and often, and it is amazing how many times we got on the score sheet early. There were many occasions when the supporters were late in taking their places and we were already one or two up. All five of us liked to score, but none of us were glory hunters. In those days, we celebrated a goal with the minimum of fuss, with maybe a quick handshake or two. Nowadays, every goal is greeted like an extra holiday – all that running about and jumping on top of each other, it just isn't manly. We, on the other hand, just wanted to get back to halfway as quickly as possible and get the game started again. The quicker the restart, the quicker we could get the ball off the opposition and the quicker we could run up the park and score another. That was what it was all about for us – scoring goals. It helped that every one of us could shoot. We never really practised shooting, but sometimes after training we would ask the boss for a ball – you practically had to plead on bended knee for one – and I would go in goal and let the four others have a go.

Though we talked about games incessantly, tactics as we know them nowadays were a rarity. Every Friday, boss Shaw would gather all the players in the boardroom and give us his pre-match speech. Then he would ask us one by one for our views, usually starting with Gordon Smith. Everyone would say their tuppence worth, and we all felt that at least we had been given a chance to have our say.

On match day, the boss would come in about five minutes before the match, and invariably he would say, 'Right, lads, go out there and give them "The Reel o' Tulloch".' Sometimes it was 'The Reels o' Bogie' or some other tune. We used to say to each other, 'What the hell is he talking about now?' It turned out that Hugh Shaw was from Islay and was a great man for the bagpipes, which he could play quite proficiently. We knew what he meant – 'Get out there and lead them a merry dance' – but it used to leave us laughing and scratching our heads.

If we had a tactic as such, it was to be always in motion about the pitch. Sometimes it looked as though we were wandering aimlessly, but in fact we were looking for the ball or for the space to run into, so that when we did get possession there was usually always someone free to receive it. So even when, say, Willie Ormond was being man-marked, that left me free to go and hunt for the ball. Or if I was being man-marked, I would make sure and draw the defender away to leave a gap for the others to exploit. We all knew each other's game so well that these things became second nature to us. There was nothing fancy to it – just pure football.

The most lethal attacks came when Gordon or Willie, or occasionally Bobby or myself, managed to hit the byline and cut the ball back. We were at our most dangerous then, because you could virtually guarantee that one of us would be on hand to accept the chance.

The interlinking passes and the quick movement upfield were a joy to watch, but it was the goals that people appreciated. We could send them whizzing in from anywhere. You cannot teach people to be goal-scorers. It is just something you are born with. I have always said that every one of the Famous Five was a goal-scorer, and each one of us was capable of scoring 20 goals in a season. It is an extraordinary fact that by the mid-1950s every one of the five of us had scored more than 100 goals for Hibs. Ultimately, that is why people came to love our style of play; football is all about goals and always should be, and the Hibs team of that era scored more than anybody else. When you see the sterile play of so many modern teams, is it any wonder that people look back to the Famous Five as the best forward line ever produced by Scotland?

It was no surprise that we often played our best football when the pitches were in good condition. All of my favourite grounds in Scotland had great playing surfaces, turf that was level and true, and on which you could pass a ball. It may sound strange coming from someone whose home ground had a notorious slope from one end to the other, but football is always better played on a flat surface, and that's why I enjoyed playing at Love Street, Pittodrie and Dens Park, the homes, respectively, of St Mirren, Aberdeen and Dundee FC. Conversely, if a pitch was brick hard or badly cut up, it seemed to affect our fluency. On those occasions, we would just grind it out, and while people recall the Five for our skills and ball play, we were also pretty tough characters and could handle things when conditions were against us.

Though attention often focused on the Five, every player was vital to the success of Hibs at that time. Every single player on the books of the club wanted to be in that first team, and everyone played for the jersey, because Hibs' management and fans made you want to do your best for them.

There was also another incentive, which was the bonus system at Easter Road. Now, Harry Swan was no rocket scientist, but he had worked out that a winning team playing good football would attract more spectators, which would mean that he could afford to pay us more money and buy better players, which in turn kept the club improving and bringing in more money at the gate. It was a virtuous circle, and we all enjoyed substantial bonuses on top of our weekly wages. The chairman really believed in what would now be called 'performance-related pay', and he and the manager always made it clear that money would be put our way if we were successful; we were, and it was.

There were times, of course, when you made the mistake of anticipating your bonus. That happened to me once in 1949, and it cured me of betting on greyhounds for life. My brother Alec had persuaded me to accompany him to the greyhound track at Falkirk. I agreed to go along for the evening because we were due to play Dunfermline in the semi-finals of the League Cup at Tynecastle the following day, and I was sure I would be collecting the win bonus, which was always paid in cash. Not being very knowledgeable about 'the dogs', I duly went home without any money, and the following day Dunfermline did us, with a former Hibs player, Gerry Mays, putting us to the sword. There were no cash machines or credit cards in those days, so that was me, absolutely broke. I had learned my lesson, and I never had another bet on the dogs.

I did enjoy an occasional punt on the horses, though, as did quite a few players. Jimmy Cairns, for instance, was a great one for the horses and always had a copy of the *Racing & Football Outlook* in his jacket pocket. But I never gambled heavily – I had worked too hard for my money to throw it away.

Apart from the dancing, our main recreation away from football was golf, a game I played right up to my 70s, with Lawrie Reilly a regular partner down at Longniddry in East Lothian. Lawrie came to Hibs from Edinburgh Thistle as a young lad. He was serving his time as an apprentice painter with his uncle when he was signed by Willie McCartney. He was a tremendous scrapper of a player. In those days of often lumbering defenders whose sole job was to tackle and clear the ball upfield, Lawrie would get in among them and cause havoc – and the bigger the better, as far as he was concerned. Big Willie Woodburn of Rangers and John McGrory of Celtic were players he loved to terrorise, and many was the defender he panicked into making mistakes.

He did not have electric pace, but over the first eight to ten yards he was very sharp and could get goalside of the defenders before they knew it. He scored most of his goals from close range, his quick reactions and stocky build ensuring that he got to the ball first more often than not. That is a skill, an instinct, you cannot teach. He scored quite a few goals with his head, but heading the ball was not his greatest attribute, as I'm sure he would admit. But when Smith or Ormond was sending in a cross, you could bet that Lawrie would either get on the end of it or snap up the rebound. He was just 17 when he made his debut for Hibs, against Kilmarnock, and he went on to earn 38 caps and score 22 goals for Scotland, both of which are Hibs club records.

Bobby Johnstone was from the Borders, and maybe he had some farming stock in him, as he was powerfully built, though small of stature. Jimmy Cairns thought he was more of a Border collie than a terrier and christened him 'Black Bob' after the collie who was the hero of a comic strip of the day. Eventually, the nickname that was settled on for him was 'Nicker' because no one was better at 'nicking', or stealing, goals.

Bobby signed for Hibs from Selkirk. He was a highly skilled player with a sharp footballing brain and had a lovely touch. We used to say he could thread a pass through the eye of the needle, and his great forte was to stroke the ball between defenders and place it in front of a colleague. He could score goals, too, and nicked a lot of them. Probably because of his lack of inches, he took some stick from defenders, but, again, he had his allies who were happy to come to his aid.

Gordon Smith began his career in Dundee. When he moved to Hibs, he lived in the centre of Edinburgh, directly opposite the old Empire Theatre, now the Festival Theatre, with his family. He was to become known as 'the Prince of Wingers', and from the start you could see that he was a very skilful player with a degree of pace. He was athletic of build, with strong legs and a powerful upper body, and he could twist and turn on a sixpence.

In those days, the winger usually only had one man to beat, the full-back, before going for his shot or making the cross. If you needed a man to beat a full-back to save your life, you would choose Smith, a maestro with a ball at his feet. But, boy, did he suffer for his art. He used to get serious punishment from his opponents, usually from full-backs trying to crock him early in the match to take the sting out of him. He was brave enough and would always get up and play on. But it was not in his nature to dish out rough stuff in revenge – that was my department!

Wingers have been a dying breed for years, and there have never been any players to match the likes of Smith, Jimmy Johnstone of Celtic or Willie Henderson of Rangers. The latter two were great wee ball-players, terriers of the dribble, while Gordon was an elegant, upright player, beautifully balanced with two great feet – he played on the right wing but could cross or shoot with his left equally well. Many's the chance he created by coming in off the wing onto his left foot and cutting infield to create confusion in the defence. The pundits of the day would often compare Gordon to England's Stanley Matthews. But, to my mind, they were completely different in style and approach, and you could not really compare them, not least because Gordon was a proven goal-scorer. His 364 goals in all competitions stand as a club record to this day.

Willie Ormond – the only one of us who cost Hibs money – was a different kind of winger altogether. He would run straight at the defence, his direct approach unsettling his opponents. He was clever, but he only had one way to beat a man – everybody in the game knew that but still couldn't do anything about it – which was to charge up to the full-back and lift the ball over his outstretched leg, then skip away, leaving the defender floundering in his wake. He would rarely waste a ball, especially if it was played in front of him, and was a lovely crosser of the ball.

At that time, we used to say that any kind of ball across the goal, even a mishit, was dangerous, because there was always the likelihood that one or more of the rest of the Five would be there to stick it away. That happened on countless occasions, when either Lawrie, Bobby or myself would snap up the cross or the rebound.

And since we are considering the merits of the Five, what about that chap Turnbull? He wasn't a bad player, could run all day, was a good passer of the long ball in particular, would shoot from anywhere, and when the others needed help, he was usually on hand. He was often called the engine room, but the boy had considerable skill, too. Aye, all things considered, Turnbull was worth his place alongside Smith, Johnstone, Reilly and Ormond.

Ultimately, I suppose, all five of us were entertainers.

One of the forgotten features of football in the late '40s and early '50s is the five-a-side tournaments played during the close season. There would often be huge crowds at these tournaments. Some were held in Ireland and some were attached to the Highland Games held around Scotland – the Oldmeldrum Games in Aberdeenshire were a particular favourite. The five-a-sides featured all the top teams and were quite lucrative for the players – you could furnish a house after a good close season as the prizes were often things like sofas and dinner sets. So popular were these 'fives' that they were usually kept to the last so that the crowd would stay at the Games. We at Hibs were masters at this form of football. The five of us would often play together, and yours truly would take the role of 'backie-in goalkeeper', which meant that I both played outfield and was the only player in the team allowed to handle the ball in goal.

I recall one particular day we were playing in front of a huge crowd of 80,000 or so at Ibrox on Rangers' sports day and reached the final against the Gers. Most of the support was for them, but, as usual, we were far too good for Rangers' five, and in truth we were coasting it, leading by two or three. Late in the game, the ball was passed back to me, and I decided to try to get them to come out of their shells and attack us. So I cheekily offered the ball to Willie Waddell, gesturing to him to come and try to take it off me. But 'Deedle' and his colleagues were not interested, so I responded by sitting on the ball. In seconds, I had 80,000 people baying for my blood. I wonder if Jim Baxter was in the crowd that day, because in the 1960s, the great Rangers player did the same thing, taunting England and their fans at Wembley. The fives died out, and later attempts to revive that kind of tournament, such as the indoor Tennent's Sixes in the '80s and '90s , have never really worked.

The Famous Five also came to a natural end. Our peak years were 1949 to 1953, and after that we did not play together every week as had been the norm. Nothing lasts for ever in football, and in 1954, after Lawrie had a dispute with the club over money – Gordon got a testimonial and none of the rest of us was offered one – he was out of the side.

Tommy D'Arcy and Tommy Preston were among those who deputised. But the Five was soon to break up permanently, as Bobby was transferred to Manchester City for the colossal sum of £22,000 in the spring of 1955.

The Famous Five was finally and absolutely no more.

We did not meet as a five too many times after our footballing days were over, largely because Bobby Johnstone was living in Manchester.

Even though I was the oldest, I have outlived three of my famous colleagues. Willie became a very successful manager and led Scotland to the World Cup in 1974. If Billy Bremner's close-range effort had gone in against Brazil in Germany, Willie would now be remembered, I suspect, for an achievement even greater than those he gained with Hibs. He later managed both Hearts and Hibs but did not keep well and died in 1984 at the age of 57.

Bobby was hugely successful at Manchester City, which is surely proof that any of the five would have prospered in any decent team.

He won an FA Cup-winner's medal with City in 1956, scoring in the final. He briefly returned to Hibs after I left, in 1959, but he had made his home in England and went back to live there, transforming the fortunes of Oldham Athletic before retiring in 1965. Bobby died at the age of 71 in August 2001.

Gordon, the Prince of Wingers, left Hibs in 1959 on a free transfer because of an ankle injury. But he got himself fit again, signed for Hearts – his boyhood heroes, it should be said – and then promptly won the League title. He then joined Dundee, and they too won the championship, making Gordon the only player in the modern era to win Scottish League honours with three different clubs. He later ran a pub called the Right Wing not far from Easter Road, and it is there under that name to this day. He died in August 2004, aged 80.

Only Lawrie and myself still survive, and it shows you how people still remember us that we are both regularly invited to Hibs functions. Indeed, while writing this book, I was privileged to attend a tribute dinner for Lawrie at Easter Road.

I am often asked how good the Famous Five were. In answer to that question, I usually reply that there are very few forward lines in world football who were known by a nickname. But I don't like to make comparisons, because football has been played differently in different eras.

I also do not make comparisons for one simple reason. We were incomparable.

7

Champions

The best match of my life came my way in the early 1950s. It was around this time that I met the girl who would become my wife.

We players used to go to the Cavendish Ballroom, which had a good reputation. In those days, the 'form' was that the men occupied one side of a dance-hall while the females sat on the other. It took a wee bit of courage – usually of the Dutch variety – to cross the floor and ask for a dance. One night at the Cavendish, I noticed this pretty lass and asked her to dance. We got talking, and eventually she agreed to go out with me on a date.

I liked Caroline McKay Gunn – she is always known as Carol – from the start. She hailed from the Highlands, from as far north as you can get on the Scottish mainland, and had come to Edinburgh to work as a secretary in the Inland Revenue. She had a lovely Highland accent – she still does – and asked me what I did for a living. I never liked boasting, but I had to tell her I was a player with Hibs. It made no impression on her; she had heard of Hibs, but she did not know that much about football. That was no bad thing in my book, as I was able to teach her, and she eventually became very knowledgeable about the game and hardly ever missed a home match when I became a manager.

We started to 'go steady' and were married in the registry office at Newington on 4 July 1953 – a good day to end my independence. We have been together through thick and thin ever since.

We started our married life in a spare room in a flat which Carol's sister Margaret rented in Gilmore Place, and, in due course, we became the proud parents of a beautiful daughter, Valerie. We are all proud Scots, but had things gone differently, Valerie might well have been born in England.

Three clubs that I know of tried to sign me during my playing career. I mentioned Bury previously, and later Middlesbrough would also enquire about my availability, but I don't think they were really serious. It was a good sum they offered for me, but I don't think Hibs needed the money. In those days of capped salaries in football, we were already near the maximum wage at Hibs – I once earned a whole £16 one week with bonuses – so moving south did not appeal that much in monetary terms, and I certainly was not interested in uprooting myself and moving south unless there was a big signing-on fee. The offer Middlesbrough made me was £750, which was a decent enough amount but simply not enough to justify me parting from my beloved Hibs.

The most serious approaches for me came from Manchester United and Matt Busby, who twice tried to sign me. The first occasion was in 1947, but that came to nothing because chairman Swan and manager McCartney wanted to keep me in the team. The second approach from Busby came when we were at the peak of our Famous Five days, in 1952. I was nearing 30 at the time, and I remember it was a Thursday when I came into training and was told that Matt Busby was upstairs in the boardroom with Swan and Hugh Shaw. Eventually, I was summoned to meet the man who had played for Hibs during the war and still had a warm relationship with the club.

I didn't know much about United – they were not the giants of world football they are now – but I liked Matt instinctively as a person. Like me, he was from a community steeped in mining, and he was a no-nonsense sort of bloke who came straight to the point. He wanted me to go to Old Trafford to be one of the senior professionals who would 'look after' the young team he was in the process of building – the legendary 'Busby Babes'. His clear implication was that if I came down as a player, there would be a position at Old Trafford for me after my playing days were over, probably as a trainer or coach.

It was a very interesting offer, especially as my basic wage would rise to £15 per week, and with bonuses I could earn up to £20 per week – a wee bit more than I was getting at Hibs. But it wasn't enough. I wanted a decent signing-on fee to ensure my security, and chairman Swan wanted as much as he could get for one of his Five. The haggling began.

It went on all day, and eventually I realised that unless Busby jumped in a taxi there and then, he would miss his train to Manchester. But I was determined to extract as much as I could and kept him talking well past the departure time. My reasoning was simple: if Matt Busby was serious about signing me, he would happily stay overnight in Edinburgh and try to clinch the deal the following day. Busby did indeed book into a hotel, and I spent a restless night wondering what the morning would bring.

The talks began again the next day, with me joining in after training. In the end, it all came down to money and none of us would budge. Busby was very disappointed, grumbling about me 'costing him two days', but we shook hands and parted with no hard feelings on either side.

I have often wondered what would have happened if I had gone south and joined in Busby's revolution at Old Trafford. I would have arrived in time to help the Babes as they began their period of domination, and I might still have been playing in 1958 – I was still doing so at Hibs – or, more probably, I would have become a trainer as Matt had indicated. I might well have been on the aeroplane which crashed at Munich, killing twenty-three people, including eight players, and almost ending Busby's life. It's a 'what if?' scenario that I don't care to think about.

Of course, like every other player, I could have been transferred against my will. It happened even to top players. We were playing Rangers in a League Cup tie in 1948. I was playing outside-left that day, and against me was none other than George Young, the very same 'Geordie' who had been my teammate in the Falkirk and District schoolboy side of 1936. We had a rare tussle between us, but by the end of the match all of the attention was focused on our goalkeeper, George Farm. He had an unusual habit of catching the ball with his arms outstretched, instead of clutching it safely to his chest, and I have to say it alarmed me.

The game had been exciting end-to-end stuff, as it nearly always was between Hibs and Rangers at that time, when suddenly the ball went high into our area, and George Farm went to grab it only to drop the ball. Rangers' predatory forward Willie Thornton needed no second invitation and slammed the ball home. We were out of a cup we might well have won, and there was nobody to blame but George.

Back at training at Easter Road in the early part of the week, there was no sign of George Farm. 'Where's George?' we asked, to be told by one of the lads that he had been transferred to Blackpool overnight. George was a good goalkeeper, but because of that one mistake he was sent packing from Hibs. He enjoyed a good career with Blackpool and won the FA Cup with them in the 1953 'Stanley Matthews' final. Later, he would return to Scotland as manager of Dunfermline Athletic and win the Scottish Cup with them in 1968. But I always suspected he wanted to beat Hibs more than most teams.

It was around the time of the Famous Five's peak years that I met a man who was to play a vital role in my later career. Tom Hart was an avid Hibs fan who ran a very successful building business in and around Edinburgh. He used to organise golfing weekends for clients and friends at Gleneagles or Turnberry or other major courses and would invite players along. No matter where we were playing, Tom would send a private car to pick up me and, usually, my friend Willie Clark to take us to the hotel at the course, and we would have dinner and drinks and then play a round the following day. It was always a fun outing.

When I was trainer at Hibs, we played AS Roma in the semi-final of the Inter-Cities Fairs Cup (matches I will tell you more about later). Tom was one of the fans who made their way to Rome to watch us in the second leg, accompanied by Jimmy Kerr, who had played for Hibs as a goalkeeper. I met them both over there and we got on well. Jimmy was a master plumber who worked for Tom Hart, and they were inseparable. With them, another former goalie, Tommy Younger, made up a trio of friends who would play a big part in my life much later on.

At the time I first met Tom, in the halcyon days of the Famous Five, injuries were the only thing that could stop us. One of the worst matches for damage was against Aberdeen at Easter Road in season 1947–48, when Willie Ormond broke his leg and Jimmy Kerr broke the scaphoid bone in his hand. He was a super keeper, who was particularly adept at cross balls. He was also a brave man, but surely no one could keep goal with a broken hand. However, with Willie stretchered off and lying in the dressing-room, Jimmy played on with his hand swollen like a balloon. We managed to keep the ball away from him for long periods, and even with ten men we won 4–2.

Jimmy also featured in one of the funniest incidents of that season. As I said, he was a brave man, and he would often dive at a player's feet or into a mêlée to grab the ball. On one such occasion, he took a real clatter on the head, and a concerned Jimmy Cairns called to him, 'Are you all right?' Kerr was completely out of it and seemed to think he was playing a different sport, because he replied, 'I'm fine, just give me the five iron out of my bag, thanks.'

One day at Third Lanark's home ground, Cathkin Park, a Polish left-winger of theirs by the name of Starosic gave Gordon Smith a very sore one indeed. To me, it was a dirty foul, a cowardly foul, and I thought, 'Right, son, I'll sort you out.' Before anyone else in our team had time to get to him I had flattened the Pole, taking him out of the game lock, stock and barrel. It was entirely justifiable in my view, but the referee didn't agree. He was a referee I knew well, an affable Glaswegian called Joe Jackson. We both knew what he had to do and went through the daft ritual.

'Right, Eddie,' he said, 'what's your name?'

'Come on, Joe, you know fine well.'

'Aye, but I've got to follow the form, Eddie.'

'OK, Joe. E. Turnbull,' I said, and off I went.

The entrance to the dressing-room at Cathkin was at one end of the pitch, and that meant an awful long walk in front of fans baying for my blood and held back only by a low wall. I kept thinking, 'What if one of them gets over the wall?' and decided to hurry along.

It was the first time I was sent off in my career, but that's not the only reason I recall my appearance in front of the 'beaks' at the Scottish Football Association. I was scheduled to be dealt with at 2.30 p.m. the following Tuesday, and that evening we were set to play in a friendly against Manchester United. It was a big game for us, and Hugh Shaw really wanted me to play in it, so I must have been one of the first players ever to turn up for a disciplinary hearing in a chauffeured limousine. The boss instructed me to ask the disciplinary panel if I could start the inevitable suspension the following day. He thought I still had a chance of playing, and he wanted me back at Easter Road as quick as possible after my hearing, so I travelled in luxury through to Glasgow to the SFA's offices in Carlton Place. Perhaps the boss thought that the fact we were playing an English team might persuade the SFA to delay the suspension for a few hours. If so, he was very wrong.

The chairman of the panel was a miserable old soul called John Robbie, of Aberdeen. He had one of those strict, sour, schoolmasterly faces, and he handed down the sentence in a voice of doom: 'Suspended for a fortnight.'

'OK, Mr Robbie,' I ventured, 'so am I still eligible to play in tonight's friendly?'

He just about exploded. 'How dare you! There is no possibility of you playing tonight! The suspension starts from now!'

So much for an appeal to the better judgement of the beaks. The Robbie family, oddly enough, would reappear in my life later, at Aberdeen . . .

The only other time I was ordered off, it was also by Joe Jackson. We were playing against Raith Rovers at Kirkcaldy, and we were on the defensive on our own 18-yard line. I was playing right-half that day and was up against Jim McEwan, who was a useful winger for the Rovers. He came running across the front of our box but pushed the ball too far in front of himself. Quick as you like, I whipped the ball away from him, but he followed through and caught me with a very sore blow. My reaction was instant – I hit him with everything bar the kitchen sink. I knew what the punishment would be and didn't bother waiting to be told.

I was already heading towards the tunnel when I heard Joe Jackson's voice shouting behind me, 'Eddie, wait a minute, I've got to take your name first!' Back I went and we went through the same ritual.

'Right, Eddie,' he said, 'what's your name?'

'E. Turnbull, Joe,' and off I went.

I am not proud of being sent off, especially as in my later career as a manager I always preached to my players that they should keep their composure at all times and always accept a referee's decision. But I know it's not easy for everyone to 'keep the heid', because no two players have the same temperament. And my only plea in mitigation is that in both cases when I was sent off, the red mist had descended, and I was out for instant revenge.

In my playing days, referees were given much more respect, and nowadays I despair when I see great teams like Manchester United or any of the big Continental sides surrounding the referee and questioning his every decision. What message does that send out to youngsters? It's not too bad in Scotland, but the problem is getting worse, and I know that referees are really worried about it.

I suppose, when I was playing for Hibs, I had a reputation as a bit of an 'enforcer'. I wouldn't let anyone kick me or any of my colleagues without letting them know that they shouldn't do that again. I would bide my time, then take my chance to 'impress upon' an opponent the error of his ways, if you catch my drift. Referees knew the game better in those days and knew what went on between players, and the Willie Brittles and the Tiny Whartons would let you know if you were going too far. They kept control with a wee word here and there, rather than by flashing cards everywhere.

One referee in particular summed up how to defuse a situation with words and humour rather than bookings. Big Bert Benzie was a fishmonger from Girvan who was renowned for his wisecracks. Once we were playing Rangers and Bert awarded us a penalty, which was not something that happened to Rangers too often. Torry Gillick was playing for Rangers that day. He had a stutter and went up to Bert to register his dissent: 'B-b-bert that wasn't a p-p-penalty!' Big Bert looked down at him and said, 'You read the Sunday papers tomorrow and you'll see if it was a p-p-penalty or not!'

I was lucky that I never broke a major bone. I did once break a bone in my foot, though, and it never healed properly. In fact, it bothers me to this day, and the break in the bone is still clearly visible on the top of my foot. The injury occurred when an opponent – I can't remember who – came down on my instep with the studs of his boots. In those days, studs were fearsome things, nailed or 'tacked' into the sole of the boot, hence the expression 'tackety boots'. That stud must have been well attached because it really hurt. I didn't think too much of it at the time and decided I could run it off. In those days before substitutes, you got a quick dab of the cold sponge, or maybe a quick rub with liniment, and then you were expected to ignore the pain and play on if you possibly could – nothing short of a cracked skull or a broken leg would see you taken off the field.

After the match, it was discovered that one of the metatarsal bones was broken. These days, everybody knows about metatarsals, thanks to the injuries suffered by David Beckham and Wayne Rooney in particular, but back then we just called it a broken foot.

Not long afterwards, maybe only a matter of days, I was down at Easter Road when Hugh Shaw called me over and said he would give me a fitness test. Within seconds, he had me gingerly kicking the ball against a retaining wall with my broken foot, and I was in absolute agony. 'Now come on, Eddie,' he said, 'the harder you kick the ball the less pain you'll feel.' Well, he was wrong. I gave the ball a thump and nearly doubled over with the pain. 'Now, Eddie,' he said, 'you didn't kick it hard enough. Try again.'

However, I was anxious to keep my place, and I had always been a quick healer. Somehow, I battled through the pain to play on the Saturday against Falkirk. We got a penalty, and I looked at my fellow members of the Famous Five. Smith, Johnstone, Reilly and Ormond – not one of them would take it, and the ball was handed to me.

There was nothing I could do. I would have to hammer the ball, broken foot and all, off the spot in my usual style. I did not hesitate. I rushed forward and gave the ball every ounce of energy I could muster – all of it going straight through the broken bone. The ball went into the net, but yours truly went straight to ground. The fracture had obviously not healed, and my shot had caused it to split open again. I was in agony once more, but Hugh Shaw still wouldn't take me off the field. 'Go and stand out on the left wing, at least you'll occupy one of their defenders,' said the boss.

These days, I would be stretchered off, given the best first aid available and taken straight to hospital for corrective surgery, with my foot put into plaster and my recovery monitored on an hourly basis, with the prospect of a long lay-off. Back then, I got a bandage and was told to report for training on the Monday.

I was still in pain during a game shortly afterwards during which the ball ran out of play and I thumped it in frustration. In those days, the fans were close to the pitch, held back only by a retaining wall. The ball flew straight at a spectator, knocking him out cold.

At that time, in the late 1940s and early 1950s, we played a whole series of games against Manchester United. Obviously, this came about because of Matt Busby's time at Easter Road during the war, and also because we were undoubtedly the best team in Scotland over that period and, I dare say, among the most entertaining teams in Europe. One of the best games was the testimonial match for Gordon Smith in 1952 to mark the fact that he had played 500 times for Hibs. United were the champions of England at that time and had many of the players who would become known as the Busby Babes. I got the first, second, fourth – the latter two from penalties – and last of our counters in a ten-goal thriller. The final score was 7–3, and it was every bit as entertaining as the scoreline suggests.

The other great English side of the time was Tottenham Hotspur. Arthur Rowe was the manager and they had players like Ted Ditchburn, Ronnie Burgess, Eddie Bailey and Alf Ramsey, who would go on to bring England glory in 1966. We used to go down there and take four or five off them, but in 1950 we won by a single goal, and that was an o.g. from Sir Alf himself. No wonder he always liked beating Scotland when he became the manager of England. Spurs played a type of game known as 'push and run', which was very effective for an attacking side. Hugh Shaw incorporated some of these tactics into our approach, and I must say we scored a lot of goals playing that way.

We also played Arsenal at Highbury, but I prefer to forget that match. It was a game to celebrate the National Playing Fields Association, the patron of which, the Duke of Edinburgh, was in attendance. There was a lot of attention focused on the match because of the fact that it was televised. Joe Mercer was playing for Arsenal at the time, and they had a wonderful player called Don Roper who played on the left. Our right-back was big Jock Govan, and he kept diving into the tackle and missing. Roper scored four and we lost 7–1, which was a rare aberration in our matches against English opposition.

In those days, the Scottish League was decided on goal average if teams were level on points, and though we would regularly score 25 or 30 goals more than Rangers per season, unfortunately we would also lose more than them. It was the time of the 'Iron Curtain' defence at Ibrox, and they very rarely conceded more goals than they scored.

Season 1949–50 saw huge crowds at Easter Road. We played in front of a record 65,850 – still the highest-ever attendance at Easter Road – for the Ne'erday Derby against Hearts and lost the match 1–2, despite a fine headed goal from Gordon Smith. In truth, Hearts deserved to win that match, as they played very well, in the second half in particular. From then on, it seemed that we had a run of defeats from Hearts by that scoreline. There was a joke going around Edinburgh that Hibs had a new phone number: Easter Road one two, one two.

But the fact is that we lost only one League match after the defeat by Hearts, and that was to Third Lanark. In February came one of my personal landmark matches. The details of it will dumbfound all those people who say that Celtic and Rangers get all the penalties going. When we played Celtic at Easter Road on 4 February 1950, we were awarded not one but three penalties against the Glasgow giants. The referee was Mr Jack Mowat, who would have a long and distinguished career in refereeing and the supervision of referees – despite, or perhaps because of, his actions that day.

During the match, Lawrie Reilly was at his unplayable best, and Celtic's centre-half, John McGrory, could only resort to kicking him to stop him. I think he gave away all three penalties, and I was delighted to give them the Turnbull treatment. I also added another goal to make my personal tally four. I sincerely doubt whether anyone else has ever scored four goals against Celtic in that manner. Perhaps somebody can check the record books and let me know! We won 4–1. Bobby Collins scored their goal, also from the penalty spot.

But the season wore on with Rangers proving that they had stamina as well. It came down to our final game of the season against Rangers after we had a magnificent run of five victories in which we scored twenty-two goals for the loss of nine. That last match took place at Ibrox Park in front of more than 100,000 people. The statistics were simple: we had to win to regain the title on goal average, whereas Rangers only needed a draw and a further point from their final match against Third Lanark. Perhaps it was the nervousness on both sides, but the match petered out into a poor goalless draw.

Even then, we came within minutes of winning the League, as Rangers only just scraped a draw against Third Lanark, who missed a late penalty with the scores even. We had lost the League by one point but had still competed superbly. The amazing thing was that both Hearts and Hibs scored 86 goals, while Rangers could manage only 58. The secret of their success was undoubtedly the Iron Curtain defence, and though we envied them their title, we preferred to play our brand of attacking football. Our philosophy was set in stone: no matter how many you score against us, we will score more.

After that last match against Rangers, we travelled down to London en route to the Continent. Jimmy Cairns had played against Rangers and was now complaining of a sore leg. No wonder – it was broken, as X-rays swiftly revealed. The injury had occurred during the match, and Jimmy wasn't quite sure exactly when it happened, but he felt the pain about an hour into the game. There were no substitutes, of course, and he played on for that last half-hour with a hairline fracture of his tibia. They bred them tough in those days.

We enjoyed the tour of Germany, Austria and Switzerland, and the playing highlight was undoubtedly our 6–1 defeat of Bayern Munich. That's right – we taught the future European champions everything they knew!

All too soon, the new season came round, and this time we were determined to realise the dreams of our supporters. We made a brilliant start in the League Cup, winning a section that included Dundee. We were so far ahead of the rest of the section that our match against Dundee, which was abandoned because of dreadful weather, did not need to be replayed. The quarter-final against Aberdeen was a classic of its kind and went to *four* matches before it was settled.

Aberdeen beat us 4–1 at Pittodrie on the Saturday, but on the following Wednesday evening, a 60,000-strong crowd at Easter Road saw us pull off a minor miracle to score three goals without reply. Away goals didn't count double, so we went into extra time. Lawrie Reilly bagged what we thought was the winner, but very late on Harry Yorston had a long shot which found the top corner of the net. The replay was set for Monday, 12 days later, at Ibrox Park in Glasgow, and I scored the opening goal in the first half of a very exciting game. But Aberdeen equalised, and there had to be another replay, which took place at Hampden Park the following day. And this was after we had played matches in the League on the Saturday. Can you imagine that happening nowadays? In the space of four days, we played three matches; it was no wonder that one of the teams tired. Fortunately for us, it was Aberdeen, and, playing with a strong wind behind us, we romped in to a 3–1 lead at half-time. They were so demoralised that we added another couple after the break. The semi-final looked to be a much easier assignment, as it was against Queen of the South, from the Second Division. Played at Tynecastle, the match was a personal triumph for me, as I scored a hat-trick in a match which actually started badly for us, with the loss of an early goal.

We were in another final at Hampden, and it seemed that surely now I would break my duck, not least because we were playing Motherwell, whom we had beaten 6–2 just a week before. But I sustained an injury in training and missed the final, and there is a good reason for me to say that my absence proved to be crucial for the team. It was not that they missed me particularly, but that Willie Ormond did not play well at inside-left. During training in the run-up to the final, Willie had been trying to vary the play by coming in off the wing. Up in the stand watching the training session was the chairman, Harry Swan. He came down from his seat with his mind made up that Willie could provide the answer to the missing Turnbull problem. So, instead of making one change and bringing in Mickey Gallagher, who was a decent player, for a straight swap, two changes were made, and Willie went to inside-left while a young lad called Jimmy Bradley took his place out on the left wing. Jimmy was a bundle of nerves, understandably, while Willie had never played inside-forward in his life and certainly not in a cup final. Still, we should have beaten them, as we had much the better of the play right up until the last quarter.

But then we conceded two goals in the space of three minutes before our goalkeeper, Tommy Younger, made a backside of a clearance and Motherwell were presented with a third and clinching goal. It is never easy to lose a final, but I can tell you it is a lot worse watching your team lose one from the stand.

Poor Tommy. He was inconsolable, and a picture of him crying appeared in the newspapers. He was known thereafter as 'the greetin' goalie', but he was vital for us. After he was called up for National Service with the Royal Scots in February 1951, chairman Swan spent a fortune on flying Tommy from army camps in Germany every weekend so that he could keep goal for Hibs.

Motherwell did the dirty on us again in the Scottish Cup, but only after one of the best games I ever took part in. In February 1951, we were drawn to play Rangers at Ibrox in the Scottish Cup. We were top of the table by several points, and Rangers were in second place. It shows you how confident we were as a team that our attitude before the match was that a win at Ibrox would leave us in pole position to win the coveted Double of League and Cup, which had never happened in the long history of Hibs.

The fans of both teams, and the Scottish footballing public in general, were hugely excited by the prospect of the two best teams in the country clashing at Ibrox, and the terracing gates were closed long before the kick-off, with a crowd of 106,000 people inside the famous stadium. You'll forgive me if I describe this match in detail, as it really was a special day, and one that would live for years in the memory of everyone connected with Hibs.

For the record, the Hibs team that day was: Younger; Govan, Ogilvie; Buchanan, Paterson, Gallagher; Smith, Johnstone, Reilly, Turnbull, Ormond.

It was a very good Rangers side and contained not only my old schoolboy colleagues Bobby Brown and George Young but also Sammy Cox, who was a friend of mine.

Rangers made the best possible start. Willie Waddell, old 'Deedle-Dawdle', as he was nicknamed, crossed from the right wing and Billy Simpson managed to beat Tommy Younger at the second attempt, after Tommy kept out his first effort. We did not panic, but I can remember thinking we were up against the best defence in the country, with Willie Woodburn at centre-half and George Young calling the shots from right-back; and if we got past them, there was still Bobby Brown to beat.

We began to play our style of football, and though Rangers nearly went further ahead through a Willie Thornton header that looped over the bar, it was Hibs who were making the better chances. Near the end of the first half, Gordon Smith went straight through the middle of that 'Iron Curtain' and played a one-two with Willie Ormond before smacking the ball past Brown.

Rangers hit us again with a sucker-punch early in the second half, though many people thought Billy Simpson was offside before he scored his and Rangers' second. But you didn't argue with referee Jack Mowat, and he had given the goal. We were behind again, but we continued to play our passing game, and Rangers were chasing shadows at times. About 15 minutes from time, I found myself with the ball in the inside-right position, but I was able to turn inside and get the ball onto my left foot. I let fly from the edge of the penalty box and the ball fairly hurtled past Bobby Brown.

As I jogged back to the halfway line, Sammy Cox called over to me, 'Aye, Eddie, looks like we're going to see you on Wednesday for the replay.' I said something like, 'I wouldn't be too sure about that, Sammy,' but even though Rangers were tiring, I wasn't too sure if I meant it.

The equaliser revitalised us, and suddenly we were all over Ibrox Park and looking for the winner. We won a free kick just outside the area, and I lined up to hit it. Rangers' towering defenders lined up to stop my shot, and in among them stood Bobby Johnstone, looking elfin in comparison to the Iron Curtain. Bobby made a wee sign to me, and I could immediately see what he was thinking. Instead of shooting, I passed the ball firmly to him, he flicked the ball up with one foot, and with the other he lobbed it over his shoulder and the wall of defenders for a quite brilliant goal.

Rangers were beaten in sensational style, and we thought that we were going to achieve the League and Cup Double after this memorable result, but Motherwell, with whom we were tied in the semi-final, had other ideas, and we also suffered a real piece of bad luck in that match. We lost an early goal, and then our full-back, Johnny Ogilvie, broke his leg. I had to drop back to cover his position, but we still managed to come back, and equalised through Lawrie Reilly. Motherwell scored twice more but Lawrie pulled one back. However, we then lost Willie Ormond with ruptured ligaments, and we missed out on the chance of the Double.

For, by that time, we were coasting in the League. We had started by beating Falkirk 6–0, and we went on to record spectacular victories over the likes of Motherwell (6–2), Airdrieonians (5–0) and Aberdeen (6–2).

The entire season was one of great football played with verve and vigour. The Famous Five of us were at our best in that year, I believe, and by the end of that season we had beaten Rangers by ten clear points. We had scored 78 goals for the loss of 26, meaning that the average scoreline in our favour was 3–1.

There were some games when the football was just unbelievable. In the League Cup, right at the start of the season we went to Brockville Park to play Falkirk, and somehow we all went to sleep and found ourselves 4–1 down with just 20 minutes to play. Then everything just clicked into gear, and we absolutely steamrollered them, scoring four goals and clinching the game 5–4 in the dying seconds. It was wonderful stuff which had our fans in raptures, and I must say that, as the season wore on, we began to become aware that a great many neutrals were really enjoying our style of play.

At the end of the season, we gave everyone who was not a fan of the Old Firm a real thrill by beating the both of them in the space of three days. We cuffed Rangers 4–1 and Celtic 3–1 in those last two matches, the former game witnessing the sight of a Rangers' goal greeted by near silence from their fans, after Willie Woodburn's free kick was deflected in. That's how far ahead we were of them.

At that time, the chairman got a bit carried away with himself and announced plans to develop Easter Road into a massive stadium which would rival Ibrox or Parkhead in size. The idea was to greatly increase the capacity of the terracing known as Hill 60, and it would have meant Easter Road would have been able to hold 98,000 people. Fortunately, wiser counsel prevailed, and the stadium remained largely as it had been before the war. But the plan showed the extent of the ambition at Hibs during that period.

Such was the demand for football in those days that there was only a short close season. As soon as season 1950–51 was all over, we went off to France, where we played Racing Club in Paris. The match ended in a draw, but I remember it for an incident in the tunnel just before we went out onto the pitch. One of their players ahead of me in the line-up suddenly dropped his shorts and began to urinate on the wall. Perhaps he just couldn't help himself or perhaps he did it for luck, but I don't recall any other player ever doing anything like that. Inevitably, one of our guys cracked 'Is he trying to take the piss or something?'

That year saw the Festival of Britain, and in July, Scottish football played its part with a one-off tournament, held in Glasgow, called the St Mungo's Cup. Once again, we reached the semi-final, but we were put out by Aberdeen, while Celtic went on to win the trophy.

We had one ambition in season 1951–52, and that was to retain our title. No team other than Celtic or Rangers had ever won back-to-back Leagues, but we were determined to have a go. I suppose it helped our cause that we did not get past the group stage of the League Cup and were knocked out of the Scottish Cup at the first time of asking when Raith Rovers beat us 4–1 in a second replay after two goalless draws. But it did not feel like a good thing at the time, because we wanted to win everything. We were unstoppable in the League, however, and, apart from one defeat by Morton at Greenock (their goalkeeper was the great Jimmy Cowan, and he beat us himself that day), we went unbeaten from the beginning of September to almost the end of December. We then lost two in a row to Motherwell and Hearts, before getting things back on track. We had beaten East Fife 4–2 to go top of the League in November, but behind us Rangers were looming.

After that defeat by our Edinburgh rivals, we went on a spree, scoring twenty goals for the loss of just the three in a five-match sequence of victories. That set us up for yet another crunch encounter with Rangers at Ibrox. It was another tough one, and a 2–2 draw was just about right. They had games in hand on us, but, by the second-last Saturday of the season, we knew that if we beat Dundee we would be champions for the second year running. Again, the nervousness showed, and we went in 1–0 down at half-time. But we rallied after the interval, and scored three without reply for a 3–1 victory that gave us the League title.

In several games that season, we had not played well, yet we had still managed to come out on top, and we were the top scorers by far, with a total of 92 goals. For a team outside of the Old Firm to win successive championships was a truly remarkable feat. Put it this way, it has only been repeated by Alex Ferguson's Aberdeen.

If season 1951–52 was a triumph, the next one was a heartbreaker. We missed out on just about everything by a whisker. In the League Cup, we reached the semi-final only to be put out by Dundee. Aberdeen accounted for us in the Scottish Cup; but the most harrowing of all was the League.

From quite early in the season, it became clear that the race for the title was going to be between three clubs: ourselves, Rangers and East Fife. The Fifers had a very good team at that time and had put up a decent challenge the previous season. This time, they looked even more formidable, and I recall one brilliant game between the two of us which we managed to win 5–3.

Five times in that season we scored seven goals, but we also lost matches to teams who should never have beaten us. For instance, we lost 4–5 to Partick Thistle and 0–2 to bottom club Third Lanark. We never managed to get far enough ahead of Rangers, and, by the time we had finished the season with forty-three points from fourteen games, they needed just three points from their remaining two games, which they duly achieved. We finished equal on points, but Rangers had the better goal average. Once again, we scored more goals than them, but we conceded twelve more than Rangers, and that was the difference at the end of a fretful year.

There was to be one final chance to win a cup. In order to celebrate the coronation of Her Majesty Queen Elizabeth II, a tournament was organised between the four best sides in England and the four best in Scotland. Apart from ourselves, the line-up was Celtic, Rangers, Aberdeen, Arsenal, Manchester United, Newcastle United and Tottenham Hotspur.

The first round saw us beat Tottenham in extra time, Lawrie scoring in the last minute, as he often did. The semi-final was against Newcastle United. We were quite brilliant that day, beating them 4–0, and I scored a hat-trick. Celtic were then in the midst of a revival, and they were our opponents in a final at Hampden Park which was attended by 117,060. We desperately wanted to win, but Celtic had a record of success in the one-off tournaments.

The teams were: Celtic – Bonnar; Haughney, Rollo; Evans, Stein, McPhail; Collins, Walsh, Mochan, Peacock, Fernie. Hibs – Younger; Govan, Paterson; Buchanan, Howie, Combe; Smith, Johnstone, Reilly, Turnbull, Ormond.

On the day, we did not perform at our best, particularly in the first half. Neilly Mochan scored for them from 35 yards after 28 minutes, with a rocket of a shot that Tommy Younger barely saw. In the second half, Johnny Bonnar defied us time and time again. I do not think the Celtic goalkeeper ever played a better game. I remember one save in particular, from a header by Bobby Johnstone, and I will never know how Bonnar got to it. He also got to one of my specials, and that took some doing, I can tell you. They also had Willie Fernie at outside-left, and he gave Jock Govan a hard time. We still should have won, though, given the chances we had. As it was, Celtic broke up the park with two minutes left, and Jimmy Walsh scored from a rebound.

We had gone through a season reaching a final and a semi-final and finishing equal top of the League, but we had nothing to show for it. It was truly disappointing, and I honestly do not think we were ever the same team again.

Still, at least there was a pleasant interlude at the end of that season. Continuing with our foreign adventures, chairman Swan sent us off to Brazil. We had been invited to take part in a competition which the Brazilian FA claimed was the first world club championship. It was called the Octagonal Rivadavia Correa Meyer, with eight teams, the only foreigners being ourselves, Olympia of Paraguay and Sporting Lisbon.

We stayed in a hotel on Copacabana Beach in Rio and thoroughly enjoyed ourselves once we had recovered from the 29-hour journey. That was the era before jet airliners, and I can tell you that spending more than a day cooped up in a cabin is no fun. Willie Ormond was one of the great pranksters in the team, and he went out from the hotel on a mysterious mission. We found out later exactly what he was up to when the fireworks were pushed under our doors.

In our first match, we gained a 3–3 draw with Vasco da Gama. It was a particular thrill to play and score against Vasco in the giant Maracaña stadium. Their third goal was a mile offside, and Bobby Johnstone and I both hit the bar in the second half, so we had a feeling of being robbed. I can also remember the crowd fighting among themselves on the terracing. Our next game was against Botafogo and was played in extreme heat, the home side winning 3–1 as we tired. We also lost our third and final game to Fluminense, by three goals to nil.

I have to say we were well treated throughout the tour, and Brazil was a superb place to visit; but it was an awful long way to travel, and further invitations to South America were declined.

There was a peculiar postscript to our visit: a football

encyclopedia published in Brazil in the 1960s contained a whole chapter devoted to the Famous Five. Yes, those lads Jairzinho, Tostão, Rivelino and Pelé had to have learned their skills from somewhere . . .

With Jimmy Kerr leaving, Jock Govan being replaced and Hugh Howie contracting tuberculosis, the team was very different from then on, especially after Gordon broke his leg in December 1953, followed by Lawrie catching pleurisy.

Not surprisingly, that was our worst season since the war. We had no success in either cup and were placed fifth in the League. As a result, only one Hibs player, Willie Ormond, went with Scotland to the World Cup of 1954 in Switzerland. In 1950, with typical arrogance, the SFA refused to attend the World Cup in Brazil because Scotland had not actually won the Home International Championship. They felt that only the champions should play, not runners-up such as Scotland had been that year. This time, they agreed to attend after finishing second behind England, but Willie was just one of the Scots who regretted that the SFA did send a team; the 7–0 hammering by Uruguay haunted the squad for years afterwards, and Willie rarely spoke about it.

The next season was memorable for me in one sense, as it was my turn to captain Hibs. I mean that literally – each of the senior players took a 'turn' as captain. It was not to be a successful tenure, and one of the main reasons for that was the emergence of Hearts as a new force in Scottish football.

With our new floodlights, Easter Road was a splendid place to play football, but we were doing so without one of the Five. The beginning of the 1954–55 season saw Lawrie Reilly's dispute with the club over the fact that Gordon Smith had been given a testimonial but no one else got one, not even Jock Govan or Archie Buchanan, who had signed before Gordon. As often happened when a player was involved in a dispute with his club, Lawrie refused to re-sign (you renewed your contract annually back then). He thus put himself out of football and went off to sell paint. He did return after a compromise was brokered by the SFA, of all people, but, by the time of his comeback, we were already struggling in the League and were out of the League Cup, which was duly won by Hearts.

And it was Hearts who put paid to our hopes in the Scottish Cup, beating us 5–0 in the second round in February 1955. That match featured the last of the many encounters between the Famous Five of Hibs and the 'Terrible Trio' of Hearts. Alfie Conn, Jimmy Wardhaugh and Willie Bauld were all magnificent footballers and were the driving force which propelled Hearts to their Scottish Cup win in 1956 and championship in 1958. We got on well with them off the pitch, but there was an intense rivalry between the two Edinburgh clubs then as now, and there was nothing we liked more than beating Hearts in a Ne'erday Derby, which actually didn't happen all that often. That 5–0 drubbing in 1955 proved to be a turning point for us, as the club needed money and Bobby Johnstone was sold to Manchester City for £22,000 very shortly afterwards.

The Famous Five was no more, and, to be honest, we were never quite the same team again. We did our best, of course, and players like Joe McLelland, John Fraser, John Grant, Johnny McLeod, Jock Paterson (father of Rangers and Hearts star Craig) and a young Joe Baker came through. But there was not the consistency of emerging talent that had been the hallmark of Hibs in the immediate post-war years, and we began to suffer accordingly.

In my last three seasons as a player at Easter Road, between 1956 and 1959, we consistently underachieved. In the League, we finished ninth, ninth and tenth respectively. We never progressed beyond the first group stage of the League Cup in any of those seasons but in 1958 we turned the clock back with a magnificent run in the Scottish Cup. The highlight for many fans was undoubtedly the third-round match at Tynecastle where we shared seven goals with our old rivals. Joe Baker at the age of 17 was outstanding that day, grabbing all four goals for us, but the defence did equally well against a Hearts forward line that was destined to score more than 100 goals and win the League that season.

Following an equally exciting 3–2 win over Third Lanark, the semi-final against Rangers was to prove perhaps the most thrilling of all our ties in the late '50s. After a 2–2 draw we returned to Hampden Park for the replay. We were leading 2–1 with minutes to go when our goalkeeper, Lawrie Leslie, failed to hold a cross and the ball appeared to cross the line. The goal was given, but referee Bobby Davidson changed his mind after consulting a linesman, and we were into the final against Clyde.

I would love to report that we ended the season on a high, and in some quarters we were favoured to beat Clyde, though I could not see why, as they had finished six places above us in the League. In front of 95,000 people, on the day we did not perform to anything like our capabilities, and a single goal by Johnny Coyle was enough to give them the Scottish Cup.

It was my second losing final as a player, and I began to wonder if that should be my swansong. However, the World Cup intervened, and, having enjoyed myself with Scotland, I decided to carry on for another season. Lawrie Reilly's enforced retirement due to injury meant that 1957–58 ended on a real downer for Hibs, and the following season was frankly forgettable. In fact, I've forgotten it!

As we toiled in mid-table and exited from the Scottish Cup in 1959 at the hands of Third Lanark, I had a real feeling that the glory days were over. The 1950s had been a great decade for Hibs, but, as the '60s approached, I felt it was time to move on. As it turned out, however, I was going nowhere.

8

Europe, Scotland and Beyond

Almost every great club, every major national league and all the
most famous tournaments in the world started from humble
beginnings. The European Cup, or Champions League as it is
now known, is the world's greatest club tournament, and tens of
millions of people tune in to their televisions to watch the best
clubs in Europe compete for that huge silver trophy. But it wasn't
always such a massive extravaganza, and many people thought the
tournament would amount to nothing when it began in 1955. The
English FA looked down their nose at it, the SFA didn't know what
to make of it, but eventually allowed us to compete, and Celtic
chairman Bob Kelly said simply that it wouldn't work. Funnily
enough, he changed his tune long before he was knighted, after his
club won the Cup 12 years later, in 1967.

So I am hugely delighted to say that I and my colleagues at
Hibernian FC were in at the beginning and did our bit to help
the European Cup get off the ground. And in so doing, I made
my own bit of British football history, as the first player from the
United Kingdom to score in any of the recognised pan-European
competitions.

As I have recorded, our chairman Harry Swan and manager
Willie McCartney were visionary men who wanted Hibs to be
the best club anywhere. They knew that European football had

caught up with the inventors of the sport in Britain and that in some countries the standard of football had already surpassed that being played in England and Scotland. Even after Mr McCartney's untimely death, Swan was determined that Willie's legacy – the team he designed – should be seen far and wide, and so Hibs began to travel to Europe each summer. I recounted our Swedish adventure earlier, and further tours to Germany, France, Australia and Switzerland were to follow, culminating in our Brazilian expedition of 1953, which I have already told you about.

It is fair to say that the exchange of football cultures didn't always go smoothly. I remember the night before a match in Cologne when we were ensconced in a bar and enjoying several refreshments. A couple of Cologne players were there, and big Jock Govan opined loudly that we would wipe the floor with them the following day. Unfortunately, one of the Germans spoke English and retorted snootily that we shouldn't be drinking, as we were due to play the following day. That was a red rag to a bull, and Jock had to be held back as an international incident was only narrowly avoided.

All that touring stood us in good stead when the idea of the European Cup was formally proposed by Gabriel Hanot, editor of French sports newspaper *L'Équipe*. UEFA had not been going long, and they, as well as a lot of national associations, did not want to get involved. Only after the success of the first tournament did Europe's football administrators sit up and take notice.

The right to enter that first tournament did not automatically go to the league champions of the various countries. The invitation to a Scottish representative came to Hibs, simply because we were much better known on the Continent than the then Scottish-title-holders Aberdeen, who in any case were not keen to be involved, no doubt because the SFA weren't enthusiastic. The English authorities did not even let their league champions Chelsea compete, and there was some heated discussion between Hibs and the SFA before chairman Swan took the momentous decision to enter the club into the inaugural European Cup.

Apart from us, strictly in alphabetical order, the other contestants were: Aarhus of Denmark; AC Milan of Italy; Anderlecht of Belgium; Djurgaarden of Sweden; Gwardia Warsaw of Poland; Partizan Belgrade of Yugoslavia; PSV Eindhoven of Holland; Rapid Vienna of Austria; Real Madrid of Spain; Reims of France; Rot-Weiss Essen of West Germany; Saarbrücken (who are, of course, today, a German side but represented the Federation of the Saar, which at that time was not part of the Federal Republic of West Germany); Servette of Switzerland; Sporting Lisbon of Portugal; and Vörös Lobogó (also known as MTK Budapest or MTK Hungária) of Hungary.

In the first round of the tournament, we were handed what appeared to be a hopeless task. Rot-Weiss Essen were the champions of West Germany, the country which had won the World Cup the previous year, and in Helmuth Rahn, they had the man who had scored the winning goal in the World Cup final.

Were we nervous? Not at all.

We were all seasoned travellers and genuinely had no fear of any team in the world. We decided we would give it our best shot and hopefully show them that Scottish football was a match for that of any country. Hugh Shaw, however, was sure we would be beaten, in Germany at least.

There was definitely an edge to that first European Cup game, because we were playing a competitive match against a team representing a country that we had been fighting in a war only ten years previously. I had lost friends in the war, and several players in the Hibs squad had lost family members. For instance, Tommy Preston's father had been killed in action in Normandy. There was a definite sense among us that we wanted to show the Germans that the war was not forgotten.

We flew to Germany, and the bus ride through that country

reminded us that they had taken one hell of a battering during the war. There were ruined buildings and bombsites to be seen everywhere.

We very much thought that we would be on our own in Essen. Perhaps a small smattering of our supporters might make it to Germany, but, in those days of still primitive air travel, there were no charter flights to cater for our fans. It did annoy us that no national newspaper saw fit to send a reporter or photographer to the match. The media shared in the general scepticism about the tournament, and only the *Edinburgh Evening News* carried a match report, which I believe was given to them by Harry Swan.

However, we need not have worried about our support on that historic day of 14 September 1955 – a date that will live in my memory for ever. For all around the ground were thousands of British servicemen, including many in Scottish regimental caps, who had come to cheer us on. No doubt it was a pleasant break from their duties in the Rhineland, and we very much appreciated their support, especially as they had to endure a downpour which turned the pitch into something of a quagmire.

That rain suited us down to the ground, though, because our game was based on short passing moves, while the Germans seemed preoccupied with trying to hoof the ball up the park. As the game wore on, the ball got heavier and heavier with rainwater, and we were in command for much of the 90 minutes. It helped that Rot-Weiss were missing Rahn, but they had other German internationalists playing. At first, we were prepared to pay them too much respect, and, fearing defeat, Hugh Shaw had told us to lie deep and soak up the attacks. Indeed, Hugh had told us that we should just try not to lose by too many. But as soon as we realised that we were technically and physically superior, we got in about them, and they certainly could not cope with our skills and direct passing play.

My moment of history came in the 35th minute, when the ball

was cleared from one of our attacks. The already soaking ball sat up nicely for me, and I gave it the treatment, fairly lashing it goalwards. Their goalkeeper, Fritz Herkenrath, could not get to it, and I was in the record books. I had become the first British footballer to score a goal in the European Cup, and indeed in any European tournament. I can assure you, I was too busy playing to worry about records; indeed, it was only many years later that I appreciated the significance of that moment.

The second half was a bit of a cakewalk, really. I scored my second fifty-three minutes in, and Lawrie Reilly made it three just seconds later. Willie Ormond added a fourth at eighty-one minutes, and we would have had another had it not been for a mysterious refereeing decision. In the final seconds, Gordon Smith cut inside from the right wing and belted the ball home with his left foot, but the referee said he had already blown his whistle for full time before the ball crossed the line. That was a first for most of us, but over the decades since then, I expect we have all become used to dodgy decisions by referees in Europe.

I would like to say that we returned to a heroes' welcome, but our achievement seemed to underwhelm people, though the newspapers finally caught on when Harry Swan announced, 'Our boys struck a great blow for the prestige of British football.'

The second leg proved to be a very strange affair because goalkeeper Tommy Younger, Gordon Smith and Lawrie Reilly all missed the game. They had been on international duty in Denmark with Scotland, and their flights home were delayed because of fog. Young Bill Adams, who was just 19, was called up to keep goal for the first team for the only time in his stay at Hibs. Jock Buchanan was also called in at the very last minute, and he had just eaten two plates of my favourite food, mince and tatties. Jock was only twenty and a useful forward, as he proved when he scored after just five minutes – the first goal on British soil in European competition, which was a special bit of history for the youngster. We should have scored more, and it was disappointing when Rot-Weiss equalised through Fritz Abromeit in the last minute. However, it was very much a consolation goal for the Germans, who were sportingly applauded from the field by our fans.

In those days, there was no such thing as undersoil heating, so we gained a terrific advantage over the Swedish side Djurgaarden in the next round, which was played in late November, when their pitch in Stockholm was already frozen. It meant they were forced to play their home leg at Firhill in Glasgow, and of course thousands of our fans made the journey to Maryhill, while virtually none of theirs could manage it.

The Swedes opened the scoring in the very first minute through Eklund, and they hit the bar after 15 minutes, but after that we realised that they did not like people running directly at them, so we switched our tactics, took control and ran out comfortable winners by 3–1, with Bobby Combe, Jimmy Mulkerrin and one of their defenders all scoring. I regret to say I missed a penalty – not something I did very often – but I made up for it five days later when we played our 'home' leg at Easter Road. A poor match was settled in the 70th minute with a penalty converted by yours truly.

We had to wait until April for the semi-final, against the French side Reims. The first match was played in Paris, possibly because Reims knew that the final would be held in the French capital and they wanted a rehearsal. If so, we were not going to make it easy for them, even though they were a quite brilliant side, who featured among their number the great Raymond Kopa, known as 'the Little General', and surely one of the finest footballers of all time.

Over in France, he set out to control the game. Even at the kick-off, he stepped back to let another player take it and pass to him so that he would be in control right from the start. But John Grant played very well that day against Kopa. We had our moments, particularly when Gordon Smith and Willie Ormond had the ball.

We also had our chances to score, and I felt that we could have been a bit more attack-minded. Even when they took the lead, after 67 minutes through Michel Leblond, I remember thinking we would 'do' them back in Edinburgh. But with seconds to go, they snatched a second, scored by René Bliard.

We had the proverbial mountain to climb at Easter Road a fortnight later, and I'm not talking about the infamous slope. The European Cup had finally caught the attention of the Scottish public, at any rate, and there was a record crowd for a floodlit match of 45,000, all cheering us on.

To this day, I still do not know how we did not win that match. We battered them silly, particularly down the slope, but somehow their goal survived intact. It was largely down to brilliant organisation by Kopa that they withstood our attack; the Little General commanded his army superbly.

In the second half, we saw a moment of pure magic from Kopa, when he sent a superb pass through for Léon Glovacki to score. There were plenty in the ground who thought Glovacki was offside, but the timing of Kopa's pass was perfect, and the goal stood. We now needed three goals to draw level, but, try as we might, we did not even manage a single counter. It was desperately disappointing to lose the semi-final, especially at the first time of asking.

Our matches were over before Real Madrid and AC Milan even played their first leg, and when the news came through that Real had reached the final, we could only wonder what might have been. What a historic game that would have been for us: Hibs versus Real Madrid in the first European Cup final. It was not to be, however, and the French side took their place against Real in the Parc des Princes in Paris on 13 June, losing 3–4 to a Madrid side inspired by Alfredo Di Stefano.

Our European adventure was over, and indeed I would never get the chance to play in Europe again, though I had many wonderful nights with Aberdeen and Hibs as a manager.

I had occasion to look back on that initial foray when the 50th anniversary of our match against Rot-Weiss Essen was celebrated in some style in September 2005. My conclusions were that Hibs thoroughly deserved to be in that first competition, and we certainly gave a very good account of ourselves. We made a bit of Scottish football history, and I personally got my name in the British record books. If our achievements were not fully recognised at the time, they have definitely been accorded due respect since. It is all part of the great history of Hibernian FC, and I know that the present manager, Tony Mowbray, is acutely aware of that past and those traditions and would ideally like to emulate them with a run in Europe. Who knows, perhaps Hibs might get that chance in seasons to come.

At the beginning of this book, I described how I was exiled from the Scottish international team for nearly eight years, but the fact is that I did play nine times for my country, as well as playing one B international. I also played four times for the Scottish League representative team and indeed captained the 'lesser internationals' on one occasion.

My last appearance on the international stage came in an inter-league match against the English Football League. It was played at Ibrox Park on 8 October 1958, and the Scottish League team included Dave Mackay and the young Bertie Auld. The match ended in a 1–1 draw, with Sammy Baird of Rangers scoring for us and a certain Brian Clough grabbing the goal for the Football League.

It had been a long ten years since I had first played in the dark blue, and I had spent most of that decade in the international wilderness because of Walter Johnston's enmity. There were five Hibs players selected for Scotland against Belgium at Hampden on 28 April 1948: Jock Govan, Davie Shaw, Gordon Smith, Bobby Combe and myself all played. The thrill of pulling on that dark-blue shirt for the first time is a memory I will always cherish. Bobby

Combe scored the first after 26 minutes and Davie Duncan of East Fife got our second after an hour, and we ended with a comfortable 2–0 win. Though I performed satisfactorily enough, I was perhaps a bit overanxious to do well and probably could have done better.

Three weeks later, I kept my place in an unchanged line-up for a friendly against Switzerland in Berne. This was a game which we all came away from saying the same thing: 'We wuz robbed.'

I was up against a very tough defender in Willi Steffen, who had been a fighter pilot and had spent a season with Chelsea. He took no prisoners, but then neither did I.

We took an early lead through Les Johnston of Clyde and looked to be cruising, but the referee was an Austrian, Alois Beranek, and he was a complete 'homer'. First of all, he disallowed a perfectly good goal by Gordon Smith, and then he annoyed us with some shenanigans just before half-time. Because it was a friendly, Switzerland were allowed a substitute, Jean Tamini, who replaced Alfred Bickel at the end of the first half. The referee obligingly played two minutes of injury time, during which René Maillard scored for them.

In the second half, the referee gave us absolutely nothing and favoured them every time in a 50:50 decision. It seemed as though he did not like our Scottish tackling, and free kick after free kick was awarded against us. Not surprisingly, Switzerland scored what proved to be the decisive goal after 78 minutes. I could not believe my eyes at what happened next: the referee actually gave a wee jump for joy and was all smiles at the Swiss players. He didn't even attempt to hide his bias, and we let him know how displeased we were at the end of a match we should never have lost.

We travelled from Berne to Paris for the match against France which I'm not supposed to have played in, as I recounted before. We were beaten 3–0, and I did not play as well as I expected to. I was due to play in the next match against Wales, but I got injured in training before the match in Cardiff. Billy Steel took my inside-left position, and that was me out of the Scotland reckoning for two years.

On 13 December 1950, I made my fourth appearance for Scotland, against Austria at Hampden, and didn't play particularly well, which led to the confrontation with Walter Johnston that I told you about. My years in the wilderness spanned the 1954 World Cup finals and that infamous 0–7 defeat by Uruguay, still Scotland's largest-ever loss, so I'm glad I missed out on that, at least. The sad thing is that I was blackballed by Johnston at the time when the Famous Five were at their peak, and we never once played together in a full international.

I have often said that, in the early 1950s, Scotland had an opportunity to play the best forward line this country ever had in front of the most famous defence. Rangers' Iron Curtain, with George Young, Ian McColl, Willie Woodburn and Sammy Cox, was the most frugal defence in the country, rarely conceding more than one goal in a match. But the Famous Five and the Iron Curtain never did play together. The vested interests of the blazers on the selection committee saw to that.

I only got back on the international scene after Matt Busby was appointed coach. Matt insisted on being given control of team matters, and the selection committee did not dare argue with the most famous Scottish manager of the day. I did not need much persuading to return to the fold.

Matt took charge of a Scottish League team that played the English League at Hampden. Their captain that day was Albert Quixall. I was in direct opposition to him. Matt said to me, 'Now, Eddie, this guy can really play.' I told him, 'He won't get a kick of the ball tonight.' I marked him out of the game.

I knew I was nearing the end of my career and would have one last chance to get back into the full international side. It duly came – in tragic circumstances. Matt had told me that I should stand by to play for Scotland in the end-of-season internationals, and, all being well, I would go to the World Cup as the senior player and perhaps help him with the coaching and training. But in February came Munich, and Matt Busby's terrible injuries in the Manchester United air crash. All of football willed Matt to recover his health, but it was to be many months before he would recover, and his absence from the Scotland managerial role proved a real loss. Dawson Walker was the Scotland trainer, and the Clyde man was asked to take over from Matt, even though he had no real experience as a manager.

Scotland then suffered a 4–0 humiliation by England at Hampden Park (they did have Bobby Charlton, Billy Wright, Johnny Haynes and Tom Finney in their ranks), after which I was recalled to the full international side for the first time in eight years, for a friendly against Hungary in May 1958. I played at right-half that day, as I had done for Hibs on occasion, and with my former colleague at Easter Road, Tommy Younger, as captain, we gave a good account of ourselves in a 1–1 draw. I played in front of Eric Caldow of Rangers and alongside Bobby Evans of Celtic, and we all did well.

That performance ensured I went with Scotland to the World Cup in Sweden. We played one more friendly, against Poland in Warsaw on 1 June, and again I was at right-half. There was a huge crowd of 70,000 that day. With Stewart Imlach playing well on the left wing, there was plenty service to the men inside him, and Bobby Collins of Celtic scored twice in a 2–1 win.

There were no weeks of acclimatisation in the host country in those days. The SFA sent us to Turnberry for two five-day periods, Monday to Friday. Then we made our way to Sweden and booked into our hotel and that was that. The SFA's organisation was pretty shambolic; while we had a trainer who doubled as a physio and were on shillings a day in expenses, sides like Brazil were there with a huge back-up team, including doctors and several physios. They spared no expense, while the SFA stinted on everything. But at least we got a team blazer each . . . and the Swedish hosts presented us with an engraved crystal vase, which I have kept to this day.

Dawson Walker was a very nice man who did his best, but during the preparations, a lot of the responsibility fell to the senior players, such as Tommy Younger and myself. In Busby's absence, we had no leader, and the preparations were pretty much non-existent. We trained every day, and on some days it was very warm, which did not suit us. Nor was there any real talk about tactics or trying to find out about the opposition. It was less professional than one of Hibs' tours of the early 1950s; it seemed the SFA had learned nothing from the debacle of the 1954 World Cup.

Sweden itself is a beautiful country, and I very much enjoyed our all-too-brief stay there. Just as we had on those Hibs tours, the players acted as ambassadors, and we went out of our way to be friendly to our Swedish hosts. Some of us gave coaching lessons to local youth players, which I enjoyed doing; it made me think I might want to do something similar again. However, I could not help reminding the people we met that I had been one of the Hibs side which had put the Swedish champions out of the inaugural European Cup.

The hotels were pleasant, but otherwise the organisation left a lot to be desired. The SFA's selection committee picked the team, and it was left to the players to discuss tactics and work out how we would play against sides we had no real knowledge of. The result was that we took the field having undergone only basic preparation which was much inferior to that of our opponents.

Our first match was against Yugoslavia, who were the second favourites behind Brazil for the tournament, and it took place on 8 June, just a week after the Poland friendly. Yugoslavia had beaten England 5–0 in their pre-tournament friendly, so we knew we were in for a tough game. Our team that day in Västeraas was: Younger (Liverpool); Caldow (Rangers), Hewie (Charlton Athletic); Turnbull (Hibernian), Evans (Celtic), Cowie (Dundee); Leggat

(Aberdeen), Murray (Heart of Midlothian), Mudie (Blackpool), Collins (Celtic), Imlach (Nottingham Forest).

I still feel we should have beaten the Yugoslavs that day, though I did not think so after six minutes when Aleksander Petakovic scored for them. My job was to mark Dragoslav Sekularac, who was their playmaker and a terrific inside-left, and we had a rare old tussle, which I know I won.

We came back into the game, indeed we had the better of it. Just before half-time, I sent in a free kick to Jimmy Murray, and the Hearts man headed home from eight yards. Scotland having drawn a blank in 1954, Murray thus became the first Scot to score in the World Cup finals, receiving his 'assist' from the first Scottish player to score in European competition. Now there's one for trivia fans . . .

We continued to press Yugoslavia, and Jackie Mudie had the ball in the net 20 minutes from time, but the referee ruled he had fouled their goalkeeper, Vladimir Beara. It was disappointing to end with a draw, but it was still a great experience to make my World Cup debut against such fine players. The draw gave us a fighting chance to qualify from the group. The next match was three days later, against the supposed minnows, Paraguay, in Norrköping.

That game turned into a disaster. They had lost 7–3 to France, and some of our team went into the match thinking it would be a walkover. But we reckoned without the fact that the South Americans were skilful and well prepared, and certainly they had more facilities than us – they had footballs to warm up with, for instance.

Again, we lost an early goal, Juan Aguero scoring after four minutes. Mudie pulled one back, but Cayetano Re and José Parodi put the Paraguayans 3–1 up before Bobby Collins got another one back in the 74th minute. Try as we might, we could not get an equaliser, and losing 3–2 was a very bad blow to us. I remember us trudging off the field with our heads down, for even though they had been a much better side than we had expected, we knew we should have beaten them.

On 15 June in Örebro, we played our final match, against France, and once again I kept my place, with Dave Mackay of Hearts and Sammy Baird of Rangers coming in. Playing for France that day was Raymond Kopa, the Little General I had so admired when he played for Reims against Hibs in the European Cup. Also in their ranks was Just Fontaine, who would set a World Cup finals record of 13 goals in a single tournament. One of them just happened to be the goal that won the match against us.

France went ahead with a penalty after 22 minutes, but we should have equalised when we were awarded a penalty. Instead, John Hewie blasted his kick against the upright and the ball rebounded over our heads and caused a mêlée which the referee had to stop. Just before half-time, Fontaine doubled their lead, but we fought tenaciously from the restart, and after about an hour, Sammy Baird pulled one back for us. We had few chances to equalise after that, but we had given France a mighty fright, and, though we were eliminated from the tournament, I think we gave a good account of ourselves in those finals.

We had run two good sides very close and drawn with a classy team, so we had nothing to be ashamed of. Playing in a World Cup finals was the highlight of my international career and a wonderful experience, one which not many players – particularly Scottish ones nowadays – are lucky enough to enjoy.

One of my major regrets about that World Cup is that I never got to see Pelé play. He was just a teenager then, but was already the sensation of the tournament. I would also love to have seen Garrincha in the flesh. Of course, we saw Brazil on film, and what an impression Garrincha made. The man that many people think was the best winger of all time was known as 'the Little Bird' and had to overcome a deformity of his legs to play. He was an inspiration to everyone, and that Brazilian team hugely deserved to win the Cup.

My biggest regret, however, is that we did not qualify from the group stage. Scotland has still to achieve that in either the World Cup or the European Championships, and I feel that we probably had our best chance to date in 1958. Instead, we came home early and a great adventure was over. So, too, was my Scotland career. But at least I got a second chance, at the age of 35, and played in the World Cup finals. I was also selected at right-half in the 'team of the tournament', as chosen by the press – proof, perhaps, that I could and should have played many more games for Scotland.

Lessons were learned in 1958, and when Scotland next played in the finals, in 1974, they were managed by my friend and fellow Famous Five member Willie Ormond, and preparations were considerably more professional.

Despite Walter Johnston and everything that happened, I remain very proud of having played for my country. I just wish I had played more games than nine in the dark blue.

9

A New Career

I played my last game for Hibs on the last day of the 1958–59 season. It was against Stirling Albion and we lost 0–1. Not a great way to finish.

When I retired, I had set a new club record of 349 League appearances which stood until Arthur Duncan beat it in an era when there were at least six more League games per season. I can assure you that I wasn't counting, but fortunately there are a lot of people who keep these statistics, and I have no reason to doubt them. All I will say is that it seemed like a lot more! I had also scored 199 goals in competitive matches, though I am sure somebody missed one somewhere, as I was pretty certain that I had got over the 200 mark. Still, I mustn't quibble, as I had an absolute ball scoring them.

Considering the manner in which I had started out in professional football, I had no complaints about the career I had enjoyed and, at the age of 36, I knew it was time to call it a day as a player. Every professional footballer knows the signs: the body taking longer to recover from injury, the reactions slowing up, the legs just not doing what they are told. Some can play on after their mid-30s if they have kept themselves exceptionally fit, but most players accept that 35 or 36 is the maximum age at which a player can perform in the senior ranks.

I went in to see Hugh Shaw to tell him of my decision and to ask for a free transfer, which would enable me to negotiate a signing fee with a new club. It was then a common way of getting a few quid in your pocket late in your career, and most clubs didn't argue when a senior pro decided it was time to go. It was clear that Falkirk were interested, and so I nearly ended my career at Brockville Park, where it had all begun back with that single match for Forth Rangers in the spring of 1946.

But Hugh Shaw had approached me while I was still playing and mentioned that I might think about becoming a trainer with Hibs. I had already been helping him unofficially in any case, and, with the chairman's backing, he now made me the offer of a permanent post, as trainer with the reserves in the first instance. I was delighted to accept, as Hibs had become like a family to me, and I also had my own family to look after. I had never had a testimonial or benefit match from Hibs, and I needed to keep on earning as I had Carol and Valerie to support.

Things went fine at first. I enjoyed working with the youngsters at Easter Road, and I ensured that Hibs' reserves, and before long their first team, remained as fit as ever. But there was one aspect of my early days as a trainer which carried on for many years and which nearly broke my heart: watching potential world-beaters learning bad habits and even dropping out of football, all because of the attitudes of the game's administrators.

During my various sojourns on the Continent, I had seen how the football clubs of Europe in those days were also homes to other sports such as athletics and basketball. They had specialist coaches for football, for running and for every aspect of sport in the club. We had nothing like that in Scotland. Our attitude was so arrogant, so blinkered. We thought, 'We taught them football, so we have nothing to learn from them,' and paid the price when countries like Hungary, Italy, Germany, Holland and France all improved their football coaching and left us behind.

Another advantage the Continental clubs had was that they could spot talent in very young kids, while boys were still in their equivalent of primary school, and then bring them on, nurturing the youths through their teenage years. It used to bother me no end that there was a school near Easter Road which had loads of young lads just desperate to play and learn about football, but, because of a set of stupid rules, we players and coaches could not go into the schools and teach them the proper skills and habits, and neither could the kids come to Easter Road.

Schools football and professional clubs just did not mix, and it was all because the Scottish Schools Football Association were at loggerheads with the SFA, bureaucrats and blazers fighting with each other to preserve their own wee patch while generations of youngsters missed out on the opportunity to be properly coached. People ask why we ended up so many light years behind the rest of Europe in terms of skill levels; well, I know where the blame can be laid.

I am convinced that the recent changes which have seen clubs and professional coaches become much more involved in younger-age-group football will pay dividends, but it won't be for a long time. Indeed, I'd like to see more former professionals getting involved in schools coaching, in particular. After all, sadly, there have been a lot of cutbacks in Scottish football in recent years, so there are a lot of them about who need a job. Back then, in the 1960s, I could only stand in silence outside the school gates and wonder at the big mistake that was being made with regard to the future of Scottish football.

My main concern, however, was the performance of the Hibs first team and reserves. We had one or two terrific results in the League in the 1960–61 season, but we never recovered from a disastrous start in which we lost eight games on the trot. A mid-table finish was our destiny. We exited the League Cup at the group stage and lost to Celtic in the quarter-finals of the Scottish Cup after a replay.

We reserved our best performances for the Inter-Cities Fairs Cup, as the UEFA Cup was then known. In the quarter-final, we met Barcelona, who were perhaps not the giants they are today but still formidable opponents. They were Spanish champions and had entered both the European Cup – in which they knocked out Real Madrid – and the Fairs Cup. They had the brilliant Hungarian Sándor Kocsis and Spain's best player, Luis Suárez, in their ranks.

After Lausanne of Switzerland pulled out, we were given a bye to meet the Catalan side. It really was a remarkable first leg. Joe Baker scored twice in the Gran Estadio, which was their home at the time. We actually led 2–0 and then 4–2, but Barça equalised in the final minutes.

A 4–4 draw gave us the advantage but we had to wait two months before Barça came to Easter Road. Our biggest crowd in years, some 50,000 plus, saw Joe Baker put us ahead in the tie on aggregate, only for Barcelona to strike back through Martinez and Kocsis. But we were not done, and, playing down the slope, we battered away at their defence, Tommy Preston getting the goal that levelled the aggregate. Now, the German referee, Johannes Malka, had already ignored a couple of penalty claims, but with seven minutes left our winger Johnny McLeod went down in the box and we were awarded a penalty.

I can still barely believe what happened next. The Barça guys surrounded Malka, screaming and shouting, and Suárez even aimed a kick at him. This went on for ages, until eventually order was restored with the help of the linesmen and police. Bobby Kinloch was the calmest man in Easter Road, and he waited patiently before slamming the ball behind the young goalkeeper, Nedrano.

The Barcelona players then lost the plot altogether. They raced after the referee, who tried to take refuge in the dressing-room tunnel, but he found himself being pummelled by the Catalans. Our guys tried to protect him, but it took the police to rescue Herr Malka. He bravely played out the last five minutes, but I spotted that, as he checked his watch just before full time, he moved himself to the touch-line right in front of the dugout, and as soon as he blew the whistle, the referee ran up the tunnel.

Even there he wasn't safe, and I can remember the screams in Spanish as the players tried to kick down the door to the referee's dressing-room. Can you imagine the outrage such scenes would cause today? Back then, Barcelona merely made a public apology and it was all forgotten about; they later came and played a friendly to show they were nice guys, really.

That victory put us into the semi-final against AS Roma. We drew 2–2 with them at Easter Road, and in the magnificent Stadio Olympico in Rome, we gained a hard-fought 3–3 draw. Away goals did not count double at that stage, and the location of the third leg was supposed to be decided on the toss of a coin.

Mystery has surrounded what happened next ever since. I can tell you what occurred. The Roma officials got hold of chairman Harry Swan, and let's just say that he was very easy to deal with. I don't know if money actually changed hands, but some deal was done and Roma also promised the squad a week's holiday in a five-star hotel. As the match could not take place until a month after our season had finished, you can imagine that our players were not exactly attuned to the task. They certainly enjoyed the Italian hospitality and were very generous in return, allowing Roma to win 6–0. There would be all sorts of inquiries if it happened now. The Italians later beat Birmingham City in the final.

The following season promised much, but the results did not go our way. We finished mid-table again, went out of the League Cup early, lost our opening Scottish Cup tie with Partick Thistle and were well beaten by Red Star Belgrade in the Fairs Cup. Hugh Shaw eventually paid the price and was sacked after nearly 15 years in charge of Hibs. It was a wrench to say goodbye to a man who had been my trainer and then manager and mentor.

I thought I had a chance of the manager's job; after all, I had spent all these years in loyal service to Hibs. But I met a local journalist, Willie Gallagher, who told me that the board considered that I wasn't ready to step up. I told him that I considered that, on the contrary, I was ready, and he passed on the message. But within a few days, Walter Galbraith had been appointed manager of Hibs.

Galbraith had played full-back for Queen's Park and Clyde, and I had never rated him highly as a player. I knew from early in his time at Easter Road that I wasn't going to get on with him. He was obsessed with his appearance, always checking in the mirror in the dressing-room to see that his hair wasn't disturbed and things like that. Apart from that, he always liked to be the centre of attention – he should have been on the stage. From the outset, he made it clear that he was going to leave the training of the players to me. He rarely came to training, and his input into that vital part of preparing a team was almost nil.

I was unhappy with things and let him know in no uncertain terms that I felt he wasn't doing his job properly. The players could see the friction between us, and things went from bad to worse. I just couldn't work with the man, because the truth was that even then I already knew far more about football and footballers than he ever would. That might sound arrogant, but it was how I felt then, and I like to think subsequent events proved me correct.

Almost the last straw came when we were preparing for the summer tour to Czechoslovakia in 1962. The tour party was to gather in the Scotia Hotel on Great King Street, and on the morning of our departure I was there supervising the loading of the kit when I was summoned to take a phone call. It was Mrs Galbraith to say that her husband had taken ill and would not be joining us. She relayed the manager's message that I was to take charge of the tour party and even wished me luck. Poor woman – she was just passing on the message. We went on the long haul to Czechoslovakia and played five games. We never lost a single match, and I thought that I hadn't done too badly for a stand-in.

When we returned to Edinburgh, Galbraith and I had another 'discussion'. I knew then that Easter Road just wasn't big enough for both of us, and the only way the impasse would end would be with one or other of us leaving. I stuck it out through almost all the next season; but after yet another spat, I had had enough and walked out. It was 21 March 1963, and, after almost 17 years with Hibernian Football Club, I was out of the door and out of a job for the first time since I left the Royal Navy. I just couldn't have stayed a minute longer working for a man I had come to dislike and in whom I had no trust – and for whom I certainly had no respect.

I then had the difficult job of telling Carol. She always remembers what happened next; it was her birthday, and I was about to hand her a most unwanted present. I took the tram home to Gilmore Place, and when I walked in, she said, 'You're home early today, dear.' I confessed what I had done, and, understandably, she hit the roof, pointing out that we had a young daughter to care for and no income.

Money was always tight in those days, and I knew I would need to get a job right away. It didn't bother me what job I took, all I knew was that I just didn't want to stay at Easter Road while Walter Galbraith was in charge. It was of no comfort to me that he didn't last long at Hibs after I left.

Leaving Hibs was the hardest thing I had ever done, but it was something I had to do to be true to myself. I know my departure caused a lot of soul-searching at the club, and maybe in the long term that was a good thing. Back then, however, I was in trouble: jobless, coming up for 40, and with no obvious prospects and far fewer vacancies to fill.

But the word soon spread around the tiny village that is Scottish football that I was available for hire. I spent a couple of days relaxing, going by tram to the Braids, the municipal golf courses on the hills to the south of the city. It was still summer, and the walking helped me to clear my mind of the turmoil of being unemployed and away from the club I considered to be almost like family to me.

I returned one evening to Carol, who handed me a note. 'You've to phone that number,' she said. It was a Glasgow number, and I vaguely recognised it. It turned out to be the number of Willie Allan, the secretary of the Scottish Football Association, who had called me from his office in Glasgow. I knew Willie from my days with the Scottish national side in the World Cup, and though many people called him dictatorial and worse, I respected the man and his work for football in Scotland, and wouldn't stand for any criticism of him.

Willie asked me what had happened and I briefly explained about Galbraith. Coming straight to the point, he asked me if I would like to take charge of the Scottish international youth teams on a special tour. He emphasised it was a temporary job, but it was a foot in the door of management, and I accepted with alacrity. Which is how I came to land an adventure in Kenya just a short while after leaving Easter Road.

The Kenyan government had decided to celebrate their independence from Great Britain in 1963 with a football tournament for young people from all over the world. I was to take charge of Scotland's representatives, and, believe me, that meant superintending every detail of the operation, from ensuring that every young player got to the airport on time to checking the kit and looking after a particularly important piece of gear – the SFA's present to the new prime minister, later president, Jomo Kenyatta. This gift was a very fine, and presumably very expensive, inscribed silver salver in a presentation box, which I carefully packed away in our luggage.

After the tiring journey to Kenya and our landing at Nairobi airport, we unloaded our luggage with the help of our Kenyan hosts. I rushed around making sure that all the lads were looked after, and then set off with our luggage in tow. We were all billeted with expatriate families, and when we got to the house at which we were staying, I carefully unloaded the luggage only to notice that something was missing – the silver salver.

I was in a panic, to put it mildly, and we rushed back to the airport, where I was sure I had last seen it. There were so many people milling around at the airport ahead of the independence celebrations, I was sure I would never find the men who had helped us unload our gear. I just couldn't picture myself going home to tell Willie Allan what had happened and began to wonder if there were any jobs for ex-footballers in Kenya. Just then, a large Kenyan chap with a big, broad smile came forward clutching the box containing the silver salver. Everything was intact. The box had slipped out of the luggage and been found on the floor.

Later, I was asked to take charge of the Scottish international amateur side which took part in the FA Centenary Tournament in England in 1963. We had players of the calibre of Peter Lorimer and Tommy McLean. We won our group quite comfortably and went straight into the final against West Germany, who were coached by none other than Helmut Schön, who would lead the full professional side to World Cup glory in 1974. We were 0–2 down at half-time before I made a couple of changes, sending on McLean and Lorimer. That turned the game, and we pulled it back to 2–2 at full time before romping away in extra time, the final score being 5–2.

After a hectic but enjoyable time, I returned home to face the prospect of unemployment again once my SFA job was finished. But within a few days, I received a call from a football writer I knew quite well, Willie Allison. Willie would later go on to be the PR officer for Rangers, but he was then reporting for a Glasgow-based newspaper and had his ear to the ground for all the developments in that city's clubs. Willie told me there was a vacancy for a trainer-coach – effectively the manager – at Queen's Park, the famous 'Spiders', the oldest club in Scotland and the only amateur club in senior football in Britain. The sole professional allowed at the club was the manager, and the whole organisation – which, don't forget, then owned what was Europe's largest football stadium, Hampden Park – was run by a committee. The club president was a man called Jackie Grant, who was a former player with the club, like many of the committee down the decades. Once a Spider always a Spider, it seems.

I went through to Glasgow for a meeting with him, and though the wages weren't grand, the post of trainer-coach did come with a house directly opposite the main stand. That was a major attraction for me and Carol after so many years sharing other people's homes. It was a semi-detached, and the other half was occupied by the Hampden groundsman, who was probably at least as important as the trainer-coach, given that the stadium hosted so many big matches.

One of the greatest club football matches, if not *the* greatest, took place at Hampden. The European Cup final of 1960 between Real Madrid and Eintracht Frankfurt was watched by many future Scottish managers, myself among them, and the 7–3 victory of the Spaniards made a huge impression on us all.

Jackie Grant was a fine man, and we got on well from the start. I knew I was joining a club that was a famous Scottish institution, and I did my best to find out how it was run; the committee structure with a president was considerably different from the company chairman and board of directors I had known at Hibs. By and large, I was allowed to get on with things in my own way. After all, I was the professional and everybody else was unpaid, though they were not amateurish. Far from it – Jackie, his committee and the players put in an effort that was professional in all but name.

The attitude of the players was very reassuring. Many of them were youngsters hoping that a spell at amateur, but senior, Queen's Park might lead to a call from a professional club. Others were men who just loved the game but preferred to keep their full-time jobs. All of them were anxious to learn from someone who had played at the top level. They all knew of Real Madrid, for instance, and I had scored my first goal in the European Cup in the same year they won the first tournament!

After moving Carol and Valerie through to Glasgow, my first priority was to sort out training schedules, and when you are dealing with part-time amateurs, that means you have to be prepared to work abnormal hours and be ready to compromise – not something I was usually ready to do. But when one of your players is a policeman, for example, whose beat doesn't start until seven o'clock at night, then you have to design a schedule that suits him. It meant that I had to make myself available to train some players during the day and others at night, so it was just as well I lived across the road from 'the shop', though we did most of the training at Lesser Hampden, the pitch next-door to the main stadium, which was also owned by the club.

I was not a qualified coach as we would understand that nowadays, and I certainly had no certificates. The SFA's famous coaching courses were only just getting under way back in the 1960s, but when I moved to Hampden, I was on my own, with only the lessons of my career at Hibs to call on. I did try to follow what was happening elsewhere in England and Europe, though, just as Hibs had gone abroad on those post-war tours.

There was one coaching manual I did use. I had picked it up after hearing that the great Hungarian sides of the '50s and '60s swore by it. I have no hesitation in saying that *Soccer: Technique, Tactics, Coaching* by Professor Árpád Csanádi was the bible I swore by for much of my career. It numbered about 680 pages, and, for years, I would study it religiously, the drawings and diagrams all laid out so that they could be understood by anyone with the slightest appreciation of football. Throughout my career as a manager, I would sit for hours at night making detailed plans for everything: training schedules, tactics, new moves to be practised. I knew from the manual that such things could be written down, and I just wish

I had kept all of my records, as I would have a manual of my own. Maybe I'll get around to writing it one of these days . . .

I will never forget those early days at Queen's Park. It was my first experience of being in complete control of a team, and though many pundits and players may wonder at this statement, given my reputation for discipline, one of the main things I learned early in my new career was tolerance. As a professional training professionals at Hibs, I had been able to say jump and a player would jump – no arguments, for you could get him dropped from the team, and that would cost him money. But when you are dealing with educated, unpaid players, who are bank managers and teachers during the week, you have to learn the art of cajolery, of persuading people through encouragement rather than threats. I did insist on a certain form of discipline – no nights out before matches, for instance – but the players accepted my ways because they knew they were coming from an experienced professional who was trying to improve them as players.

I found that I preferred this way of working and that being positive with players was a whole lot more productive than being overly critical. Not that I ever let anyone make mistakes and not get told about it – that would have been unprofessional, and unproductive in the long term. But I quickly learned that there are ways of talking to men which will get you better results, and indeed things did begin to improve for Queen's Park.

It helped that we already had signed, or managed to acquire, some pretty decent players. There was Bert Cromer, who was a bank manager for a living, and a good and thoughtful player. Davie Letham, who would later turn professional, was a very good wing-half, and we had other players, such as Willie Hastie and Junior Omand, who were all technically competent.

One of the goalkeepers in the squad was a young lad called Robert Clark, better known as Bobby but always called Robert by me, even to this day. I'll tell you more about him later, as he was one of the first players I took to Aberdeen. He and two fine players, Alex Ingram and David Millar, were inseparable, as they had played together for the local Victoria Park juvenile team before joining Queen's Park. I always felt a bit guilty about splitting up the trio when I went to Aberdeen, but Clark was always that bit special.

When I joined Queen's Park, they were languishing deep in the Second Division, but I was determined to see us rise up that table. I remember calling the players together for an early 'council of war'. I told them bluntly that I was prepared to give 100 per cent to the cause and I expected nothing less from them. Anyone who was not prepared to commit themselves to the club could leave. No one did, and soon I could sense that the players were beginning to get the message and were enjoying the more professional attitude around the place. We began to put together a string of decent results, and funnily enough our record away from Hampden was better than our results at the old place.

In those days, the Glasgow Cup – a charity tournament in which all the city's senior clubs competed – was sometimes a chance for Queen's Park to measure themselves against the might of Celtic and Rangers. Invariably, we would lose. But in the Scottish Cup in 1965, we nearly pulled off a major shock. We were drawn against Celtic at Hampden Park, and, though this was just before Jock Stein joined the Parkhead club and transformed them into champions, they were still a very strong side – in fact, they went on to win the Cup that year. We gave a good account of ourselves and, while we lost 0–1, I was delighted with the way our lads played, and we could have scored with a bit of luck.

Bertie Auld, who played for Celtic in my old position of inside-left, was good enough to say how well we had done. I had known Bertie before, and the two of us always got on well – even after he came to work for me later at Hibs!

That Celtic match proved a very good calling card for me. We did not win anything but respect in my two years at Hampden, but as I neared the end of my time there, we were going well. For the first time in years, Queen's Park were serious promotion candidates.

But during February 1965, one of Scotland's most famous clubs was in turmoil. Aberdeen FC were heading for relegation after a series of dismal results. Dropping down to the Second Division was unthinkable for this proud club, and their manager, Tommy Pearson, resigned.

Once again, Willie Allison came on the telephone. He asked me if I had considered going for the job at Pittodrie, and I answered truthfully that I had not. He suggested that I should do so, and, more in hope than anticipation, I sent off an application. My feeling was that I had nothing to lose, as I was sure Queen's Park would not stand in my way. How different from nowadays, when even the greatest managers, such as José Mourinho or Sven-Göran Eriksson, cannot just apply for a job 'on the quiet' without somebody crying foul and demanding an inquiry. Football really was a much more simple game back then.

It was not long before I heard from Aberdeen. Within a few days, I received a written reply inviting me north for an interview. Some people were surprised that the club would send for a man with relatively little experience as a manager and none at all in the top flight of Scottish football. But I had trained Hibs for two years and more, and had shown what I could do with a squad of amateurs, so I felt no anxiety about being considered for what was one of the prime managerial jobs in Scotland.

Aberdeen were, after all, in some disarray. It had been ten years since the Dons had won their one and only Scottish League championship, and things had been pretty much downhill from then on. Indeed, Aberdeen had not finished in the top five since the year after their title win, and in season 1964–65 they were really struggling. Relegation was a real possibility, and the club had not been out of the top division since joining it in 1905.

Aberdeen had a great history. The club was formed in 1903 from the amalgamation of three clubs in the city. Apart from the League title, they had won the Scottish League Cup in season 1955–56 to add to their sole Scottish Cup win in 1947. One of the first teams to tour abroad, they were always reckoned to be a go-ahead club but were also curiously old-fashioned in some ways.

Football was much more gentlemanly in those days, so to be sure that nobody's working week was disturbed, my interview took place on a Sunday – just after our narrow Cup loss to Celtic. But a Sunday interview brought its own problems, as there was only one train north from Glasgow to Aberdeen and only one return train later. What if the interview ran on too long? I decided I would just have to cross that bridge if and when I came to it, like Matt Busby all those years before when he had come to Easter Road to seek my signature.

It was arranged that I would be interviewed in the city-centre office of the vice-chairman of the club, Dick Donald. The Donald family were very well known and respected in Aberdeen. They owned cinemas and theatres and had interests in other local businesses. They were known for running a tight ship, and were all keen supporters of the Dons, in whom they had invested considerable sums. Indeed, they owned the largest single shareholding and 'spoke for' other shareholders. I found his office and was introduced to the four members of the board: chairman Charlie Forbes, John Duncan, Douglas Philip and Dick Donald.

My attitude was simple. If they wanted me to do the job, they would have to find out from the start just how I would go about things. I wanted total control of their club, and I was going to demand it.

The interview went well, but then they asked me if I had any questions. My first query was straightforward: 'What measure of success are you looking for? What do you want to win?' They were flabbergasted, struck dumb. They simply couldn't answer. Who was this man asking them serious questions about winning? Who was this fellow talking about success when the club was on the brink of relegation? But I wanted to know the extent of their ambition, and I deliberately set them a 'tester'; it was like probing a defence on the football field, trying to see if there were any weaknesses.

The conversation took off from there, and in no time at all they were asking me what I wanted to do, how far I thought Aberdeen could go. I told them that the most important thing for me was that I should have complete control of the playing staff and the selection of the team. I knew only too well that chairmen and directors even at the biggest clubs liked to interfere with playing matters, and I simply was not prepared to tolerate that. Sure, I would listen to the board, and of course I would need to talk money – transfers and salaries – with them. But I wanted no one telling me which players I could and couldn't pick. I then told them that it might take time, but I would have Aberdeen back at the top rather than struggling to avoid relegation. You may think I was arrogant, but I would say I was confident in my own ability.

The board talked among themselves about my conditions, and eventually the four of them called a halt. They said they would call me back in a few minutes, and I didn't know if that was a good sign or not. But when they called me in after a short while and asked if I could come back later in the afternoon, as I was on the short leet, I was happy to oblige, especially when they suggested I repair to a nearby hotel for a refreshment. But I felt I had to make a point and told them categorically that I had to be on the only train back to Glasgow, at six o'clock. They suggested I come back at four, and when I did so, I found the four men waiting for me.

I do not know to this day how many applicants there were or how many interviews were conducted, but their verdict was in my favour. 'The job is yours if you want it,' said the chairman. There was no hesitation on my part: 'Thank you very much, gentlemen, I accept.'

That was it. I had become manager of one of Scotland's top clubs in the space of half a day.

There was the formality of Queen's Park having to release me from my position, but I had been assured that the committee would not stand in my way, and, on 1 March 1965, they met at Hampden and agreed to release me after the following Saturday's match at home against East Fife. I got a terrific send-off from everyone at Hampden, and the lads did me proud by winning 3–0.

James Logan, the club secretary, was good enough to tell the press: 'He has done a great deal towards putting the club back on top.' And when I left them, Queen's Park were challenging for promotion. Was I swapping a club that was set to go into the First Division for one that was heading down to the Second? Only time would tell.

Now, those who persist in portraying Aberdonians as tight-fisted will no doubt delight in my revealing that the salary I was going to earn at Pittodrie was not actually much higher than that which I had 'enjoyed' at Queen's Park. There were certainly no vast sums of cash flowing my way – we're talking about £30 per week plus bonuses.

But with the job there was a car! Which was great, except for one wee problem: I didn't want a car. And there was a very good reason for me not wanting a car: I couldn't drive. Having lived so close to 'the shop' at Hibs and then having lived literally across the road from Hampden, I had never needed to drive for work purposes, and I couldn't really afford a motor for leisure purposes. The Aberdeen board were insistent, however. 'You'll need a car to go and see players and opposition teams,' they said. The manager of Aberdeen might not earn a king's ransom, but he had the status to deserve a car.

'But I can take the train,' I said. They would hear none of it, which is why, when I moved to Aberdeen, I enlisted the help of the team bus driver to give me lessons and shortly afterwards passed my driving test – which might have been the worst thing ever to happen to me, as I then spent hundreds of hours driving thousands of miles on club business. Those were the days when it took four hours to drive from Edinburgh or Glasgow to Aberdeen – there was no motorway north of the Central Belt – and Stirling became my personal black spot, as it was the original speed trap, without the cameras. The traffic police would just wait at night for you and give you a warning, thank goodness. And in the next chapter, I'll tell you how a late-night trip almost ended my career . . .

10

The Northern Light

I very nearly didn't see any success at Aberdeen. Early in my time there, I was down at a midweek game in Glasgow in the middle of winter and was making my way home. It may seem strange in this world of satellite television, when every game seems to get covered, but, with few exceptions, the only way to watch a match back then was to go to it. I would often have to go down to Glasgow or elsewhere in central Scotland to watch an evening match and then return home afterwards. Sometimes I would not get home till 2 a.m. and then have to be up to open the stadium for training first thing the following morning.

That night, it was a lonely drive as usual, and as I hurried along through Perthshire, I did not notice that black ice had formed on the roads. Those were the days before special road surfaces and anti-lock brake systems. Driving at speed, I just lost control, and the car drifted over to the grass verge. I didn't know what to do, whether to brake or not, but matters were out of my hands in an instant. When I touched the brakes, I just kept going and going, hit the verge and then bounced along the wire fence which was the only barrier between the road and the fields alongside.

Somehow, the fence held as the car bounced along and around, and miraculously I found myself back on the road proper with the car on all four wheels.

Even more miraculously, the engine was still running and the car was more or less intact, so I just carried on to Aberdeen. The following morning, I went to see Aberdeen's Mr Fix-It, John Murray, who had quickly become a good friend, and told him about the incident and the state of the car. He arranged for the local police to test the vehicle, and they found that I had had a very lucky escape, as the steering had been damaged. I could have gone off the road at any time after the accident. I had the car discreetly repaired and nobody at Pittodrie was any the wiser – except for me, as I resolved not to drive on ice again!

But that was all in the future. After I got the job, my first task was to get to Aberdeen and get things sorted, as the club really was in danger of relegation. It was just ten years since Aberdeen had been League champions, and, you will recall, Hibs took 'their' place in the European Cup. There was no resentment about a man from that same Hibs side coming north to take over at Pittodrie, though. I was taking the reins from Tommy Pearson at a critical period, and time was of the essence, so it might seem strange that I actually took a few days 'off' between leaving Queen's Park and joining Aberdeen. However, it was a busman's holiday, because I went down to London to Stamford Bridge to see an old pal, Tommy Docherty.

That brief visit came about because 'the Doc' and I had kept in touch ever since our days playing together for Scotland. I called him to tell him I was going to Aberdeen and asked if I could come down to see him. The word on the grapevine was that Chelsea were on the verge of great things, largely because the Doc was using some revolutionary new training methods. As always, I was eager to learn about anything new in the game, and so I was delighted when Tommy said, 'Come on down.' The Doc was already successful and would go on to greater things, but not a lot of people realise that one of the secrets of his success was that he, too, was always willing to go places and learn things, as well as pass on his knowledge. Later, he and I would go on coaching courses in West Germany, as it then was, and he also asked me to help out when he was manager of Scotland.

The Doc greeted me warmly, and, after seeing round Stamford Bridge, I went with him to a training session. Chelsea had some fine players at that time – Terry Venables and Peter Osgood, to name but two.

One of the first things I learned was that the Doc liked to have an eagle's-eye view of everything. He took me high up into the stand, where he had a special platform from which he could look down and see the whole field of play. From then on, I too would always sit in the stand to watch a match, rather than crouch down in the dugout with its limited view of the action.

I was impressed with the way he had Chelsea playing a direct passing game and noted the various methods he used to get his players into that mould. What particularly enthused me was the fact that so many of the Chelsea side had come up through their youth system. As many as nine of their starting line-up were products of it, and I resolved that I would try to replicate that success at Aberdeen. There was already a youth coaching class at Pittodrie, and I decided it would become a much more important part of the club. But, again, that initiative was in the future.

I enjoyed my all-too-brief trip to London, especially as the Doc and I did manage 'a wee sherry' or two in between training sessions. The visit also had another benefit, as a year or so later, when Aberdeen had a much better side, I called Tommy and asked if Chelsea would make a visit to Pittodrie one of their pre-season friendlies. This was in the days when Chelsea could pick and choose who they played – they played the German national team, for instance – and they could demand top money for an appearance. The Doc consulted his chairman, a wonderful man called Joe Mears, who was the godfather of English football at that time, and they agreed to come up to Aberdeen – and we beat them 2–1! They had been doing us a big favour, and Tommy was none too pleased, I can tell you.

I left Stamford Bridge to head north to my new position on the afternoon of Wednesday, 10 March. I took the overnight sleeper to Aberdeen, going straight from the station to the stadium to begin work. I soon found out that a fairly colossal task lay before me.

There was an overwhelming lack of confidence about the place. Aberdeen had been ejected from the Scottish Cup after a replay by East Fife. They had also been humiliated 8–0 by Celtic at Parkhead – and this was before Jock Stein had taken over the Glasgow club.

Avoiding relegation was our sole aim. Between Pearson's departure and my arrival, the team had taken five points out of a possible six to make things slightly easier for me. I knew that if we could achieve safety, it would get the Aberdeen footballing public on our side. We could then rebuild the team in the close season.

I didn't have time to waste, as our first game could not have been tougher. We would be playing Rangers, then the reigning league champions, at Pittodrie. Two points from that game, or even a draw, would be a big step towards safety, but it would also be a huge blow to Rangers' chances of the title, so I expected them to go for everything – it would be one helluva game.

On that Thursday morning of my arrival at Pittodrie, one of the first people I met was the trainer, who was none other than Davie Shaw, who had once been captain of the Hibs side when I played at Easter Road. He had gone to Aberdeen as a trainer and then become manager for a short spell but was back as trainer again. His assistant was a fine lad called Teddy Scott, who over the years played a great part in helping men and boys to settle in at Pittodrie. I asked Teddy where the training gear was kept, and he replied that it was kept in the boilerhouse, where the heating system was located. In this room was a furnace which powered the stadium heating, and when I walked in and saw the state of the training gear, I ordered Teddy to open up the furnace.

'Right, Teddy,' I told him, 'throw all this in there.'

'But what will the players train in, boss?'

I got him to show me the cupboard where the playing gear was kept and told him, 'Use these.'

He looked at me as if I was daft. But I was determined to set standards right away. 'From now on, they will train with fresh gear in the morning and with fresh gear in the afternoon,' I said. This was the practice at Easter Road, and I was not going to accept second best for my new club.

Next, I checked the store of footballs. Aberdeen had just six for their entire staff. I sent somebody to Peter Craigmyle's excellent sports shop in the city to buy new training gear and enough footballs to give the players one each.

Those tactics made sure I was getting off on the right foot with the trainers. They saw immediately that there would be no messing about and that only the best would do. And hang the expense!

I took my first training session with the full-time players later in the morning, and I marched straight onto the Pittodrie pitch, though they were reluctant to do so. I think it was big Ernie Winchester who said, 'The groundsman won't like us being on here.' I blew my top, suggesting we could always get another groundsman, but we were all stuffed if we got relegated – though my language may have been a bit more basic than that. The players, too, were getting the message that things were going to be different.

Like many clubs, Aberdeen had a fair sprinkling of part-time players, mostly the young apprentices, so I ordered every one of these to attend in the evening and organised a practice match along with the full-timers. It was immediately clear to me that I had a problem on my hands. Some of them just were not good enough to be professional footballers, and in my judgement they would never make the grade. Others were unfit or did not have a clue about playing in a team, while others still just did not have the attitude I was looking for.

In all, there was a staff of about 40 players, and in the next few days I looked at every one of them. I had to assess which of

The earliest picture of me in football gear, with the Carronshore Primary School team which won the Henderson Cup in 1936. I am second from right in the front row, behind the Cup.

With the Falkirk and District Schools team. I am fourth from right in the front row, with Davie Lapsley, later of St Mirren, second from right. George Young, later of Rangers and Scotland, is fifth from the right in the middle row, wearing his schoolboy international cap, while Bobby Brown, who both played for and managed Scotland, is third from left in the middle.

Left: Having a lark in the Navy: with some friends from HMS *Bulldog*.

Below: The unstoppable Hibs team of the post-war era. I am seated on the ground on the right, in front of Willie Ormond.

A fine figure of a man – and, honestly, that really is lemonade.

Lying down on the job: my famous goal against Dundee in 1947.

Shaking hands with Harry Haddock of Clyde before the
Scottish Cup final of 1958, as referee Jack Mowat looks on.

With the Scotland World Cup squad of 1958, during training at Turnberry.

We had great encouragement from the locals in Sweden.

At home with Carol and a young Valerie.

The fabulous Baker boy: giving Joe Baker a lift during training.

The most powerful man in the world and
President Lyndon Baines Johnson.

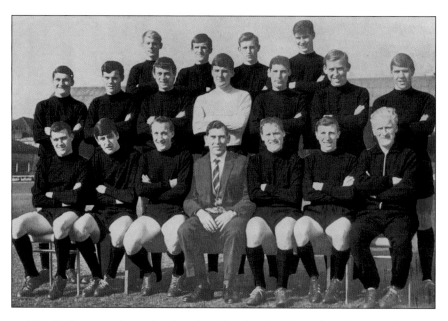

The Reds: an early outing for the all-red strip I introduced at Aberdeen.

Well done, lads! Greeting Joe Harper and Jim Forrest at
the end of the 1970 Scottish Cup final.

Holding the Scottish Cup with Martin Buchan.

Giving Arthur Duncan of Hibs a bit of 'inspiration' before extra time in the 1972 Drybrough Cup final. It worked, as he scored our fifth and final goal in that 5–3 win over Celtic.

Me with the League Cup in 1973. Spot the champagne stains on my suit.

With Alan Gordon. Yes, his brains really were in his head.

With Martin Buchan on one of Ian Taylor's golf days.

Capped at last! Wearing the Scotland cap I received at Hampden in 2006. (Courtesy of Frances Anderson)

them were needed to achieve the main aim of survival in the First Division and also decide which of the youngsters could make a go of it in the future. In a very short space of time, I concluded that the club could do without several players, and I gave them all free transfers, meaning they could all leave immediately and sign for another club without Aberdeen receiving any cash. If they found a new club, they would be able to negotiate their own signing-on fee as well, so for some of them it was not as if they were facing the dole right away.

In those days, things were so much easier when it came to getting rid of a player. There was no messing about with contracts or agents. I would just ask the club secretary to make their wages up with what they were due, then put their P45 certificate in the envelope alongside the cash. It was straightforward and simple, and you just would not get away with it nowadays.

Throughout my career as a manager, whenever possible I always told the players myself, face to face, that they no longer had a job with the club. It was always hardest with the youths. It was not a pleasant task to tell young lads that you did not think they were up to scratch and that they would have to move on. Most of them were trying to make a career in football and to be told they were surplus to requirements was always a bitter blow. But it had to be done for the sake of the club, and I did not shirk from the task, especially in those early days at Aberdeen.

There were times when I had to take the same action with established professionals. One of the first people to go out of the door was a former Rangers player called Bobby Hume. Having played at Ibrox, he had an air about him – a big-time Charlie, or so he thought. He had played 13 games for Aberdeen that season, and it was to prove unlucky for him.

In one of my first training sessions, I asked Hume to do something which I knew was simplicity itself for a player of his quality and experience. I asked him to play the ball forward into a space for a colleague to run onto, but he was pig-headed and deliberately miscued the pass. I asked him to do the same again, but again he laid the pass off skew-whiff. When he did it a third time, I knew exactly what he was doing: showing me that he would not kowtow and that he thought he knew more about football than me.

Big mistake. This was a challenge to my authority in front of the other players, including young apprentices, and I knew I had to act because if you let such behaviour go, it becomes a cancer in a squad, and eventually everyone thinks they can defy the manager's authority.

I told him to report for training the following morning but to come and see me at the club office first. When he arrived at the front door, I intercepted Hume and handed him an envelope with his wages and P45 already made up.

'You know what that is?' I said loudly.

He nodded dumbly in reply.

'Right then,' I said, 'f*** off out of here and don't ever come back again.'

He turned and left, and I never saw Hume again. I know from speaking to his friend Eddie Thompson, chairman of Dundee United, that Bobby Hume was a decent enough fellow. I'm sure he regretted his mistake, but there could be no return for him. He moved to South Africa, where, tragically, he was shot and murdered in a robbery of a shop he owned.

I had a good idea that the players would have heard me sacking Hume in what I admit was a peremptory fashion. And, yes, I did set out to make an example of him. From early in my time at Aberdeen, I was determined to lay down the law and dictate the way forward. There would be discipline and hard work, and I promised the players that if they accepted my way of doing things they would see the rewards. Hume was just one of the people who couldn't see things my way, so he had to go. It was tough, but that was football in those days. And it worked. From that day until I left Pittodrie I never experienced anything of that sort again.

My reputation as a disciplinarian – thoroughly deserved, even though I say so myself – stems from those early days at Aberdeen, but in truth, as trainer at Hibs and manager at Queen's Park, I had usually taken a firm approach to keeping players in line. I had learned discipline in the Navy, after all. It was just that, at first, Aberdeen needed more of the stick than the carrot.

After all the departures, I was left with the semblance of a team. At first, the goalie was a big fellow called John Ogston, who was known as 'Tubby' – when I heard that nickname I knew exactly what that signified. David Bennett was the right-back, and the experienced Ally Shewan was left-back. Ian Burns was at right-half, and at centre-half was either John McCormick or a giant of a lad called Doug Coutts, 6 ft plus, while Dave Smith was at left-half. At outside-right, we had Billy Little; Leif Mortensen was at outside-left, while the front three were usually Jorgen Ravn, Ernie Winchester and Don Kerrigan.

I soon made changes, but only minimal ones, bringing in Tony Fraser on the right wing and moving Billy Little to inside-right. Mortensen, Ravn and Jens Petersen were three Scandinavian imports signed by Tommy Pearson, and two of them had a good, professional attitude, which Mortensen and a few others in the squad did not share. After one game near the start of my time at Aberdeen, when Mortensen came off at the end I pulled him aside and showed him that there was no mud on his shorts, while everybody else was covered in the stuff. 'How do you explain that?' I asked. He just shrugged, and that was the beginning of the end for him. Mortensen was on his way by the summer of the following season, and sadly he took Ravn with him. Jens Petersen, thankfully, stayed and is still recalled fondly by fans.

But by and large, I had to work with the players Tommy Pearson left me. I could see at once that they were used to playing in a particular pattern, and I realised that I didn't have time to change their style; I couldn't beat them so I joined them. But what I did do, from day one, was emphasise that their work rate would have to improve considerably.

In the second training session, I called all the players together and gave them the gospel according to Turnbull. I did not have coaching badges at that time, and I had only managed one club, but I told them that I had played the game a long time and had played with and against the best players in the world. 'So don't try and mess me about,' was my parting shot. It didn't go down well with some of the squad. 'Who does he think he is?' was their attitude. But I had no time to quibble. We were 24 hours away from my first match in charge, and I was not in a mood to argue, as I knew I had to get the best out of them if we were to survive in the top division.

In that first match against Rangers, I was determined that they would give their all and more. I let them know in no uncertain terms what I expected. I was also very gratified that a crowd of 25,000 turned up to see the match, the highest attendance for a League match that season. There was a terrific atmosphere inside Pittodrie. The match was hard fought, as expected, and it all passed in a bit of a blur, to be honest. Rangers had their chances, but goals from Don Kerrigan and Ernie Winchester gave us a 2–0 victory.

I was on my way, with a good start, and, after a draw away to Morton, we thumped fellow strugglers Airdrieonians 5–2, with Ernie Winchester grabbing the club's only hat-trick of the season. I could breathe more easily, as survival was all but assured, and indeed we notched up a couple more victories – at home against Dundee United and Airdrie – eventually finishing 12th of 18, Airdrie and Third Lanark being the relegated sides. Kilmarnock (yes, you read that correctly) won the League on the final day, beating Hearts on goal average, both sides having 50 points. Dunfermline were third, a point behind the top two, with Hibs in fourth. Rangers and Celtic finished fifth and eighth respectively – no Old Firm domination that year.

Our First Division status had been preserved, and I felt I had changed attitudes at Pittodrie in a short space of time. But I was also determined to change the way Aberdeen worked from top to bottom, and the scouting system seemed to me to be pretty poor. Our chief scout was Bobby Calder, who was rightly a legend in scouting circles. He had been a top-class referee and had managed Dunfermline. A former railwayman, he spent countless hours searching for the best talent Glasgow and district could produce. He also had his henchmen everywhere, tipping him off about potential talent. Bobby was going to be the key man in the new scouting system I was about to introduce. I wanted the best of talent to come to Aberdeen, and Bobby was the man to find it. Rangers had tried to poach Bobby, but he had given his word to Aberdeen and kept it. Over the decades, he found talents such as Ian MacFarlane, Charlie Cooke, Jim Smith, Willie Young and many, many more. Two he found for me would make the grade at the highest level – Tommy Craig and Arthur Graham. But more of them later.

The way we worked together was simple. If I heard of a player or saw someone I liked the look of, I would ask Bobby to watch him play, and vice versa. If the two of us agreed, we would try to sign the player. Many of them were teenagers, and it was here that the personal approach invariably paid off.

Now, I know that over the years I developed a reputation as a tough taskmaster with a fierce air about me, but when dealing with the parents of a potential signing, I was charm personified. I would address my remarks mostly to the mother, since I had long since worked out that if a woman didn't want her teenaged son to leave home, he would not be leaving. I would say to her, 'If your laddie goes off the rails, it will not be him that's to blame, it'll be me, because I am responsible to you for his well-being. I will be doing for him what I think you would be doing.' I meant every word, too.

One of the innovations we introduced was a forerunner of the summer football academies which are commonplace nowadays. With Bobby's men working overtime, we found just about every youngster in the Central Belt worth a look at and brought 24 or 25 of them by train to Aberdeen. A local hotelier, a Mr Esslemont, had a huge, barn-like complex to the rear of his hotel, and we accommodated the lads there on mattresses on the floor. They were getting well fed and trained at Pittodrie, so they didn't mind roughing it. They got to mix with senior players and were given tuition they had never had before, so they had a whale of a time, especially when I went along at the weekend and gave them all a five-pound note. For some of the boys from Glasgow, it was the most money they had ever had in their hand at once. Most major clubs now run summer schools for budding young footballers, but we were among the first to do so, and we did find some fine players over the years, especially from Glasgow.

I always preferred the Glasgow boys. They were usually sharper than the rest, because the environment in which they were brought up meant they learned a lot about life early on – when they crossed a road, they crossed it quick. Lads from country towns took a bit longer to adjust.

We signed a lot of youngsters in my years at Aberdeen and had to find digs for them all. It helped that the city had a host of landladies who lived near Pittodrie, all of whom took personal pride in looking after the young lads. Not once did I ever have a landlady come to me and say that one of their lodgers had stepped out of line.

In my first few weeks at Aberdeen, I myself was fortunate to find a good lodging in a hotel called the Gushet Neuk, which was comfortable and well run. It was near the stadium, and I could get peace and quiet to concentrate on the task ahead, which was nothing more nor less than the rebuilding of a football club which had fallen on hard times. Only later did I reflect on what a huge task I had taken on, because at the time I was too engrossed in every minute detail of the job in hand.

Avoiding relegation had given me the time I needed, and I knew I had the fans behind me. They had drifted away, but now they were interested again, though it would be some time before attendances – then down to an average of 7,000 to 8,000 – rose to five figures regularly again.

There had been constant vituperation in the local papers, the *Aberdeen Press and Journal* (known in the area as the *P&J*) and the *Evening Express*, and it had become so bad that the directors stopped travelling to away matches for fear of a press-inspired fans' revolt. Only Douglas Philip would come on the bus, which was fine by me, as I always got on well with him.

I remember telling him that the thing which was standing me in good stead even at that perilous time was the experience I had gained at Hibs. I had learned from Harry Swan, Willie McCartney and Hugh Shaw how a club should be properly run. I had made Hibs my benchmark, and I was sure that if I could re-create at Pittodrie the same atmosphere and commitment that I had seen at Easter Road, then Aberdeen would prosper again. And I did achieve my aim, to everybody's surprise – except, of course, my own.

By the end of that first portion of a season in charge I had freed or sold 17 players, of whom probably the best known was Don Kerrigan, who was joint top scorer in season 1964–65. I had not fancied him as a player when I arrived at Pittodrie. I was told he was a guitarist. 'I hope he's a better guitar player than he is a footballer,' I recall saying. He further blotted his copybook in one match in which he played a long pass back straight from the kick-off when it would have been easier to go forward. That was an attitude I did not like, so I let him go in a swap deal for Tom White of Hearts, which was a good piece of business for me.

By the start of pre-season training, I was confident that I was building the team along the right lines, but there was still a shortage of experience. Remedying that meant paying decent money, something the Aberdeen board were reluctant to do, as the club's finances were in poor condition. But I knew what needed to be done, and I was determined to get my way, even if it meant putting my head on the block.

Over that summer of 1965, I had three main tasks in mind for the club, though the most important personal job was quickly accomplished when Carol, Valerie and I moved into a rented house near the ground.

My first task was to get in the players I thought we needed for the new season ahead; the second was to impose more disciplined methods; and the third was to try to build some club spirit at a place where it had been at a premium in previous years. One point I had learned in the Navy was that you could be very good at your job, but if you didn't all work together and get on with each other as best you could, well, you could end up with a very unhappy ship.

It really was a root-and-branch rebuilding of the club. In fact, I would say I started virtually from scratch, with just a few good professionals in the squad and on the staff to help me.

I thought signing players would be straightforward enough; that was my first mistake. I knew that we would be bringing on youngsters and that to do that we needed experienced professionals to show them the ropes. Having cut the wage bill so spectacularly with those 17 departures, I supposed there was a bit of money to spend. But I was told by the board there was nothing extra to spend on transfers, as the club's bank accounts were bare. I didn't really believe that. In any case, I persuaded them to allow me to bring in Jimmy Wilson from Greenock Morton.

But then came the signing which almost ended my Aberdeen career before it had started. It happened just a few weeks into the season. Dunfermline Athletic had a player I had always admired, Harry Melrose. Now, Harry was an inside-forward with a good goal-scoring record, and, just as importantly, he was a clean-living model professional whom I was sure would be a good example to the youngsters. He was married with two children, and that meant we could offer him one of the houses which the club owned or leased. Harry was also well respected within football generally, so I knew he would be an asset to the club. But signing him caused my first real confrontation with the board.

I went to see chairman Forbes and told him that I wanted to sign Harry. He asked me, 'What do you want him for?' and I explained that we needed such men to help bring on the youngsters. But approval came there none . . .

It was Douglas Philip who suggested my next move. On the way home from a match which we had lost, with none of the rest of the board present, as usual, he said, 'There's something bothering you, Mr Manager.' I told him my plan, and he replied that if I really wanted Melrose, I should call an emergency board meeting the following day. 'Go home tonight and get on the phone to the chairman and vice-chairman, and call the meeting for 11.30 a.m. tomorrow at Pittodrie. I'll see you there.'

I went home from the stadium and told Valerie that the phone would ring in five or ten minutes' time and that she was to answer it. By that time, I could already tell the chairman's habits. He would pop into Pittodrie at the same time after each match, and if I wasn't there, he would call me at home. I just knew he was going to call, and, sure enough, five minutes after I was in the door, Valerie was answering the phone to Charlie Forbes. Her doing so gave me enough time to gather my thoughts and steel myself for what I knew would be an unpleasant conversation.

'Not so good today,' he said, and I could not disagree.

I then asked him to be at Pittodrie at 11 a.m. the following morning.

'What for?' he asked. 'I'm playing golf at that time.' He was a member at the prestigious Royal Aberdeen club, where tee-off times were hard to come by, but I needed to press my point.

'I want an emergency board meeting at that time,' I said. 'And if you and the board are not there, you can get a new manager.'

I put the phone down on him, then called vice-chairman Dick Donald at his country retreat outside Aberdeen. I made the same request, and he tried to make his excuses, so I gave him the same ultimatum: 'Be there or I'm away.' The other director, John Duncan, was quite happy to attend.

I didn't sleep well, but I was determined to force the issue, to resolve it once and for all. I went to Pittodrie in plenty time for eleven and then waited a bit before marching along to the boardroom. Sure enough, the board were all there.

This time, I explained at length what was needed to get Aberdeen FC out of the mire. 'If you want this ship back on an even keel, then you'll have to realise it's a huge task. You will have to go along with my plan, and that means giving me money to sign Harry Melrose.' I then clearly implied that if I didn't get the cash, I would be on my way.

I should explain at this point that the sum involved was just £4,000 – less than a day's wages for a modern star like Rio Ferdinand. In view of the sums that were being bandied about for players even back then in 1965, it was relatively small beer.

The directors were clearly taken aback, but since I had enjoyed such a good start with the club and had the backing of the fans, they knew they could not risk losing me. I got my money, and the real business of restructuring Aberdeen was under way.

I had won one battle, but in a sense I had won the war, too. For though we would all have to work like Trojans and it would take longer than I thought, nothing would ever be the same again at Pittodrie. I would make sure of that!

11

How to Build a Football Club
in Several Uneasy Lessons

In my first encounter with directors who might have opposed me, I had won hands down. In modern parlance, I had said it was 'my way or the highway', and I meant it. I knew I had plenty to give Aberdeen, but I could not succeed with directors' shackles round me and with no access to some of the money that I knew the club had tucked away, not least because I had freed 17 players.

Signings went easily after that meeting. Tommy McMillan was brought in from Neilston Juniors to be centre-half after Bobby Calder spotted him, and, from Queen's Park, I cajoled Davie Millar and Robert Clark into turning full-time professional and joining their old boss at Pittodrie.

It was at Queen's Park that I first implemented a rule which I also enforced at Aberdeen and Hibs. When I arrived at Hampden, I found they only had one or two balls for training, so I insisted that each player be given a ball; after all, a bricklayer doesn't learn to build walls without using bricks and mortar. This made an impression on young Robert Clark in particular, and he happily followed me to Aberdeen, where he quickly displaced Tubby Ogston, whom I later sold to Bill Shankly at Liverpool for £12,000. Shanks probably owed me a favour, as I had earlier taken young George Scott off his hands. An Aberdonian 'loon', George had been homesick at Liverpool and was happy to move back north, though, sadly, he picked up a terrible knee injury soon afterwards and never played for us again.

The sale of Ogston was a good bit of business for me, if not for Bill Shankly. He never got a first-team game for Liverpool. I had not taken to the goalie, especially as he seemed less than committed to the regime I had introduced. I remember one training session during which he was tiring fast when he suddenly said, 'That's enough for me.' I gave him the verbals. 'Who's the boss around here?' I shouted. 'I'll tell you when you've had enough.'

I told him that he 'had had enough' in no uncertain terms after he gave me a really solid reason to transfer him. I found out that a local newspaperman, Ronald Main, was getting regular briefings from someone inside the first-team squad. I discovered this while reading the newspaper in the toilet of Aboyne Golf Club, where I had taken the squad on an outing. It was very upsetting to be on 'the throne' reading an extremely accurate account of some new systems I had been trying at recent training sessions. You could have heard my roars of anger back in Aberdeen, but I kept my temper in check until the day out was over.

As soon as I could, I ordered all the players back to Pittodrie, where I locked them in the dressing-room and let rip. 'You'll be wondering what's going on and why you are all here,' I said. 'Well, there's a rat in here and I'm going to find him, and when I do, he's finished here.' Sure enough, it was the goalkeeper, and Ogston's days at Aberdeen were numbered from that instant. It may have seemed harmless, but what he did was a form of industrial espionage, giving away things that were secret to the squad and maybe creating an advantage for our opponents. It was also a breach of the discipline I was trying to instil in the players, so he had to go.

In any case, Robert Clark would have kept the gloves permanently, so impressive was his start at Pittodrie. I had been so determined to sign Robert that, even though it meant a lot of travel back and forth to Glasgow for him, I allowed this clever young man to carry on his studies in physical education at Jordanhill College, effectively making him a part-time professional during term time. I knew such a grounding would stand him in good stead in later life, though it did cause a problem, which I'll explain later.

Robert came from good footballing stock, his father being a director of Clyde, and he had made such an impression at Queen's Park that he could have had his pick of senior clubs – Rangers, Chelsea and Tottenham Hotspur were all after his signature – but he opted to follow me to Pittodrie, and we were both grateful for that in the long run. He would go on to set a British record for games without losing a goal and would break the Aberdeen record for Scottish caps. He later became a distinguished coach in places as far apart as the USA and New Zealand, where he coached the national team. He keeps in touch and very kindly always acknowledges that I was his best manager; of course, I would not disagree!

Davie Millar did not have the kind of career I thought he would have, for various reasons, principally because he had a poor start in the first team and the fans didn't take to him. Sadly, if that happens, you do not often last long at a club.

But we gave Davie and Robert every opportunity, and indeed I actually brought them to live with Carol, Valerie and me in our rented house in order to make them feel as at home as possible. They just about ate us out of house and home, and I had a renewed appreciation for the work landladies did for the club.

Two other youngsters who joined the club during that period became major stars for Aberdeen. Jimmy Smith and Tommy Craig joined at about the same time, both the products of Bobby Calder's researches in Glasgow.

Jimmy Smith was a fine boy from Glasgow, who, despite being tall for his age, had developed tremendous footwork and ball control. His nickname was 'Jinky', and I suspect only the other Jinky – the late, great Jimmy Johnstone of Celtic and Scotland – matched or bettered the close control of our Jim. Bobby Calder later signed up his brother Joe, who would also play for Aberdeen.

Tommy Craig was another Glasgow lad, short of stature and with a shock of reddish hair, who had a good left foot. Later, we would sign his brother John, and the entire Craig family then moved to Aberdeen – mum, dad and sister too. They were a lovely family, and Tommy became one of my favourite players.

I have had no greater reward in football than seeing a youngster I have trained go on to make a successful career in the game, and Tommy is a prime example, as he had a long and varied career before moving into coaching. When he arrived at Pittodrie, he was a bundle of raw talent, but I could see right away he was special. I got to work on him, forcing him to practise his skills and positioning, and he was such a good learner and had such good basic ability that within a short space of time he was knocking on the door of the first team.

The squad I wanted to build was coming together nicely, with a mixture of older professionals and exciting young talent, and, having changed the training system to my satisfaction, with a lot of emphasis on fitness and ball work, I was full of anticipation for season 1965–66.

The second task was to sort out the discipline at Pittodrie. Imposing discipline was not hard for me to do, as I was used to it myself from my Royal Navy days. I used to say to the players that discipline was the key to everything. 'If there had been no discipline in the Navy, Air Force and Army, you would all be speaking German today' was one of my regular lines. At the start of pre-season training, I called the entire playing staff together for a final warning: 'There is going to be discipline here, and those of you who are not prepared to knuckle down and work hard will be shown the door.' And by now, they knew I meant every single word . . .

Some pundits and footballers have reported that I got my way by ranting and raving at players. Sure, there were times when I shouted at players, and over the years I did grab a couple of them by the scruff of the neck – you may sense I'm using a euphemism there – but any dressing-down was given behind closed doors. Nobody outside those four walls needed to know what went on between me and a player.

Greater emphasis on discipline went hand in hand with better training. I had started changing the training routines almost as soon as I arrived, and during pre-season training, I stepped up the fitness work and introduced much more practice with the ball. In essence, what I did was make them train hard for fitness and then do ball work as their muscles were recovering. With alterations and additions inspired by my coaching courses, that simple format was maintained ever afterwards.

It was hard work, but we did have some laughs. I remember one occasion during my time at Pittodrie when we were working on some routines at Linksfield training ground. I had made it a cardinal rule that the training ground was off limits to all personnel other than players and coaches, but I didn't account for dogs. All of a sudden, a white French poodle appeared on the pitch. Now, the dog couldn't help itself and ran around barking and yelping. I was incensed, and if I had caught the mutt, I would have kicked it where the sun doesn't shine. Cursing at it to get off the pitch, I suddenly heard a voice calling, 'Fifi! Fifi!'

'FIFI?' I roared. 'I'll give it f***ing Fifi! If I get that dog it's mincemeat!'

It turned out that the poodle belonged to one of the newer directors, Dick Spain, and was used to being allowed to run free. Fifi the poodle was escorted off and never reappeared at training again – lucky for it.

From the start, because they were professionals and had to do what I told them, most players buckled down and responded to my urgings. The young ones in particular were loving it and would turn up early for training. They enjoyed the tuition they were getting from me, and I suspect that was the first formal skills coaching many of them had received since their schooldays.

I was able to put into practice the theories I had developed at Hibs and Queen's Park. I wanted the team to get forward quickly, and I emphasised that players should pass the ball ahead of their colleagues. Later in my time at Aberdeen, I brought in a system in which the defence was to press up the field and every player was to give their opponent no time on the ball. Some pundits called this 'the offside trap', but I always disagreed. I remember having a heated discussion with Bill Shankly after the 1970 Scottish Cup final when he said we had tried to play an offside trap, but I flatly denied it. To try to predict that someone will be caught offside is always dangerous; what we did practise was moving the ball as quickly as possible from defence into attack, changing wings if necessary. It was not rocket science, just the application of the many lessons I had learned in my years at Hibs, where we hustled our opposite numbers all the time. And if they were caught offside, that was their fault.

Within weeks, the improvement in fitness and teamwork was visible, though it was very hard going for all of us at times. Personally, I don't think there was a harder-working manager in Britain at the time. I worked round the clock, from early in the morning to last thing at night. I quite literally used to be the last man out, locking up the stadium when everybody else had gone. I would work late into the evening on programmes for training and pre-match activities, and I would go into the tiniest detail because I knew that attention to detail would be the key to success. Then I would go round the place, turning off the lights and locking all the doors before turning the key in the main door and heading home.

It was tiring, occasionally exhausting, work but I loved it. I loved the job and the whole idea of being in charge and putting my stamp on the club. The only sad aspect of my time at Aberdeen, I now realise, is that I didn't see as much of Carol and Valerie as I should have, but I can only plead that I became totally involved in the job.

It was a job I was sure I could do well. I never suffered a moment of self-doubt, because I felt that each individual was given a talent of some sort, and, while I had obviously been given some gifts as a footballer, from the moment I began coaching, I knew this was the role I was born for. I just took to it naturally, though obviously I had listened and learned a lot as a player. Now here I was, managing a prestigious club, and, while I still had things to learn, I knew I could get the club where I wanted it to go as long as everybody worked hard.

As well as hard work, I was determined there was going to be fun as well. From my background – in Carronshore's close-knit community, in the Navy and at Hibs – I had learned the importance of working together for the common good. I felt strongly that a family atmosphere at a club was conducive to building good relationships on the pitch. After all, if you actually care for your colleagues, you are more likely to work with them and for them; whereas if you can't stand them, you won't be motivated to lift a leg for the team. Even the most professional of professional footballers works better when he is genuinely a member of a team rather than an individual among other individuals.

There are many ways of building team spirit and a family atmosphere. Remembering many happy nights at Hibs, I plumped for the idea of a club dance involving players, staff and their partners. The notion seemed alien to those in charge, but I was determined to see it happen, though it took me a season to get my way. By that time, Harry Melrose was captain, and I took him aside and said, 'Harry, you're my right-hand man, and I want you to organise this dance. Get all the wives and girlfriends in, and let's have a hooley.' The directors turned up their noses at first, but Harry did a great job, and I'm glad to say the evening later that season was a terrific success. I dare say even some of the board enjoyed it.

I knew from the outset it would take time to build a family atmosphere and real club spirit at Pittodrie, and, as I had guessed that he was the real power in the club, I had already deduced that vice-chairman Dick Donald would be the key director in the rebuilding process in the years ahead.

His family held the largest shareholding and were wealthy from their various businesses, though Dick drove an ordinary enough Mercedes and was never, ever flashy about his riches. I felt that Charlie Forbes was their 'placeman' and that Dick would eventually take over as chairman. Forbes was a perfectly pleasant, well-spoken and well-educated man, but he was not always easy to get on with; occasionally I felt he talked down to me, like a headmaster – not surprising, as he was indeed a head teacher in the city. I used to get annoyed with the way he talked to me, and on occasion I would pull him up. 'I'm no' one of your pupils,' I would say, 'I'm the 40-odd-year-old guy that's managing your club!' He would also expect things to be done for him, as in school where his word was law, and I had to point out to him that running a football club was different from running a school and that the manager was the most important person in the club. But for the most part we got along in perfectly civil fashion, though I suspect he didn't always see it that way!

Dick Donald did eventually take the chairman's seat, and he would become a legend at Aberdeen; but, being frank, Dick wasn't always the wise leader he turned into. Now, I'm not claiming any credit for Dick's achievements, but I do like to think I taught him a thing or two, just as I learned from him.

He was a jovial character, perpetually whistling away to himself, and you could tell he had a background in show business, as he knew all the best tunes. Like Charlie Forbes, he was a former Aberdeen player. He had been a professional in the '30s and '40s, and had played both for Aberdeen and briefly at Dunfermline Athletic. Dick had been no more than a moderately good player, but off the field he was a spectacular success as a businessman, and he and his family owned theatres, cinemas, a hotel and a car sales firm. Dick became a director in 1949, and by the time I came to know him, the Donald family was so successful that he was preparing to spend more and more time on the club which he undoubtedly loved.

I'm glad to say that Dick saw eye to eye with me on the need to rebuild Aberdeen as a 'family', a club which developed its own talent and looked after it, and which enjoyed a special relationship with its fans. It was his background in the entertainment business that led Dick to promote the idea that fans wanted to watch games in comfort. We could do nothing about the Aberdonian weather, but Dick didn't see why the fans should suffer, and that is largely why the enclosure was converted to a stand in 1968 and Pittodrie went on to become the first all-seated, all-covered senior football stadium in Britain. The massive stand at the Beach End at Pittodrie is named after Dick, and a fitting tribute it is, too.

At first, I got on better with Doug Philip and John Duncan than with Charlie Forbes and Dick Donald. Perhaps I rubbed them up the wrong way, as I could be quite fierce in my pursuit of success – and that was the thing that remained to be achieved for Aberdeen. We needed solid progress, and that meant higher League placings and trophies. I now realise that I was determined nothing would get in my way. Hopefully, I didn't offend too many people in that quest for success, but I won't apologise for my actions, as Aberdeen FC needed to be shaken up.

Which, unfortunately, is what happened early in season 1965–66. We had made a reasonable start, beating Rangers 2–1 in August in the sectional games of the Scottish League Cup. But in September, we went to Ibrox and were beaten 4–0, and three weeks later, we visited Parkhead and were trounced 7–1, with big John Hughes running riot for the team that Jock Stein was starting to build. It was a humiliating result, yet I used it to our advantage, basically telling the board and the players that we now knew the size of our task, and we had all better get working.

The players responded, and we beat St Mirren at the start of a ten-match unbeaten run which hauled us well up the League table and ensured that there would certainly not be any talk of relegation that season.

But I was concerned about our form away from home. For nearly four months, from the end of November to 21 March, we did not win a single League match away from Pittodrie. We had also gone out of the League Cup at the qualifying stages after losses at Tynecastle and Ibrox. Conversely, we were making Pittodrie a very difficult place to visit, as it had been during my playing days, and I particularly recall beating Jock Stein's new Celtic.

I had played against Jock in the '50s, and he was a big awkward sod who was, frankly, a bit slow. But my first serious confrontation with Jock Stein as a manager almost ended in a boxing match. In what was for both of us our first full season in charge of our respective clubs, his Celtic side were flying high when they came to Pittodrie on 15 January 1966. We were coming off the back of four straight League defeats, and they had beaten us 7–1 earlier in the season, but we raised our game magnificently that day and ran out 3–1 winners, with goals from Billy Little, Ernie Winchester and Jorgen Ravn, the latter playing particularly well. Big Jock was livid at the end, and I anticipated there would be fun and games during the small talk between us afterwards.

As I made my way towards the dressing-room, I could hear Jock trying to keep up behind me. Jock had a distinctive way of walking, thanks to a limp from the ankle injury which finished his career, and I could hear him approaching, so I slowed down to let him catch up. He was not in a good mood, and his first remark was unforgivable. 'Aye,' he growled, 'if we had been wearing blue jerseys the day you wouldn't have played so hard.' I stopped myself from clocking him and hit back verbally: 'Come off it, Jock, you know me. And I know what you're up to. You can say that to some lesser mortal, but it will not influence me one bit!' And it did not – Celtic or Rangers, it didn't bother me which one we beat!

That exchange was Jock up to his psychological tricks, at which he was a master. But as the only manager to beat his great Celtic side in four cup finals with two different teams, I think I gave as good as I got. Over the years, we certainly developed a very warm respect for each other, so much so that when he became Scotland manager, he got me to come and help him at the start with the coaching of our national squads, which of course I was delighted to do.

His sudden death in Cardiff in 1985 in the minutes after a World Cup qualifying match shocked me as it did everyone in football. We were roughly the same age, and here am I some 21 years later remembering the jousts we had. Aye, we had our tussles, but we each appreciated what the other tried to do with our respective teams: play good attacking football.

That victory over Celtic was some recompense for the hiding they had given us earlier in the season, but it did not stop Celtic from going on to win the championship by two points from Rangers, while we finished eighth, which was respectable enough, though, frankly, I was disappointed overall.

However, we did embark on a good run in the Scottish Cup, which included a 5–0 drubbing of Dundee United. The semi-final was against Rangers, and after a 0–0 draw we suffered the heartbreak of losing by the odd goal in three in the replay. Missing out on a final was tough to bear, but I told the players that their improvement had been consistently demonstrated in season 1965–66 and that it would not be long before the team was challenging for honours.

Certain players had shown such improvement that they became targets for bigger clubs. Dave Smith became the first player from Aberdeen to be capped in six years when he played for Scotland against Holland at the end of the season. But he was already bound for Rangers, and the Aberdeen fans were not best pleased at losing such a fine and influential player. I was not too concerned, though, as I knew we had a couple of promising youngsters on our books. Also, I had already identified a possible replacement elsewhere, and that was Francis Munro.

I had spotted him as a youngster playing with the Scottish international youth team that I had briefly coached and had waited to see him make his breakthrough with Dundee United. I would check their team lines to see if their then manager Jerry Kerr was giving Munro a run in the team, but I rarely saw his name, and I wondered what was wrong.

One of my friends in the press was Tommy Gallagher of the *Dundee Courier*. I called him and asked about Munro, and he told me that Munro was not getting on with his manager. I took the plunge and called Jerry Kerr direct.

'I was just wondering about Francis Munro, Jerry, as I had him with me in the youth team.'

Jerry replied that Francis was not yet fulfilling his promise, and, suspecting there was more to that remark than met the ear, I left things a few weeks and made some discreet enquiries. It turned out that there had been some family difficulties, so I twisted Jerry Kerr's arm and said, 'Let me talk to him.'

I could see immediately that I was dealing with an unhappy young man, who was also carrying some excess weight. But I was sure that I could get the best out of this skilful footballer, so I persuaded the board to stump up £12,000 for him and talked Francis into coming to Pittodrie.

'You're a big lad, but you're carrying too much weight, son. I'll get that off you, and I know you can play, so come and join

Aberdeen, because we're going places,' I told him. How could he turn down such an approach?

I made sure he went into good digs with a caring landlady and then got to work on his weight problem. The excess flab did not last long, especially after I gave him the 'hothouse' treatment. Poor Francis would spend hours in the stadium's boiler room wreathed in tracksuit and jerseys, until he had lost sufficient weight to allow him to take a full part in training. And to encourage Francis, I joined him in the hothouse – I was soon wasting away to a shadow. I also enrolled Francis with a local fitness trainer, and as he got fitter, it was gratifying to see this young man blossom as a footballer. Indeed, I would say that once he gained full fitness, he was possibly the best all-round player I ever worked with.

Another lad I signed at that time was Davie Johnston. He was another hugely talented player, but, sadly, he never hit the heights. He was a country lad, never happier than when he was playing for his local Highland League side, Nairn County, for whom he had scored a league record of 72 goals in a season. He worked in a smelly laundry before moving to Edinburgh and Hearts, but he got homesick and went back to the laundry and his local club. I knew that Tommy Walker, then manager of Hearts, had let him go on condition that he did not sign for another senior team, but I called Tommy and cajoled him into relaxing that stipulation.

Everyone at the club did their best to help Davie settle in, and for a couple of seasons he did his best. At times he reminded me of a young Bobby Charlton, as he was two-footed, had a terrific shot, was great in the air and could send passes 30 or 40 yards from wing to wing. We tried settling him with his wife near other players, and Ally Shewan became his great friend and confidant. But nothing could bring Davie out of his shell. When I met Ally last year in Aberdeen, we talked about Davie, and he told me how he had tried and tried to get Davie to be more confident as a player.

A gentle boy, sadly he never could overcome what I think was basically shyness, and he only lasted three seasons with us. If he had possessed just a bit more self-belief, he could have been one of the greatest of Dons, but at least we did see some periods when he played to his potential. Davie spent his latter days quietly in Auldearn, where he died tragically young in 2004 after a long and brave battle with cancer.

By the start of season 1966–67, we had lost two of our Scandinavian contingent, Jorgen Ravn and Leif Mortensen. More significantly for Aberdeen's future, we had already identified Jim Hermiston, whom I'd signed from Bonnyrigg Rose juniors, as a future first-team player, though I felt he needed a long run in the reserves to prepare him for the top level. By contrast, Jimmy Smith was ready to make his step up, and he was joined by Martin Buchan.

I have no words of praise high enough for this wonderful footballer and fine human being. To this day, some 35 years after I last worked with him, Martin still keeps in touch and goes out of his way to visit me whenever he is north of the border. But he was always like that – a decent and honourable lad, whose qualities of selflessness and commitment shone through from the start.

The son of a former Aberdeen player, it was probably his destiny to play for the club. When I brought him to Aberdeen, he was playing for local juvenile side Banks o' Dee, where I watched him perform more than creditably. He was very clever educationally speaking, well dressed, well mannered and well spoken, and seemed destined to go to college or university. He was only 16, but I could not delay, and I called at his house to ask him to try full-time football for a few months; if he didn't like it, then he could always carry on with his education.

He decided to come with me to Pittodrie, and it was soon clear to me that this was a very special youngster. He had a highly astute football brain and was a natural leader, with a steeliness about him. He spoke his mind, yes, but he also accepted the occasional rap on the knuckles in the proper spirit. Even when he was a teenager, I had marked him down as a future captain of Aberdeen. He was that good.

Martin said to me, 'Can you make me a professional footballer?' and I told him that if he listened to me, I could show him how to overcome any obstacles in his path. In return, he promised to learn and work hard. They were big promises to make, but I think I kept my side of the bargain, and the man who went on to captain Manchester United and Scotland certainly kept his. Seeing him reach the heights of football has been one of the greatest satisfactions in my life.

He would be joined at Pittodrie by his younger brother George, who was also clever, and who enjoyed a decent enough career before going on to be a teacher. I wonder if his pupils know about the time George was whizzing along in training and I shouted, 'Hold the ball,' only for George to stop and pick it up . . .

I wanted to educate Martin about the demands of top-rank football, so I gave him a taste of the first-team game in October 1966, in a drawn League match against Dunfermline. A week later, I gave Jim Hermiston and Francis Munro their debuts, but all three would not become first-team regulars until some time later, three seasons in Jim's case. I'm sure that early experience convinced them of their desire to play for Aberdeen's 1st XI and also that they needed to work harder to get there.

By that October, we had already gone unbeaten through our League Cup section and had qualified for the knockout stages – the first time Aberdeen had done so in eight years. By beating Morton over two legs in the quarter-finals, we had earned a semi-final against Rangers. Sadly, the semi-final of the League Cup mirrored the semi-final of the previous season's Scottish Cup, and again we lost in the replay.

The first match, on 19 October 1966, was remarkable for one reason. As the game went into extra time, I noticed that Billy Little was tiring, and I wanted to change the attacking formation, so I sent on Pat Wilson to become Aberdeen's first-ever substitute in a competitive match. Rangers also made a substitution, and after the match, all hell broke loose. In making the substitutions, I and my managerial opponent – the hugely respected Scot Symon, one of football's true gentlemen – had apparently broken some 'unwritten rule' that substitutes could only be used to replace genuinely injured players. Well, I had checked the new substitute law and nowhere was there any mention of that 'rule' about the seriousness of the injury. I had told the players that if I wanted them to come off, I would send on word and they were to hit the ground or start limping. 'No Oscar performances,' I said, 'but make it look good.' Billy duly bit the dust, and we carted him off to be replaced by Pat.

As far as I was concerned, sending on Pat Wilson was entirely legitimate, as Billy Little was not fully fit, but the powers-that-were and the press tut-tutted. Scot Symon and I had an 'understanding' about the issue, so we were basically accused of cheating. Scot was upset, but my attitude was 'stuff them'. Though I used substitutes rarely – seven in total all season – just ten days later I sent on Ernie Winchester in a match against Hibs, and he scored the winner. I felt fully justified in making such tactical changes, as they were within the law – that's the important point. Nowadays, of course, tactical substitutions are so much part of the modern game that nobody gives them a second thought. Another first for Turnbull, I would say!

By the time of our League Cup exit, I already knew we were on the brink of something special. At the start of the 1966–67 season, I had made a small but significant cosmetic change, something which is now part of Aberdeen's history. I had long admired Real Madrid and felt that their all-white strip was a football icon which should be copied by any team that was determined to make it to the very top. So I threw out the white shorts and brought in Aberdeen's all-red strip, which, give or take the occasional lapse in taste, they have worn ever since. How could I possibly have known that one night almost 18 years later, the All Reds would beat the All Whites in the European Cup-Winners' Cup final on the greatest night in the history of Aberdeen?

By the end of October 1966, the team was relatively settled, with Bobby Clark in goal and Jim 'Chalky' Whyte and Ally Shewan at full-back. The latter man was a model of consistency, a fine professional who set a club record of 162 consecutive appearances in League matches.

The three across the middle featured Tommy McMillan as a stalwart centre-half, while Francis Munro, Davie Millar and Jens Petersen scrapped for the half-back positions, with Jens often dropping into the role of sweeper. Up front, I mixed it between Billy Little, Harry Melrose, Ernie Winchester, Ian Taylor, Dave Johnston and Jimmy Wilson, whom I signed from Morton. Jimmy was a winger, a typical Glasgow sharpie, and the fans took to him after he scored a cracker on his debut against Dundee.

Basically, I wanted to keep the defence solid by playing a regular formation, but I was prepared to make changes up front in search of goals. The formula worked, as the side gelled marvellously, and from October to December we went on a spree, winning eight League matches in succession and reaching the unheard-of heights of second place in the League. Most gratifyingly, the attendances began to creep up, with 28,000 and 31,000 for our home matches against Celtic and Rangers respectively. We lost that latter match, which sparked a period of what I can only describe as baffling inconsistency.

We put five past Ayr United, seven past Airdrie, and six past Falkirk, but lost to Dunfermline and Motherwell. Our home form held up, but we conceded some daft goals away from Pittodrie, and our initial challenge for the title faded as the Old Firm raced away to fight it out among themselves, Celtic eventually prevailing in a race that went to the wire.

The League championship had proved beyond us, but there was still massive excitement around Pittodrie as the season neared its close. For by then we had enjoyed our best Scottish Cup run in eight years and had reached the final to play Celtic.

It was the greatest day of the 1960s for the club – and I wasn't even there.

I had won the League championship as a player, and I knew the great satisfaction that it gave you. I had been so close to winning the Cup as a player that I had always wondered how it would have felt to have won. But for most of April 1967, I was wondering how it would feel to win as a manager and how the players would feel to gain their first medals by beating Celtic in the Scottish Cup final.

We had reached the final after a run which started with two terrific 5–0 victories, the first of them away to Dundee, in which we played some of our best football of the season, with Jim Smith running riot. He and Davie Johnston scored twice, and Jim Wilson added the other. St Johnstone were beaten by the same score, with the same three players grabbing four between them and Harry Melrose scoring the fifth. My old teammate from my schooldays and Scotland days Bobby Brown managed St Johnstone then, and he said to me, 'Some crowd here at Pittodrie today, Ned,' to which I replied, 'Aye, and all Aberdeen supporters.' And they were – cup fever was hitting the city already.

The quarter-final against Hibs at Easter Road was a nail-biter. The weather was atrocious, and skill was not greatly evident, in a good old-fashioned cup tie. Hibs had taken the lead after 15 minutes, and, try as we might, we just could not break them down. In the very last move of the match, we won a corner, and Jim Smith jumped at the back post to head home the equaliser.

Afterwards, because that late goal had devastated Hibs, I told Stewart Brown, the Edinburgh sportswriter, that 'Hibs should not bother coming up to Aberdeen for the replay'. It was some statement to make, but I wanted to pile the pressure on my old club, and I think it worked.

The replay presented two real problems for us, however. One was that Robert Clark had an important exam on that day, and in that era you turned up for the exam on time and stayed until the period for the test was over. That was going to give Robert an almost impossible task to reach Pittodrie on time, but the course chief, Roy Small, who was deeply involved in football and would help set up the SFA's famous coaching courses at Largs, agreed to let Bobby sit the exam an hour earlier, on condition he did not reveal the questions. He kept that promise – his father was waiting outside the college to drive him to Aberdeen as soon as he'd finished to ensure he made it to Pittodrie in time.

Jim Smith had picked up an injury on the Saturday and couldn't play, and it was here that my memories of earlier matches came into play. Ernie Winchester was no longer a first-choice player and was looking for a transfer, but I remembered that he had played very well against the Hibs centre-half John Madsen when that player was at Morton the previous season. I took Ernie aside and told him he would be playing in the Hibs match against a player he had bested previously and that it was an ideal opportunity to put himself in the shop window for clubs looking for a centre-forward. I told Ernie beforehand that Madsen would not like being given 'the treatment' and instructed him that at the very first opportunity he should try and draw the centre-half out to the wing and show him who was boss in a physical challenge. 'Thump him,' I said. Well, something like that . . .

Ernie Winchester duly proceeded to give Madsen a doing in the corner and that was the Hibs player finished. Ernie gave the rest of the defence a torrid time and scored two goals in a 3–0 victory. That earned us a semi-final against Dundee United at Dens Park and such was the excitement among our support that some queued all night to make sure they got tickets. Ernie did his transfer value a power of good – he went to Hearts shortly afterwards.

The previous season I had won a small but important strategic victory over Dundee United in the Scottish Cup. We were due to play them on 19 February 1966 at Pittodrie in a second round match, but it snowed all day and the game was called off late by the referee. There were no mobiles then, and we could not contact the United bus to tell them to turn around. They eventually arrived at Pittodrie, and manager Jerry Kerr and his directors went to the boardroom, where our chairman Forbes dispensed hospitality. But they began to talk about replaying the game, and while I was briefly out of the room, the United crew ganged up and persuaded our directors that the game should be played on the following Monday. Jerry Kerr said to me as I came back into the room, 'That's it settled, then, see you on Monday.' But I was having none of it.

'This is the SFA's cup, and its secretary Mr Willie Allan will decide when the game is played,' I said, giving Charlie Forbes one of those looks I kept in the locker for people who had let the side down. I wanted more time to prepare my players and allowing United to set the date for our home fixture would also have given them a psychological advantage. As I thought, Willie Allan decreed that the postponed match would go ahead on the normal day, i.e. the following Wednesday, and I had won my little battle. We promptly ran out 5–0 winners, with big Ernie Winchester bagging a couple. As we came up the tunnel, I couldn't resist saying to Jerry Kerr, 'Aye, we would have stuffed you on Monday anyway.'

A year or so on, and I still felt we had an edge, but United put up a real fight, and the semi turned out to be another match that tested every nerve in my body. We got a bit of luck when Tommy Millar scored an own goal and then had to suffer when we were awarded a penalty which Jim Storrie, whom I had signed a few weeks before, unfortunately missed. After that, our defence was sorely tested but we clung on, and though injury time seemed to last for ever, the final whistle was eventually sounded and we were in the final – my first as a manager.

However, I did not see it as the culmination of all the hard work. That would come when we won the Cup, for I was determined that we could and would beat Celtic at Hampden.

Before the final, there was an important date for Scottish football: Saturday, 15 April 1967, at Wembley. England were the world champions but we all knew that Scotland had a great team in 1967. Now the two 'Auld Enemies' would meet at Wembley in the annual Home International Championship fixture, the world's oldest international match, between the two countries which invented football.

I was keen to be at the match, as all Scots were, and I thought about going down by train. But eventually I travelled down with a friend from Edinburgh, John Russell, in his car, to watch as Scotland became the world champions – well, if you beat the world champions it stands to reason that you are the new world champs, or so our theory went – winning 3–2 with a wonderful display of attacking football.

On the way home, I became unwell, and I just could not shrug off the feeling that I was suffering from something distinctly unpleasant. The pain in my insides was excruciating, and I felt as though I had been punched silly. I knew I was suffering from something a lot more serious than food poisoning. I was not wrong; my doctor, Dr Hugh Falconer, contacted the local hospital, where I was diagnosed with hepatitis.

I was soon doped to the eyeballs with medicine. Taking the training became increasingly painful, and eventually I was just going through the motions, going down to Pittodrie each day but barely moving from my chair. I drove to and from the stadium, and still do not know how I managed it. If the police had seen me, I would have been done for dangerous driving.

By the next Thursday, it was time to take the team down to Gleneagles to allow the players to relax away from all the media hype and to finalise our training plans. Two nights previously, Celtic had qualified for the European Cup final by drawing with Dukla Prague in Czechoslovakia. I genuinely hoped that they would win Europe's premier trophy (as they did, on 25 May in Lisbon, beating Inter Milan), but in the meantime, we were going to do our damnedest to stop them earning a clean sweep of trophies. It shouldn't be forgotten, either, that Rangers had reached the final of the European Cup-Winners' Cup, where they would lose to Bayern Munich – we were mixing it in the best of European company that season.

But, try as I might, I just could not gee myself up, and by Friday I was a wreck, utterly listless and unable to move an inch. The team bus was delayed until the last possible minute on the Saturday, but eventually I had to concede defeat and send them on their way, while I stayed in my hotel room listening to the final on the radio. The bus was so late it needed a police escort, and the players had to hurry to get changed after arriving with less than half an hour till kick-off.

Basing it on the experience of playing Celtic in the League only ten days before the final, when we defended well to secure a 0–0 draw at Parkhead, I had prepared a plan which saw Harry Melrose and Jimmy Smith dropping back to counter Celtic's midfield, but it was to no avail. Perhaps if I had been there, I might have been able to influence things and maybe change the game plan, but on the day Celtic were the better side, and their two wingers, Bobby Lennox and Jimmy Johnstone, set up Willie Wallace for two goals either side of the interval. Our loyal supporters stayed to cheer the boys to the end and showed their appreciation for a revitalised club.

It was heartbreaking to meet the team when they returned to Gleneagles, but they had done everything they could in the circumstances and had shown we were able to compete against the best. After all, less than a month later, Celtic were European champions.

There was still plenty to play for. Two days later, we went to Rugby Park to play Kilmarnock in the final match of season 1966–67. We needed a point to guarantee our place in the Fairs Cup, and secured it with a 1–1 draw. We had finished fourth in the league, behind Celtic, Rangers and Clyde (next time you meet a fan of the 'Bully Wee' remind them of those days). Because Celtic won both the championship and the Cup, as losing Cup finalists, we were promoted to the Cup-Winners' Cup, Europe's second-most-prestigious tournament. At the end of a long hard season, our efforts had been enough to guarantee European football for Aberdeen for the first time.

Yet I was acutely aware that, although we had come a long way in a relatively short space of time, we had not won anything. Only a trophy would suffice to crown our improvement.

12

Winners at Last

We were in Europe at last, but it was another continent which saw Aberdeen first. In America, football looked as if it could take off as a spectator sport, and, with the backing of FIFA, the US Soccer Football Association was trying to boost the game by involving foreign teams in a tournament. Aberdeen FC were invited, but quite a few people argued that a six- or seven-week trip would be too arduous and we would be tired the following season. But I remembered how foreign trips had helped the Hibs squad to bond and 'cement friendships'. Following my strong pleading that we should go, the board accepted the invitation to participate, and I'm glad they did, as it led to an unforgettable experience and a meeting I had never thought possible.

Each of the 12 teams was to represent a major city, with the idea that the local citizens would get behind 'their' club. The visiting clubs would effectively act as surrogates for the various city sides, so, for a brief period in 1967, the Dons of Aberdeen, Scotland, became the Whips of Washington, DC. Hibs represented Toronto, Dundee United became the Dallas Tornadoes, while, from England, clubs such as Sunderland, Stoke City and Wolverhampton Wanderers were among the others who took part in this experiment. There was a mixed bag of other foreign teams. Bangu of Brazil competed, as did Glentoran of Belfast and Shamrock Rovers of Dublin, the latter representing the Irish-dominated city of Boston. The great Roberto Boninsegna, who scored for Italy in the 1970 World Cup finals, was there with Cagliari, while the Stoke City side included one of the world's greatest goalkeepers, who would also make his mark in Mexico – Gordon Banks.

The team departed for Washington on 23 May while I was still officially on the sick list. I distinctly recall sitting around the house before they left wondering how the boys would cope without me. Just at that moment, a telephone call came from one of the tournament organisers, a PR man called Jerry. I told him I was still under the supervision of my doctor, and he expressed his disappointment that I could not make what for them was a most important ceremony – an official reception for the Washington Whips at the White House.

Americans being 'can do' people, Jerry promptly offered to fly Dr Falconer and myself to Washington for the reception. He asked me if the doctor was near by, and I said he was just across the road, so I left Carol chatting to this complete stranger ('It's Jerry from America, keep him talking,' I said), while I jumped across to the surgery to check that Dr Falconer was able to go. 'Fancy a weekend trip to America to meet the President of the United States?' I asked. He thought I was joking at first, but then he realised the offer was genuine and went off to sort out a visa and make the travel arrangements for his patient.

Dr Falconer and I had an uneventful trip across the pond, though I was still pretty weak. The Washington club officials could not do enough for me, and we were whisked off to meet the President. Now, I don't know whether President Lyndon Baines Johnson knew anything about football, but he personally supported the tournament and had agreed to let it be contested for the President's Cup. It was pretty extraordinary stuff, this wee lad from Carronshore getting to meet the President of the United States. We had a brief tour of the White House before being ushered in to meet President Johnson.

He was, of course, familiar to me from the television. A big, tall man with a strong Texan accent, he was very friendly and charming when I was introduced to him as 'coach' of the famous Aberdeen club. He had done his homework and talked knowledgeably about 'soccer'. I have very clear recall of our conversation, in which he said he was delighted that we had come across to represent Washington. I replied, 'We'll try our best, Mr President, and I'm sure we'll make you happy.' We presented him with a gold football and had our photographs taken, and all too soon it was over.

I do have one souvenir: a couple of black-and-white pictures of the president and myself. They have pride of place in my home in Edinburgh, and one bears the cheeky caption, put there by the photographer: 'The most powerful man in the world with the President of the United States.'

I went home for a fortnight to recover fully and then flew back to join the squad. The team did well, beating Sunderland and becoming the first Scottish team to play on artificial turf when we played in the Houston Astrodome. The Astrodome was quite amazing. With the touch of a button, the seating could be changed from football-match stands to boxing ringside seats. The spectators were kept informed by giant scoreboards, and everything was done to make the fans comfortable.

We were treated a bit like royalty in Washington, especially as we were doing so well for the city. We were taken to meet the Washington Redskins American football team, and we all got on famously. Too famously, almost, as Jens Petersen had a very successful try at kicking field goals, and at the end of the session, one of the Washington coaches asked me if he was available for signing! The coach reckoned Jens had the look of Charlie Gogolak about him. Only later did I find out that Gogolak was their star kicker, who was earning probably about 50 or 100 times what our man did. But I was not for letting our Danish star go: 'He'll do all his kicking for Aberdeen,' I said, 'and hopefully some of it will go *under* the bar.'

We travelled first class everywhere, stayed in the best hotels with swimming pools, and the initial stages ended with us winning five and drawing five of our twelve matches to top the eastern section of the tournament and reach the final against western section winners Wolves. If the organisers wanted a match full of incident to show the Americans the excitement of football, they could not have asked for a better game.

The final in Los Angeles' Olympic Stadium before a crowd of 18,000 featured a bonanza of goals and a bizarre sending-off, when Jimmy Smith was given his marching orders for clattering Dave Wagstaffe, who Jimmy claimed had spat on him.

Our ten men were heroic, and it was 4–4 at full time. In extra time, both sides scored once more, and, this being America, there could be no replays and had to be a finish. In 'extra' extra time, Ally Shewan unfortunately put through his own goal to make the final score 6–5 in favour of the Englishmen. It was a real shame for Ally, as he had been one of the players of the tournament; the Americans called him 'the Iron Man' because they loved the way he got stuck into big players such as Derek Dougan of Wolves. Robert Clark and Tommy McMillan were named in the All Star XI, which also featured Pat Stanton of Hibs and the great former Ranger Jim Baxter of Sunderland.

The final was widely reported, and the tournament did help to establish soccer as a sport in the States. It was also a great experience for the players, who not only played their hearts out but also got to see a lot of that great country while enjoying the best hotels and hospitality.

Ronnie Allen was the manager of Wolves at the time, and later he would join Sporting Lisbon, where I would have a memorable joust with him in my time managing Hibs. But back in 1967, there was only one thought in Allen's mind: how could he get his hands on Francis Munro? During the tournament and especially in the final, Francis had played very well, showing the considerable skill he had for a big man. He was also one of the finest long passers I've ever seen, and it was no wonder that Wolves wanted to sign him.

At first, they did not match our valuation, but nearly eight months later, when Allen made the very substantial offer of £50,000, we could not turn it down; it was four times more than we had paid for him just 18 months previously. It was also a chance for Francis to play in top-flight English football and earn considerably more than he was getting at Aberdeen.

I could not be sure, however, that he would be willing to leave, so I used the same ruse on him that Willie McCartney had used on Jock Weir all those years ago at Hibs. I went to club secretary Bert Whyte and told him to get a one-way flight to Birmingham for Francis Munro, and when the lad came down for training, I handed him his ticket and his boots in a parcel and told him the car was waiting to take him to Dyce Airport. Off he went to sign for Wolves, and while I was really sorry to lose him, the money from his transfer was critical for the club's finances.

This happened midway through the 1967–68 season, which had started with Pittodrie buzzing with anticipation, not least because we had beaten Chelsea in a pre-season friendly. A crowd of 36,000 turned up for the opening competitive match, in the League Cup, which we drew 1–1 with Rangers. Sadly, that was to be our best home crowd of a season which was a bit of an anticlimax compared to the achievements of the previous one, not least because we performed dismally in the Scottish Cup, losing by a late goal at Dunfermline in the second round. We were equally woeful in the League Cup, finishing bottom of a very tough section which featured Celtic, Rangers and Dundee United.

It was around that time that I had a personal crisis, when I had the opportunity of moving to the mighty Rangers. The outcome is obvious – I stayed at Aberdeen, of course – but I came very, very close to taking over at Ibrox. Yes, you read it correctly – I turned down the biggest managerial job in Scotland. Only now will I reveal why I did not go there. It's a secret I've kept for nearly 40 years, but all the other principals are dead and can't be harmed by what I write.

Despite the fact that he'd taken Rangers to the European Cup-Winners' Cup final in 1967, everyone knew that Scot Symon's time as Rangers manager was coming to an end. In conditions of great secrecy – or so I thought – I was invited down to Glasgow to meet the then Rangers chairman John Lawrence and members of the board, including John Wilson Jr and Matt Taylor.

We met at the St Enoch Hotel in Glasgow, and talked in general terms about football before getting down to brass tacks. Basically they wanted to kick Scot 'upstairs' and make him general manager while I would be brought in as manager under him, benefiting from his experience. That seemed perfectly logical to me and I said, yes, I would consider taking the job, and yes, the money and conditions were fine; but there was something I knew about the manager's role at Ibrox, and I wanted a clear commitment from the board on the matter.

'I understand that your managers in the past have had to submit the team sheet to directors for their approval,' I said. 'Directors have sometimes said that such-and-such a player must be left out or put in. Is that still the case?'

John Lawrence suddenly became very uncomfortable, and the rest of the board members squirmed. The chairman tried to explain that directors sometimes had a legitimate reason for wanting a player to play or be left out. I couldn't believe that – I'd heard that Rangers' board sometimes left a player out because they didn't like his manners – and I was having none of it. They also controlled transfers in and out. 'If you want me to be your manager, those practices will have to cease immediately,' I told them. My chances of managing Rangers ended right there and then. There was a lot of humming and hawing, but Lawrence and his directors were not ready to dispense with their veto on team selection. They thanked me for my time, and I left.

I made my exit from St Enoch and went back to the hotel at Queen Street Station, where I ran into a couple of football writers who 'just happened' to be at the hotel and seemed to know what was going on. One was Jim Rodger, who was known for his connections across football, and the other was Willie 'Deedle' Waddell, my old Rangers adversary from playing days, who had managed Kilmarnock before joining the ranks of the press. They knew perfectly well why I was in Glasgow. Deedle said, 'Come on, Ned, what's the score?' so I told them that I had not taken the job. I did not give them the details of what had happened, but I made it clear that I was not going to Ibrox. Waddell said, 'Aye, you've done the right thing, Ned,' and we had a wee drink.

After I turned down the job, former Clyde player and manager Davie White was brought in to Rangers, but this young and relatively inexperienced manager did not make his mark. The Deedle then spent many columns giving White a hard time, until the Rangers board eventually dispensed with his services and appointed Waddell himself to the manager's job. I thought that was a bit unfair of the Deedle, but football is like that.

So I went back to Pittodrie and an up-and-down struggle. Once again, inconsistency was our main problem. For example, in October we hammered Dundee United 6–0 in the League, but we had earlier lost 0–5 to them in the League Cup. We did well at Pittodrie but lost key matches away.

However, I had spotted a couple of things in the USA which I thought could help. One was a terrific Danish player called Henning Boel, about whom I'll tell you more later, and the other was something I had seen in American football. During our visit to the Washington Redskins, I noticed how much more identifiable each player was, thanks simply to the large squad numbers they wore on their shirts. I decided to try that with Aberdeen and ordered a set of shirts with outsized numbers on the back. It was purely to help spectators identify players, and there was no advantage to Aberdeen that I could think of. But the SFA had a nitpicking rule stating the maximum size of numbers, and the beaks stepped in after we had played a couple of games in the shirts and banned us from wearing them. I was furious. If it was good enough for American football, it should be good enough for Scottish football, was my reply. But we had to abide by their silly rules. Nowadays, of course, all shirts carry big numbers and names. Another first for Turnbull, but I was too far ahead of my time, again.

That season saw Aberdeen play in Europe for the first time. We had an all-too-brief but nonetheless spectacular adventure in the European Cup-Winners' Cup. We had been drawn against KR Reykjavik of Iceland in the first round, and though they had the advantage of being near the end of their season, which was played in the summer months, we were just far too good for them. Francis Munro got a hat-trick, and we ran out 10–0 winners at Pittodrie. The second leg was a formality which we won 4–1. That first-leg score and the aggregate remain Aberdeen's best tallies in Europe.

The second round paired us with Standard Liège of Belgium, whom we played away first. I knew they were a very good side with lots of European experience – they had reached the semi-finals of the Cup-Winners' Cup the previous season, losing to eventual winners Bayern Munich. We did our homework, but nothing could have prepared us for our early defensive lapses as we let in two goals from corner-kick moves.

A third goal seemed to confirm our exit, but what a fight we put up when we got them back to Pittodrie. There had been snow early in the evening, and the crowd was reduced as a result, but the fans got behind the team as Francis Munro and Harry Melrose scored to bring us within a goal of levelling the tie. But Chalky Whyte missed a good chance late on, and the Belgians held out.

It had been a steep learning curve for us, and it gave me the taste for European football as a manager which I had always had as a player.

Out of three cups and bumbling along in the League, it looked as though it would be at least a season and a half before we played in Europe again; but from the middle of March, we found consistency and lost only two of our final ten matches. Approaching the last match of the season, we knew we could secure a place in the Fairs Cup if we gained both points. The trouble was that our final opponents, on 27 April 1968, were Rangers at Ibrox. Nobody gave us a chance. We had not won there for seven years, while Rangers had not lost a game all season and were level on points at the top of the League with Celtic, who had a superior goal average but were still to play Dunfermline. If Rangers won, that would put pressure on Celtic, who would then need to beat Dunfermline to lift their third successive title. For us, the prize was European football. And I'm glad to say that with a little 'prompting' from yours truly, my guys rose to the task.

The match did not start well for us. Of all people, it had to be our former player Dave Smith who put them ahead. Davie Johnston levelled, but Alex Ferguson put them ahead before Johnston equalised again. We were being pummelled, but I had spotted that they were vulnerable to a quick break. For once, I came down from the stand to the dugout to make a change. I had signed Ian Taylor from Martin Buchan's old side, Banks o' Dee, and he had proven his worth several times thanks to his pace. I sent him on with instructions to run at their defence if he got the chance, and in the final seconds of the 90 minutes he raced upfield and scored.

To this day, Rangers fans still think we robbed them of the League, but Celtic beat Dunfermline in any case. There is a rare photograph of me leaping up and down in front of Rangers' main stand at the final whistle – rare because I never normally went to the pitch side. I took pelters from the Rangers fans, who thought I was celebrating the fact that they had lost the League. Nothing could be further from the truth; my joy came from the fact that Aberdeen had qualified for Europe in the most unlikely circumstances.

The season ended on a high note, with recognition of our improvement as two of our players, Robert Clark and Jim Smith, were both selected for Scotland against Holland in May, Robert having won his first cap against Wales in November.

I was not happy with the overall squad, however, and decided we needed a proven goal-scorer. I let Jimmy Wilson go to Motherwell, while Pat Wilson and Davie Millar had gone to Raith Rovers and Jim Storrie to Rotherham. With the money for Francis Munro in the bank, I felt justified in asking the board for a serious investment. The man I wanted was a Scottish internationalist and former Rangers player who I knew would be virtually guaranteed to get us goals.

Jim Forrest was at Preston North End, and I had heard on the grapevine that he wasn't happy. I decided to check out the rumours, and I recount this story as an example of how managers sometimes get their information. I knew that former Rangers centre-forward Jimmy Millar, who owned a pub in Leith, was close to Forrest. I drove down to see Jimmy and went into the small snug bar with him, where I immediately turned the conversation to Jim Forrest, who was a smart and sharp player but who appeared to have lost something along the way. I figured that if I could get him back to Scotland and back on the rails, he could do a job for us. And when Jimmy said he was a good lad who had just fallen out of favour with his former manager at Rangers, Scot Symon, I knew it was time to act. Such things happen all the time in football, and I was sure I could overcome any problem to gain us a pacy goal-scorer.

I went to the board with my request, and we broke the club transfer record to sign Jim for £25,000. In the space of a couple of seasons, I had gone from haggling about £4,000 for Harry Melrose to signing players for six times that sum – and there were more big signings to come. Meanwhile, Jim went straight into the first team and straight onto the score sheet, as I had predicted he would.

During the season, I had strengthened our Danish connection by making Jens Petersen captain, and now I went after Henning Boel. I had seen him playing in America for Washington Whips, and he was just the sort of big, quick defender I wanted for a new system I was working on, which involved full-backs getting up and down the pitch – forerunners of what we now call wing-backs.

I liked Henning from the start. Big and genuine, he was to become a real hero with the Aberdeen fans and was known as 'the Great Dane'. His popularity no doubt stemmed from the fact that he was always committed to the cause. Capped 17 times for Denmark, his Aberdeen career would end prematurely when his ankle was broken against Borussia Mönchengladbach in 1974. He ended his career back in the USA, playing against the likes of Pelé.

Apart from those vital additions to the squad, I would prefer to draw a veil over season 1968–69, as, frankly, it was a time of turmoil which I have tried to forget.

Even our trips to Europe were unusually turbulent. We were drawn against Slavia Sofia in the first round and were poised to meet them when the Soviet Union invaded Czechoslovakia five days before our first-leg match in neighbouring Bulgaria. With real tension between East and West, European football was thrown into disarray overnight, and UEFA eventually redrew the European Cup and Cup-Winners' Cup so that clubs from Western Europe did not have to travel behind the Iron Curtain.

But the Fairs Cup was left unaltered, and it gave us a nightmare trip to Bulgaria. Very much under Soviet control, the Bulgarians went out of their way to make us feel unwelcome. We arrived at the airport and were held for hours as each passport and visa was checked and rechecked and our luggage was inspected several times over. In another innovation for Scottish football, we had taken all our own food with us – standard practice now. The Bulgarians went through the hampers with a fine-tooth comb.

We had been well warned by the British Foreign Office not to make any trouble, so we just sat there and let the officials get on with it. Then we were taken to our hotel in a vehicle which was more like a prison van than a team bus, the windows blanked out so that only the driver could see anything. I swear I went to Bulgaria and never saw the country – the only things we saw were the insides of the bus, the hotel and the stadium.

Slavia were the second team in Sofia, CSKA being the Communist Party's favourites and therefore the perennial winners. All the Slavia players were also soldiers, and we kept wondering what would happen if during the match they were called away to some real 'action'.

I had decided to defend in depth on a very hot day, and set out a 5-3-2 formation. I also played a trick on the Bulgarians, sending out Martin Buchan in the number 11 jersey. I liked the look of confusion on their faces when we kicked off and he ran back to join Tommy McMillan as an extra centre-back in a defensive formation. It was not a new trick; I had persuaded Hugh Shaw to do the same number exchange with Joe Baker against Roma some years previously. And Martin was a revelation as he mopped up attack after attack. I had told Ally Shewan to keep showing Bulgaria's players the inside channel, and they bought it every time, charging in to the centre, where Martin was waiting.

We overcame the heat, the intimidating atmosphere and their soldier players. We drew 0–0, and in the return leg, in front of 29,000 fans at Pittodrie, we excelled ourselves in blitzing the Bulgarians, attacking in waves and scoring two fine goals through Ian Taylor and Davie Robb.

Unfortunately, our next opponents were even tougher, but had we held Real Zaragoza to 2–0 at Pittodrie, things might have been different. But Tommy McMillan put through his own net to give them a vital away goal, and in any case the Spaniards dominated the return leg, winning 3–0.

More European lessons had been learned – such as avoid Iron Curtain clubs if you can – but it was our domestic form which gave me most concern in the winter of '68 and '69. We had failed to qualify from a League Cup section which was won by Clyde, and a sequence of five defeats in a row early in the league doomed us to be also-rans. Sometimes this happens with a club. A malaise sets in, confidence disappears and individuals in the squad and on the staff lose focus and direction. It happens no matter how hard you work. I used to call meetings and we would try to talk things out. But it was to no avail. There were some press reports at the time that I was in serous ill health but that was not the case – I didn't get my ulcer till much later! I did worry that perhaps I was putting too much stress on details to the point where it became desperate.

You have to act to alter this negative state of mind, so I chopped and changed the team, trying to find the blend that would save us from the drop. After he lost eleven goals in two matches, I thought even Robert Clark had been affected by the poor run, and I heard that he was sitting in his house in the suburb of Milltimber brooding over results when he should have been on his way to join the Scotland international squad. I had decided to drop him and give Ernie McGarr a chance, but I wanted Robert to hear the news from me. So I drove over and told Robert in no uncertain terms that I would drive him to Glasgow for the team gathering myself first thing in the morning.

We had a good talk – well, it was mostly me doing the talking – and I reminded Robert that hard times could be the making of us. Then I dropped it on him that he was going to have a spell in the reserves. Of course, Ernie came in and was outstanding, and Robert spent nearly a year in the reserves, which led to the then unique situation whereby we had two Scottish international goalkeepers on our books at the same time, as Ernie was also capped shortly afterwards. Robert has said that the 'time out' was the making of him, and it also gave young Mr Clark the chance to fulfil an ambition.

Both he and big Ernie liked nothing better than to play outfield positions in practice matches, but later Robert actually turned out for the reserves, and did well, at centre-half. He was so good, in fact, that I sat him on the first-team bench against Rangers, and he even made the team to play St Johnstone once. But all this outfield stuff appeared to have gone to his head and he seemed to fancy himself in a new job. So one day in the dressing-room, I told him to stick to the gloves: 'What were you doing out there? You're a bloody goalkeeper and don't forget it.'

In 1968–69, we spent most of the season looking over our shoulders at the relegation zone. It is not an excuse, but around that time there was a major distraction off the pitch, which I had to do my best to shield from the players. There was considerable disquiet among some businessmen in Aberdeen, who included former player Don Emery and a former club secretary, Gordon McIver. They were concerned about the way the club was being run by the board and mounted a takeover battle. Rumours about the plans went on for months and they included a story that Jock Stein might be offered my job – frankly ludicrous, given Stein's powerful position at Celtic. I told Charlie Forbes it was none of my concern but he said, 'This affects you too, Mr Manager,' and from then on my main aim was to conceal the goings-on from the players. It was bad enough battling relegation without them knowing what was happening behind the scenes.

Crucial to defeating the bid was Dick Spain – the owner of Fifi the poodle – and three women who all held sizeable shareholdings. One of them was Mrs Flora Duncan, widow of the former director John, who had died not long before that. Another of the 'petticoat brigade' was Mrs Mabel Callender, the daughter of John Robbie, the very same Mr Robbie who had given me no quarter at the SFA disciplinary hearing all those years before. Dick Spain sided with the board and became a director, and the three women refused to sell their shares and also sided with the board, which effectively finished the takeover battle.

We were still suffering on the pitch. It was only in April, after wins over Morton and Airdrie and a draw with Rangers, that we were truly safe. That draw, at Pittodrie on 9 April 1969, once again dented Rangers' chances of the championship, which went to Celtic for the fourth time in a row. Gaining that point was sweet revenge for the events of 22 March when Rangers hammered us 6–1 in the semi-final of the Scottish Cup, bringing to an end a run which had seen us twice win replays away from home, against Dundee United and Dunfermline. If only we could have maintained that away record in the League, we would have had no relegation worries at all.

The tie against Dunfermline was particularly memorable. We played them at Pittodrie in a second-round match that had previously been postponed. They had a good side at the time, with the likes of Ron Barry, so I was pleased we were leading 2–1 with just minutes to go. They had a big centre-half called Jim Fraser, and I was concerned that he could be dangerous in the air from a dead-ball situation. During the week, I had worked with the team to drill into them the danger that Dunfermline posed from corners and free kicks. I told them that Alex Edwards would take any free kick on the right and would ping the ball into the left side of the penalty box, looking for Fraser, who would come up for such moves. Jim Smith was detailed to pick up Fraser on those occasions, but when Dunfermline won the late free kick and Edwards swung the ball in, Jinky was nowhere to be seen, and they duly scored to equalise.

We were now faced with a very difficult task in the replay, which was held the following evening, 26 February 1969, because the quarter-finals were due later that week. In the dressing-room after the draw, I lambasted Jim Smith: 'If we go down there tomorrow night and lose, then you have cost this team money. It might not matter too much to you as a single guy, but look at these married men with kids. You will have cost them hard cash, you will have robbed their families of real money.' I wasn't as polite as that, I might add. Smith was suitably embarrassed, especially when I added: 'And if I find out you are at the dance-hall tonight you'll be finished at Aberdeen!'

Later that night, I was sitting at home when the phone rang and a female voice enquired why Jim Smith was 'under house arrest'. The lady turned out to be the aunt of Smith's girlfriend, who was herself the daughter of a businessman with an interest in the club. Apparently the girlfriend was very, very keen on Jinky, who was a handsome chap. She was seriously upset that he had not made it on their big date, and her aunt wanted to know if I could let him out for an hour or so. 'I'll tell you what I told him,' I said to the aunt. 'If Jimmy Smith is at the ballroom tonight, he's finished at Aberdeen.' He stayed in.

On the train down to Fife, I learned that Dunfermline had pulled a fast one by booking the dining car for the first sitting. I got hold of the conductor and said, 'We give you business every fortnight, and now you allow Dunfermline in for first sitting. You won't get another penny from us!' It let the team know I was sticking up for them, but the truth was that I had not reckoned on Dunfermline catching the same train and had simply forgotten to book for the meal. Sometimes a manager has to cover up his mistakes!

That night at East End Park, Jim Smith ran riot and could just about have beaten them himself, though he needed Davie Robb to actually score the two goals by which we won. It was surely the thought of missing out on future dates with his girl which spurred Jim's efforts that night . . . now there's motivation for you!

It was nothing to do with the Dunfermline incident, but I sold Jim to Newcastle United that summer for £80,000 – they had made us the proverbial offer we couldn't refuse. I have no hesitation in saying that on his day, Jimmy was the most skilful footballer I ever worked with, and losing him was not easy. Nor was it easy to say goodbye to Ally Shewan, who had set several appearance records and become known as Mr Consistency. He could not agree to a new deal and left.

I also sold Tommy Craig, who had been a star for us for the best part of two seasons. I had wanted to play him out on the left wing to keep him out of trouble, but he was determined to mix it in midfield. I told him that despite my tutoring, he was still not fully developed as a player, but eventually I had to let him play in his favoured position, where he was a revelation, though I also played him on the wing again. He had an educated left foot, and I have always said that a player with a good left peg is better than a right-footer.

His talents were obvious, and it was no surprise when Sheffield Wednesday came in with an offer in that close season. It did not match our valuation, but I decided to go down with him to Sheffield and negotiate a better deal for both him and the club. I went face to face with their secretary, Eric Taylor, and he soon upped the fee to just short of £100,000, which was a British and, for all I know, a world record for a teenager. It was a crying shame to lose him, and the fans were very unhappy, but we just could not afford to turn down that sort of money. Tommy went on to enjoy a great career with Wednesday, Newcastle United, Aston Villa and Swansea and later returned to Pittodrie as assistant coach to Roy Aitken. At the time of writing, he is still in football, working as a coach with Newcastle United.

I didn't want Jim or Tommy to leave, but the combined income of £180,000 meant that the club's finances could be put on an even keel. The Aberdeen fans, or at least those with typewriters, in the press, were incensed at the sale of both players, but they did not realise that when I went to Pittodrie the club was heading for a pauper's grave. Now, with money from young players who had cost nothing, we were in good order at last. The money for Jimmy and Tommy balanced the books, and I had some of the cash for strengthening the squad. And I knew that we had men like Henning Boel, Martin Buchan, George Murray, Jim Hermiston and Jim Hamilton coming to a peak.

Davie Robb was another I had signed who I felt sure would consolidate his first-team place. He came from a well-known Fife family, and his parents were very decent people. As with the families of so many youngsters, I had to assure them that Davie would be very well looked after at Pittodrie, and they then agreed to let him sign. I'm very glad they did, as Davie became an important player for Aberdeen. He was big, honest and strong, and had a will to win, but let's just say that on occasion his ball control let him down. He was a great asset to the club for many years.

We also had a couple of youngsters in the youth team and reserves who I knew would be major players for us, such as Derek McKay and Arthur Graham, so I felt that the departures of Shewan, Craig and Smith were acceptable risks. What's more, I had signed Alec Willoughby from Rangers (he was Jim Forrest's cousin and the two formed a good partnership), and I had already identified the player I really wanted. His name was Joe Harper, and he played for Morton.

Joe was a winger-cum-striker, and he had impressed me greatly when we played Morton. At the start of season 1969–70, we made a generous offer to Hal Stewart, Morton's legendary chairman and manager. Hal was a law unto himself, though, and knocked us back. But I wanted Joe Harper and knew I would get my man eventually.

We did well in the League Cup, qualifying from our section only to lose to Celtic over two legs in the quarter-final. Our start to the League could not have been better, as we thumped Clyde 6–0 in the opening match. But we won only one of our next five matches, and I went back to the board about Joe Harper.

Joe had started his career down in Huddersfield before returning to Scotland to play for Morton, and I thought he was being wasted on the wing there, as he seemed to me to have all the natural attributes of a striker. We needed someone to score goals, and I thought Joe could be that man. Bobby Calder and I went to see him at Ibrox. It was a very wet day and the pitch was muddy, and Joe was running around with his stockings about his ankles, which Bobby did not like. But I was convinced he was a natural goal-scorer, so I went to see Hal and did the deal for £40,000 – and only then did I tell the board! That was a club-record fee, but it was arguably the best money Aberdeen ever spent.

Joey, as he was known, was a real character, who was always getting into scrapes. He was funny – he once cracked that he was the only footballer with 20,000 budgies named after him. One night, I got a call to tell me that he and Ernie McGarr were in a wee bit of trouble – they had somehow commandeered a snowplough and taken it for a ride. It wasn't the first or last time the phone rang with an Ernie McGarr or Joe Harper story . . . and I have to say it was big Ernie who was in trouble more often than any other player!

But there was no malice in Ernie or Joe, and, as with a lot of the players, I was willing to forgive them the odd scrape, as they more than repaid the faith I invested in them. I also knew they were young men in a lucky situation; it often seemed to me that there were three women to every man in the city at that time, and, of course, playing for the club made them something of a catch. There was no serious bother, however, and I don't think I ever fined Joey Harper or any other player at that time – my bark was enough to frighten them.

We also knew that Joe wasn't the best of trainers. The players would be sent on a run of three laps round nearby Seaton Park. Joe would hide in the bushes on the first lap and come out when the lads were approaching the end of the final lap – and he thought we didn't know! But I didn't care as long as he banged in the goals.

Joe joined us in the first week of October 1969, and scored his first goal, against Partick Thistle, the following week. He would go on to score more than 200 goals for Aberdeen in two periods with the Dons, and, between them, he and I would be reacquainted at Hibs. His career was ended with a bad knee injury. Joe is rightly remembered as one of the greatest heroes to grace Pittodrie. He had a stroke a couple of years ago but has recovered well and still writes a column for the *Aberdeen Evening Express*.

With Joe leading the attack, we embarked on a Scottish Cup campaign with a 4–0 win over Clyde, in which Joe scored twice. We then struggled to beat a stuffy Clydebank 2–1 on a night when I made Martin Buchan captain for the first time. It had been a cold night, and we were, frankly, lucky to win, but I was annoyed with our fans that night. They had expected an easy win and gave the team some jeers, but the conditions and the visitors did not make it easy for us.

The quarter-final against Falkirk was memorable for a medical reason and for the Cup debut of another player. In the week before the match, our players started to fall ill with flu. They went down like ninepins, and soon we were struggling to find a full squad. I asked for the game to be postponed but the SFA refused. I called in Jim Hermiston and Derek McKay, a striker from Banffshire whom I had signed on a free transfer from Dundee, and in doing so, I inadvertently created a legend.

For Derek duly scored our only goal against Falkirk and then did the same in the semi-final against Kilmarnock at Muirton Park in Perth. There had been a dispute over the venue for the semi, as Kilmarnock wanted the game played in Glasgow, but this time the SFA favoured us, and more than 25,000 people crowded into Muirton, the home of St Johnstone. The pitch was wide, which suited us, and McKay did the business again.

While we were at Muirton, I was thinking about completing a bit of business. Stevie Murray was the captain of Dundee and a player I hugely admired. I had heard on the football grapevine that he might be available. So I met Dundee's officials secretly and secured the promise of his signature for £50,000 – breaking the club transfer record again. The problem was how to tell the board.

I solved this by calling in Jimmy Forbes and giving him the exclusive for the Saturday green edition of the *Evening Express*. Sure enough, on the Saturday evening I got a call from chairman Forbes.

'What's this about you signing Stevie Murray?' he asked.

'Aye,' I said, 'it's in the bag. Just needs a signature.'

'But we weren't told,' he complained.

'No,' I said, 'it had to be done in secret. But I'll tell you what – the fans are going to love a chairman who is looking to strengthen the team for the future after reaching the Scottish Cup final. They'll be very happy with such a forward-looking move.'

'Do you really think they will?'

'Of course,' I replied.

I got my money and Aberdeen got a classy player.

By then, our League form was inconsistent, but we were still in with a chance of qualifying for Europe, while Celtic were romping away with the League and would be our opponents in the Scottish Cup final. They were also destined for the European Cup final and were in pursuit of another Treble.

I knew that our game against them at Parkhead on 25 March 1970 would be hugely important psychologically. If Celtic beat us that night, they would win the League title, but I felt we had to give them a battle to show that we would not be cowed.

Just before going in to give my final team talk, I spotted some bottles in crates along the tunnel outside Celtic's dressing-room. I asked a passing photographer what was in the bottles, and he replied that it was the champagne to celebrate winning the League. I was furious. They were openly parading the champers before the match, almost taunting us. I thought it was another of Jock Stein's psychological ploys, and so I marched into our dressing-room and asked the team if they had seen the crates. They had not realised the significance of them, but I told the boys in no uncertain terms that that big 'eat-the-breid (bread)' – a slang term for a person who's gotten too big for their boots – had already bought the champers because he thought his team were going to win the League. 'We are going to make them choke on it,' was one of my more polite encouragements.

We worked like Trojans and won 2–1 that night, one of the goals being scored by Arthur Graham, who was having his first 90 minutes for the club. Known as 'Bumper' after the Glasgow name for the kind of plimsoll he wore, Arthur was just 17 when he was spotted by Bobby Calder and we snatched him from under the noses of Celtic, who were his boyhood heroes. Arthur was from Castlemilk and was playing for junior side Cambuslang Rangers while earning good money at a steelworks. Bobby persuaded me we should go for him but added that Sean Fallon, Celtic's assistant manager, who recruited so many of their talents, was due to meet Arthur soon. I jumped in the car and drove to Glasgow early in the morning, picking up Bobby and making our way to the Graham house in Castlemilk, which was a very tough area. Arthur's father welcomed us in and asked us if the car outside was ours, 'Because if it is, you better make this quick or you'll have no tyres when you go back out.'

We took the hint and signed Arthur there and then, a decent signing-on fee clinching the deal. I'm told Sean Fallon was none too pleased that we landed him. Arthur went on to be a real hero for the Dons, playing more than 300 games before moving to Leeds United and later Manchester United. He had to wait until 1977 for his first Scotland cap, as he was one of the players banned and later reprieved by the SFA after an infamous incident in Copenhagen. I feel he should have had more caps, as he was certainly one of the best players of his era.

After he had done so well against Celtic, I had to decide whether this teenager had the temperament to play in the Scottish Cup final at Hampden Park. To a certain extent, my hand was forced by an injury to Alec Willoughby and the fact that Stevie Murray could not play as he was cup-tied.

In the days leading up to the final, there were all sorts of media hype and publicity, and while people admired our style, nobody gave us an earthly. That suited me, as I preferred us to be the underdogs.

Once again, we based ourselves at Gleneagles Hotel where a rich American guest took a shine to the lads. Apparently, he thought this smartly dressed crew was a choir. Who could see Joe Harper and Arthur Graham as choirboys? He was soon told the truth, though, and he promised the squad a party if they won. That was in stark contrast to the board, who had only bought champagne for the lads following their semi-final win after I reminded the directors just how much they would earn the club. And it was a very tidy sum indeed, for an astonishing 108,000 people crowded into Hampden Park for the final.

The preparations had gone well, and apart from Alec Willoughby and Jim Whyte, who had only recently returned from injury, I had a fully fit squad to choose from. The Aberdeen team that day was Robert Clark, Henning Boel, George Murray, Jim Hermiston, Tommy McMillan, Martin Buchan, Derek McKay, Davie Robb, Jim Forrest, Joe Harper and Arthur Graham, with George Buchan as substitute.

Celtic had seven of their 1967 European championship side in their line-up, which read Evan Williams, Davie Hay, Tommy Gemmell, Bobby Murdoch, Billy McNeill, Jim Brogan, Jimmy Johnstone, Willie Wallace, George Connelly, Bobby Lennox and John Hughes, with Bertie Auld on the bench.

With two such talented sides, a great game was in prospect, and as I took my seat, I was feeling confident in my tactics. Celtic were due to meet Leeds United in the semi-final of the European Cup, but I knew Jock Stein would not let them relax. It was a Cup final, after all, and Celtic would attack. So I decided that I would trust to our defence and hit them with quick breaks upfield. I also told Joe Harper to move around and try to draw Billy McNeill and Jim Brogan out of defence to make room for Jim Forrest and our wingers. I also emphasised the need to play the ball on the ground and pass to feet, as Celtic had some big men in defence.

I had tried to keep the players relaxed all week, but before my final team talk, George Murray said, 'Give us that "eat-the-breid" stuff again,' and I gave them an address that would have roused the dead.

Sure enough, Celtic started fast and furious as I predicted, but our defence held out well, and, in the 27th minute, Derek McKay thumped in a cross which hit Bobby Murdoch on the arm.

The referee gave a penalty kick and Celtic went ballistic. The ref, Mr R.H. 'Bobby' Davidson, had a 'history' with Celtic, and their players crowded round him trying to get him to change his mind. Tommy Gemmell even flung the ball at Davidson and was booked for his pains. Meantime, Joe Harper had grabbed the ball and was waiting on the spot to take the penalty. Out of the corner of my eye I could see him playing keepie-uppie. When order was restored several minutes later, the coolest man in Hampden sent Celtic's goalkeeper Evan Williams the wrong way, and we were one up.

Within minutes, we looked to be level again as Bobby Lennox dispossessed Robert Clark and scored. Now, the 'Buzz Bomb' Lennox was one of the fastest players in the world, but he was not quick enough to fool referee Davidson, who had spotted him using a hand to rob our keeper. Funnily enough, Lennox had done the same thing to Robert in a League game, and that time he got away with it and scored!

But in the Cup final, he did not escape, though it was ourselves who got a break when Bobby Lennox went down in the box, apparently tripped by Martin Buchan. The Celtic fans and players screamed for a penalty. Mr Davidson was having none of it, so we got to half-time still in the lead.

I told the team that they were 45 minutes from victory and hadn't won anything yet. Celtic threw everything at us, bringing in Auld for Hughes and swapping Jimmy Johnstone to the left wing, but Jim Hermiston had the game of his life that day, along with Henning Boel, and they were the rocks in our defence.

With seven minutes remaining, we broke away and Derek McKay fired in a cross which Jim Forrest diverted at Williams, who could only parry it away. Who should be there to score but McKay. His extraordinary record of cup goals was continuing. But Celtic scored in the final minute through Lennox. Surely not even that great fighting squad could now equalise against us?

What followed were the longest seconds of my life, until, in injury time, Arthur Graham and Joe Harper combined to give Derek McKay a golden chance, which he took with glee. It is a fact that Derek McKay played 13 League games for Aberdeen and never once scored. He played in three Scottish Cup games and scored four, including the goals that won the Cup. The legend of 'Cup Tie McKay' was born, and though he left Aberdeen not much later, that enigmatic player will always have his place among the legends of Pittodrie.

We had won the Cup for only the second time in Aberdeen's history and had done it in style, becoming the only club to score three goals against Celtic that season. I watched as proud as a peacock as the team accepted the adulation of the thousands of fans who had come down from Aberdeen and elsewhere to support them. Martin Buchan became the youngest-ever captain to lift the Cup, and the lap of honour was wonderful to see.

How our fans deserved it. They had stuck by the club through thick and thin, and now it was their turn to savour success. The directors also revelled in the celebrations – they were fans, too. Charlie Forbes would later say it was the proudest moment of his life.

For me, I could only reflect that I had played in and lost two Scottish Cup finals in my career, but now I had played two and won one as a manager. It was a sweet, sweet feeling – the pinnacle of my time in football, though I was not to know it then.

Jock Stein had plenty to say about the referee, but he was entirely gracious to me and the Aberdeen players, shaking each one of us by the hand. He also sent in a crate of champagne to our dressing-room. I suspected it was the same champers I had spotted at Parkhead. It was Jock's way of saying, 'Well done, you out-thought me,' and that gesture was the true mark of the man.

After the celebrations, I was standing in the foyer of Hampden when Tommy Gallagher of the *Dundee Courier* spotted me and came over.

'Ned, you look like the calmest man here,' he said.

'That might be how I look on the outside, Tommy,' I replied, 'but inside I'm dancing!'

We went back to Gleneagles where the American was as good as his word, and we all had a whale of a time.

During the evening, young Arthur Graham – just 17 remember, and from that rough, tough part of Glasgow – went over to Bobby Calder and handed over his winner's medal. 'I want you to have this, Mr Calder,' he said. Bobby was deeply moved by the gesture, as was I. But he insisted that Arthur keep his medal, though he was as sure as I was that it would not be the last to be won by this remarkable lad.

The following day, we took the team bus back to Aberdeen, stopping at Stonehaven to accept the congratulations of the town's provost. Then it was onto an open-topped bus for an amazing procession through Aberdeen to the Town House. Tens of thousands of people surrounded us all the way through the city. I remember Robert Clark pointing at them and saying, 'Only a few weeks ago we got jeered off the pitch against Clydebank and look at us now.' I looked at him and said, 'That's fitba, son.'

The Lord Provost of Aberdeen was Robert Lennox, uncle of the famous singer Annie. He greeted us, and we made our way onto the balcony. It was 12 April 1970, and it was my 47th birthday, as the Lord Provost announced. To have 100,000 people sing 'Happy Birthday' to you is pretty special, I can tell you.

Then it was off back to Pittodrie, where the fans were allowed in to see us parade with the Cup.

Eventually, everyone departed the stadium, directors and all, leaving me with the Cup. I couldn't get the keys to the trophy room and didn't know where to put it, so I took it home with me. And that is how the Scottish Cup spent the first night of its second stay in Aberdeen – by the bedside of Mr and Mrs Turnbull.

13

Turnbull's Tornadoes

After such a splendid end to the season, there was every chance that 1970–71 would be an anticlimax. Indeed that eventually proved to be the case, but not before we put up an incredible fight which saw us come very, very close to being champions of Scotland.

We did so without Ernie McGarr. He had been picked for Scotland, and so we were in the almost unbelievable position of having two international goalkeepers on our staff. Robert was always going to be my first choice, barring injury, but Ernie wanted first-team football, and I could not stand in his way, so we sold him to Dunfermline Athletic. Jim 'Chalky' Whyte also moved, to Kilmarnock. We made one big signing – and 'big' was the operative word. Willie Young was a raw, red-headed giant of a lad, and, over the coming months, we gradually blooded him until he took his place in the squad. He would go on to be one of the great Dons.

Stevie Murray was now coming into his own as a thinking midfielder, and overall the team had a settled look. I had brought in Jimmy Bonthrone as a coach, and his quieter style worked well alongside my own rather more voluble presence. It was the old 'good cop, bad cop' routine, and guess who was the baddie? Jimmy was a marvellous friend and colleague, whose support I greatly appreciated. He went on to take over from me as manager, and I feel his achievements between 1971 and 1975 are underrated.

I had given the players a pep talk early in the season about the need to make Pittodrie the place that other teams feared to visit – Fortress Pittodrie – and I am proud to say we were not defeated at home all that season. I told the players that it was a matter of pride for them as professionals to compete in every minute of every game, and they did so in that memorable season.

But things did not go swimmingly at first. We blew a real chance to qualify from our League Cup section when Hibs beat us 4–0 in the final match, this despite Joe Harper having scored four on his own in the 7–3 win over Airdrie in the previous match.

We made history in the European Cup-Winners' Cup, but it was of the wrong sort. We had been drawn against Honvéd of Hungary in the first round, and, as a student of Hungarian football, I knew they would be tough.

On the Sunday before the match, I was relaxing at home when the doorbell rang. Valerie answered it and came in to say, 'Dad, it's Joey.' Uh-oh, I thought, here comes trouble, and his name is Harper.

'Sorry about this, gaffer,' he said, 'but you know the glass door in my digs?'

'Aye,' said I, knowing what was coming next.

'Well, I had a wee accident with it, and I've had to get three stitches in my back.'

His face was so angelic I could tell he was guilty.

'Aye, Joey, so you stumbled and fell into a glass door . . .'

'Honest, boss.'

'And who do you think you're trying to kid?'

He had obviously had a few the night before and perhaps had a wee 'fall' on the way home – or maybe three falls and a submission in a wrestling match.

I gave him the full blast: 'Stitches or no stitches, son, you are playing on Wednesday night!'

Sure enough, in the first leg at Pittodrie, Joe played through his pain and scored our second in one of the best European performances by Aberdeen. Honvéd went ahead early, but goals from Arthur Graham and then Joey had us in front by half-time, before Stevie Murray made it 3–1 seven minutes from time. I eventually took pity on Joe Harper and substituted him, but he had done his stuff, stitches or no.

Over in Hungary on 30 September 1970, they attacked from the start, with their playmaker Sándor Kocsis on fire. His first goal looked offside, and the linesman had his flag raised, but the referee gave the goal. In those days, it was very difficult to bend and dip the ball from a free kick, as it was of a different texture then, but Kocsis did it, with a lovely, swerving chip shot, which gave Robert Clark no chance.

Kozma scored what looked to be the clincher for them. I urged our guys to get forward, and, again, it was Stevie Murray who did the business, with a speculative shot that hit a defender on the way in.

It was 4–4 on aggregate, and the away goals had cancelled each other out. Up until then, European ties which finished level in such a way were decided on the toss of a coin, but UEFA had introduced the penalty shoot-out, and that night Aberdeen and Honvéd contested the first one in a major European tournament.

It was all new to us. Joe Harper or Jim Hermiston normally took our penalties, and finding another three to shoot from the spot took a few minutes. We never thought the tie would go to penalties and had not practised. Indeed, some of our guys had probably never taken a penalty in their life. The excitable Italian referee, Concetto Lo Bello, did not help matters, and the players were understandably nervous. Jim Forrest hit the bar with our third kick, and we needed them to miss. When their goalkeeper Bertalan Bicskei stepped forward to take the fifth and final kick, I thought we had a chance; however, a goalkeeper taking a penalty was not an unusual sight on the Continent, though I'd never seen it in Scotland. He slammed the ball home, and we were out of Europe in an unfortunately historic manner.

No doubt as a reaction to midweek events, we promptly lost our League match against Morton. But then something quite amazing happened. Everything I had preached about a solid defence allowing our players to press up the field and play a swift passing game suddenly came to wonderful fruition. We were simply unstoppable, as we went on a run of 15 wins from 15 matches which included 12 consecutive games in which we did not concede a goal – a British record. Robert Clark also set a record of 19 hours and 15 minutes without losing a goal. In that 12-match run, we scored 31 goals, 7 of them against Cowdenbeath.

I had always said that if we could beat both halves of the Old Firm in Glasgow, we could win the title, and we achieved that feat. When Joe Harper beat John Fallon with a header at Parkhead for the only goal of the game, we overtook Celtic to sit top of the table. It wasn't just the fact of the results which astonished people, it was the way we did it, with Joe Harper at his exciting best.

The run ended on 16 January with a 1–2 defeat at Hibs, Pat Stanton ending Robert's goalless record in the 64th minute, but we bounced back to beat Morton and were still looking good for the title. But all our dreams turned to ashes, almost literally so, on the night of 5–6 February 1971, when Pittodrie was hit by a massive blaze.

It was the middle of the night when the phone rang. I grabbed the receiver, and though I was barely awake, I registered that it was the club secretary, Bert Whyte, and he was saying, 'Boss, the place is on fire.' I sort of mumbled to him 'OK' and put the phone down. I must confess that at this point I did something very strange: I went back to sleep. It seemed to me that I was dreaming the whole experience, and I have since spoken to people who have had the same reaction to bad news. But then something inside my sleep-filled mind must have registered the import of what I'd been told. I sprang to life and was awake and fully conscious in an instant. I dressed hurriedly and drove to the stadium. From a fair distance away, I could see the glow in the dark; the place was well and truly alight. The fire had started deep in the main stand and had spread quickly through the largely wooden structure.

The firefighters did a terrific job and saved the Scottish Cup, but lots of club souvenirs and written records were lost, as were my golf clubs. The dressing-rooms were also destroyed, as well as many seats in the stand. In the morning light, it looked as though a stick of bombs had hit the place. Apart from the Cup, only two large metal trunks full of the players' gear were saved. They had been packed and made ready for the match later that day against Dunfermline down in Fife. The players were already staying in a hotel and learned the news by telephone.

I had a real dilemma facing me. I was pretty certain the Scottish League would allow us to postpone the game, but we were going so well in the League that I feared an interruption could stop our run to the title that was within our grasp. Sure enough, we were offered the chance to postpone, but I worried about how the players would react if, having got themselves prepared for such a vital match, it was then called off. On the other hand, how would they react to the news that their place of work – a second home to some of them – had burned down?

I thought that some would be bothered by the news and others would not, so, at first, I decided to cancel the game. But as the morning wore on, I changed my mind and decided that we would play. It is a decision that has haunted me ever since, and will do so until the grave. As I feared, some minds were elsewhere, and in goal for Dunfermline was none other than Ernie McGarr. He did a good job for his new team, who had gone ahead in the first half through Hugh Robertson. We just could not get an equaliser, but fortunately Celtic lost to St Johnstone and we were still top. But the defeat coupled with the fire seemed to demoralise some of our lads. Joe Harper's goal-scoring feats dried up, and he only scored one goal after that, though others stepped into the breach.

We had to change our training arrangements, which was also

unsettling, and Pittodrie was not the place it used to be. We drew with both Rangers and St Mirren at Pittodrie, where the wind now whistled through the burned-out stand and made skilful play difficult. But we had to ignore the surroundings, and I hammered it home to the players that they had to keep grinding out the results, which they did. We got back on track and remained top of the League until the beginning of April. It was nip and tuck between us and Celtic, with both of us dropping points.

It all came down to our home match against Celtic on 17 April 1971. We were three points ahead, but Stein's team had two games in hand. In the programme notes for that match, Stein graciously wrote, 'We don't intend to give up our title as champions easily. If, however, we do, I can see no club more worthy of being champions than the Dons.' In my contribution, I went back to Churchill for inspiration and wrote, 'After nine months of blood, sweat and tears, the crunch comes today for the Dons.' I added, 'This is the moment for supreme effort. Gone are the days of an inferiority complex presenting too big a burden. The players are full of confidence but not arrogance.' And I had plenty more to say in similar vein in the dressing-room.

It was as tough as I thought it would be. Harry Hood scored from a Jimmy Johnstone corner, but Alec Willoughby equalised after 38 minutes. We both had chances, and it looked as though we were going to win when Arthur Graham rounded goalkeeper Evan Williams, only for Billy McNeill to somehow get back and clear off the line.

The match ended 1–1, Celtic were on a roll, our heads went down, and the following week we went to Brockville and lost by a single goal. Had we beaten Falkirk, we might still have won the League, but our momentum was extinguished against Celtic, who became champions and would eventually win nine titles in a row, while our brave and sometimes brilliant challenge had ended with failure at the final hurdle.

Looking back at the end of the season, I singled out the fire and that loss to Dunfermline as the turning point for us. Yes, I know that a season does not revolve around a single match or incident, but that devastating fire hurt us so much, and I will always ask myself, 'What if I had postponed the Dunfermline match?' We had set new club records – longest winning run, fewest losses in a post-war season, fewest goals conceded ever – so I should have been proud; but we came so close to the championship that I will always feel a sense of loss.

We had given Celtic a mighty scare, however, and Jock Stein himself predicted we could do even better the following season. Aberdeen would have to accomplish things without me, however. For, in the close season of 1971, I received a call which would take me back to my first love, Hibernian FC.

I had already started pre-season training with Aberdeen and was very much looking forward to the following months, as I felt we had a very strong team who were now battle-hardened.

Dave Ewing was manager of Hibs at that time, but when Tom Hart took over the club in 1970, the two apparently did not get on. Tom Hart wanted to find out if I was interested in the job, but it wasn't 'the done thing' for a chairman to 'tap up' the manager of another club. I had had little contact with Tom in previous years, though on one occasion I had fixed him up with tickets for an Aberdeen–Hibs cup tie. But now he was in control of Hibs, and he wanted changes.

Hart was determined to try to get Hibs back to the very top of Scottish football. There was no doubting his love of the club. He had spent a great deal of money travelling to support the team over the years, and I knew of his generosity to players like myself, with those admirable golfing weekends he'd arranged.

Sportswriter Stewart Brown of the *Edinburgh Evening News* acted as a go-between, calling me to see if I would be interested in a meeting with the chairman. The invitation, via Stewart, was unusual: Hart wanted Carol and me to come to lunch at the Old

Course Hotel at St Andrews. Now, I knew perfectly well why he wanted to meet me, but I couldn't work out why he wanted my wife to come along.

I took a day off pre-season training, and Carol and I motored down to meet Tom, who was accompanied by his wife, Sheila. As always, Tom had things well organised, and lunch was served in a private room overlooking the Old Course.

Sheila Hart was a lovely person, and Carol and she went off for a chat while Tom and I got down to talking about the job. It was made easy by the fact that we had long been friendly, and he emphasised how much he wanted me to return to Easter Road. He had big plans for the future and was prepared to invest money, but he wanted me at the helm first and foremost. It was flattering, but I could see he was sincere. Friend or no, however, I was determined to drive a hard bargain financially, and, of course, I insisted on complete control of playing matters.

Tom agreed to this and made a good money offer – but you never accept the first offer! I assured him I would make my mind up quickly, but I had a lot to consider, not the least of which was uprooting my family. I wanted Carol's opinion before I made any decision.

Carol and Sheila Hart had got on famously, and in the car returning to Aberdeen, we talked about moving. We both loved Edinburgh, and Carol had, after all, spent most of her working life in the city. I do not think she had really settled that well in Aberdeen, and her sister and most of her friends still lived in Edinburgh. In a sense, it was easy for me to live in Aberdeen because I was always preoccupied with the business of the club. I knew that at times it was hard for Carol, as I spent so much time on club matters. I suspected that it was more difficult for women to integrate into a community, though Valerie was certainly enjoying school and had acquired a boyfriend, Alistair Low. They really were childhood sweethearts and not even her moving to Edinburgh could split them up. In fact, they're still together all this time later.

As we talked, we decided that it would be a wrench, but we would move.

It was also going to be really upsetting to leave the Dons. I had been there six years and had managed to at least start building the family atmosphere I so craved, helped by Dick Donald, who was now chairman, and other directors such as Chris Anderson, who had joined the board in 1967 and had become a very influential figure.

Above all, could I leave the players? They were mostly young men whom I had either signed or brought through the ranks, and I was sure they would shortly reach their full potential. The thought of walking away from a team with guys like Robert Clark, Henning Boel, Jim Hermiston, Willie Young, Joey Harper, Davie Robb, Stevie Murray and Arthur Graham was very troubling. I had everything I wanted in a squad. We had grown together, and those lads would run through hell and high water for the club.

Though we had not won any trophies, Aberdeen had enjoyed a successful season by anybody's standards. Hibs, by contrast, were in decline and had finished a full 24 points behind the Dons. Could I, should I, leave a club which was possibly on the verge of greatness for one which might be failing?

But Tom Hart was very convincing, and the lure of Easter Road, above all, made up my mind for me. I was going 'home'.

I went back to Tom and he stated that I could name my terms. I then had to tell the Aberdeen board, staff and players. No one had an inkling as to what was going on, and I think it came as a big surprise to most people at Pittodrie. The Aberdeen directors tried everything to make me change my mind, but I had decided to go to Hibs and nothing was going to divert me. The biggest wrench was leaving the players. I went down to the final training session and gathered them around. I knew it would be bad news for some of them, though one or two would be glad to see the back of me. It was a very emotional session, especially for some of the lads who had been with me from the very start, back in 1965. There were other players whom I had trained and encouraged in their careers, and I could see that one or two of them were close to tears. I was upset myself but was determined not to show it.

I recall very well the lecture that I gave them at the end of the session.

'There comes a time in everyone's life when you have to make a decision. Then you have to stick by that decision for good or ill. This is the situation that I find myself in at present. I have made a decision, and whether it is going to be successful or not, I cannot tell. This will happen to you all at one time or another in your life. What you must learn to do is stick by your decisions, as I must do now.'

It was done. My time at Aberdeen was over. The truth is that I had always considered Hibs to be a bigger club than Aberdeen. I felt that Hibs were the sleeping giants of Scottish football, and if I could get the right players, I knew I could make the club great again. In my playing days, all the top Continental clubs knew the name of Hibs, and I wanted that to be the case again.

It was also a good move financially; at that stage in my life, money was important to me, although never to a great degree. Suffice to say I was well paid at Aberdeen, but I was going to be significantly better off at Hibs. I suspected I would be the highest-paid manager in Scotland outside of the Old Firm, and I might be getting even more than Jock Stein at Celtic.

Nevertheless, the most important thing to me was the assurance that I would be in complete control of team matters, and that included the signing or transferring of players. Much later on, I would come to regret not sticking to that principle. Obviously, I would have to go to the board for approval of what I was intending to do, but since the board eventually consisted of people who had been placed there by Tom Hart, in reality I was dealing entirely with him.

My move to Edinburgh was announced at Gleneagles Hotel. Typically, Tom did things in style, and there were plenty of journalists on hand as soon as I had signed the deal. Tom also insisted that I be accommodated in the five-star North British Hotel in the early weeks of my new tenure. But that was far too fancy for me. I preferred the family-run Scotia Hotel, which I had used in my days as a player. It was off the beaten track, and that was fine by me. I left Carol and Valerie to start arranging a move and arrived at Easter Road the day before training started. It was a very good feeling to know that I was there as gaffer at last.

I was met by Tom McNiven, who was on the coaching staff. I said to Tom that I wanted to take a tour of the place to remind myself of the layout after all these years away from Easter Road. But in fact there was really only one place that I had never seen, and that was the away dressing-room. In we went, and the first thing I saw was an ashtray sitting on a window sill. I had just left a place where such a sight was common, and I hoped it would not be the same at Hibs. I then told Tom I would need a new tracksuit and that I wanted it ready in time for the following day's training session. The one that he brought me had a hole in it, and I blew my top when I saw this. 'I am the manager here, and we are starting training tomorrow. I want us all to be spick and span, and I personally want to set a good example for the players, because I intend to change things at Easter Road.'

I had heard on the grapevine that there had been a certain amount of slacking under the previous manager. Above all, I demanded fitness from players, and I knew some of them were lacking in that department. The players were about to get a rude awakening!

Tom told me that the only other tracksuits they had were dress tracksuits – the kind that were retained for match days and photo sessions. I told Tom to fetch me one of these. It was a point of principle with me that I should look my best on my first day as manager. I duly took the field the following morning in my best bib and tucker, and the players were suitably impressed. Unfortunately, I could not say I felt the same about them.

It was not plain sailing at all. There was a lack of discipline about the establishment, and I found out that the players had not been able to reach their full potential principally because they had not been properly trained. The methods I introduced at that time were entirely new to them. Having proved at Aberdeen that they worked, I was not prepared to compromise in any way at Easter Road.

Once again, I had to tell a group of players that if they did not knuckle down to hard work and if they in any way disobeyed my instructions, then they would be out the door. My reputation for tough discipline had obviously preceded me, and I am delighted to say that with very few exceptions, the players accepted my rule and the results on the pitch were obvious almost from the start.

I have to say, however, that I was very depressed by what I found, and after a fortnight or so, I was asking myself whether I had made the right move. Jimmy Bonthrone had been installed as manager at Aberdeen in my place, and I began to envy him, as he had some tremendous young players on his hands. But I soon realised that there was indeed talent in the ranks at Easter Road and that it had merely been badly used up until that point.

The lessons that had been learned in the time during and after the heyday of the Famous Five had all been forgotten, and it was a surprise even to the 1970s generation when I introduced training sessions which consisted entirely of working with the ball.

As I had done at Aberdeen, I began to build the team from the back forwards. There were only two goalkeepers on the books, and after pre-season training and friendlies, I did not think either was suitable for the job. I looked around and spotted that Jim Herriot, a former Scotland international who had played for Dunfermline and Birmingham City, was languishing in South Africa. But apparently his family had not settled, and the word was that he might want to return to Scotland. I persuaded Jim to return from the Durban

City club in South Africa to replace our regular goalkeeper for one 'trial' game at York City. At this point I have to confess to breaking football's rules. I was concerned that if other clubs learned of his availability, Jim might be snaffled up, so I played him under a false name. The 'trialist' A.N. Other in that match was Jim Herriot of Scotland – well, the beaks can hardly discipline me now!

Jim was signed that night, and the game had also given me a chance to show I meant business about discipline. We were staying at a hotel in Harrogate not far from York and some of the players wanted to do a bit of sightseeing or whatever before the match. I told them to report to York City's ground at 2 p.m., and I made sure I was there dead on time. Some were there on time, some a little late and the last of them drifted in at 2.20 p.m. I gave them a verbal roasting: 'If I say be at a place by two o'clock, then you will be there at two o'clock, otherwise you'll suffer the consequences.' I may not have been quite as diplomatic as that, and they certainly got my message.

I also impressed upon the players the fact that Hibernian FC was a club with a great history, and, by chance, there was an early opportunity to show the squad exactly what I meant by that.

We had agreed to meet German cracks FC Schalke 04 in a pre-season friendly. Hibs were making a presentation to old Jimmy McColl, the veteran former player and trainer, to mark his decades of service at Easter Road. Schalke were one of the teams we beat on our tour of Germany in 1950. So, for the first time since we stopped playing, the Famous Five met up to mark the occasion of this new clash with the German side, and also because we all knew and greatly respected Jimmy. Gordon Smith, Bobby Johnstone, Lawrie Reilly and Willie Ormond joined me on the pitch, and we received a long and loud standing ovation from the fans. If the players didn't know before then that Hibs had a wonderful history, they were well aware from that moment on. Perhaps it was that history lesson which encouraged the players to redouble their efforts and start playing together in the way that I wanted.

With Hibs in those early days, I was able to put into place the philosophy I had developed at Queen's Park and Aberdeen. The only part of the team which a manager can develop and control is the defence. The remainder of the team must play to a pattern, but within that system they must be encouraged to express themselves. I was able to implement this strategy very quickly at Hibs.

Jim Herriot brought a lot of experience to the team, but the rest of the defence was mainly young blood. John Brownlie, Jim Black, John Blackley and Eric Schaedler were impressive talents to work with, and soon the defensive organisation began to take shape. Brownlie was all skill and flair, and was one of the best attacking full-backs I ever saw. By contrast, Eric Schaedler was all speed and strength. He had not been rated by the previous administration at Easter Road, but I took him under my wing and he prospered as a result, largely because he was a good listener and prepared to learn lessons. At centre-back we had Jim Black and John Blackley. Jim was one of the least mentioned but also one of the most effective players in that team. Blackley was a magnificent footballer who liked to beat players, even in defence. The important thing was that they all played together as a unit and they were the bedrock on which I built the team. The subsequent success of 'Turnbull's Tornadoes', as the team became known, stemmed from that early work with the defence.

What amazes people is that I was able to take a bunch who had underachieved and turn them round so quickly. It didn't surprise me. I spotted what was wrong and corrected it, and then added just a few more players to the mix, chopping and changing until I was sure I had the right blend.

I bought only a handful of players at first, but all of them were experienced men. I got Alex Edwards from Dunfermline and brought Alan Gordon in from Dundee United. Jerry Kerr was manager of United at that time, and Jim McLean was his understudy and was about to take over. Jim did not want Alan to be sold, and he came down to Easter Road with Jerry, perhaps hoping to stop the sale. But I managed to get the deal, and we had acquired the kind of goal-scoring, good-in-the-air forward I needed for the team I was trying to construct.

Like Jim Herriot, Alan had stuck in my mind from when he was a young lad. He had played for Hearts with the likes of Willie Bauld and was a more-than-useful player. At this point, I would like to confirm the famous story concerning myself and Alan. He was a very clever man, who had gone to university and had graduated with a degree in the arts. He had also studied accountancy, and I often remarked that he and I were always the cleverest people in the dressing-room – at least that is how I saw it. There was no doubt whatsoever that he was very much better educated than I was, but I liked to let him know that I was in possession of superior football knowledge – my brains were in my feet, you might say. It was often reported that we did not get on, and there was an element of truth in that, but, really, it was just a case of two people being from entirely different backgrounds.

I cannot recall the exact circumstances, but, after one match or training session, the dressing-room banter was in full swing. Alan had perhaps tried to be too clever, so I went back at him, saying, 'The trouble with you, Gordon, is that your brains are all in your head.' I meant it as a joke, a reference to his considerable learning but occasional tendency to let the side down by trying something on a football pitch which he was not capable of doing. I dare say that the only two people in the room who got the joke were Alan and I. It has somehow been misrepresented that I was making a mistake and that I did not know what I was saying, but nothing could be further from the truth. It was a witticism which has gone down in football history, and I have been amazed to find that quotation repeated in magazines, newspapers and books ever since – and that remark was made more than 30 years ago.

One Scottish journalist recently used it and attributed the

remark to 'the late Eddie Turnbull'. Sorry to disappoint the writer, but, in the immortal words of Mark Twain, reports of my death have been greatly exaggerated. Mind you, that story did encourage me to hurry up with this book!

As we began season 1971–72, things soon began to gel, helped by the buzz among the lads. You can always tell a happy dressing-room: everyone has a good friendly slanging at everyone else. At Easter Road, this process was encouraged by the bewildering set of nicknames which they had all acquired over the years.

Some of the derivations were obvious. Alan Gordon was 'Tosh' because he was good in the air, like Liverpool's John Toshack. Blackley was 'Sloop' after the old Beach Boys song 'Sloop John B'. Jim Black was called 'Cilla' after the singer and TV-show hostess. John Brownlie was 'Onion' because his hair was always a mess. Pat Stanton was known as 'Niddrie' because that was where he hailed from. Arthur Duncan was 'Flyer' because of his speed. Perhaps the most of bizarre of all was 'Sodjer' – Alex Cropley, who was born at the Army headquarters in Aldershot. I never did find out why the Dunfermline players had nicknamed Alex Edwards 'Mickey' after Mickey Mouse, but the name had stuck. Personally, I could not see a resemblance between Jim Herriot and Robert Mitchum, the American actor who lent Jim his nickname 'Bob' because they both apparently had sleepy eyes. Nor did I ever find out what the players called me behind my back. I had always been known as 'Ed', 'Eddie' or 'Ned', but I suspect I was called a fair few other names in my time . . .

By and large, the players all got on well, but just as important in the creation of a successful team was the backroom staff. Wilson Humphries had been a good player in his day, and I had met him and become friends with him on a coaching course down at Largs. I suppose I was looking for someone like Jimmy Bonthrone, a quieter man who could pour oil on troubled waters after I had stirred them up. That is the role Wilson played at Hibs, and he did it very well. In many ways, Wilson was just like Jimmy and was just too nice for his own good. But he and I worked well together, and I know the players greatly respected him.

Tom McNiven had stayed as trainer, and my old mate John Fraser was coach. Tom had not played professional football, but he had a background in physiotherapy and had also been a talented runner. It was largely due to him that we had so few problems with muscular injuries in my time at Easter Road. He would conduct warm-ups that lasted for 40 minutes, and he emphasised to the players the need to remain supple at all times. 'Have you ever seen a cat after it has been out chasing mice?' he would ask. 'Or maybe you have seen a lion on television? They are always stretching, always trying to relax their muscles. That's why you don't see cats with cramp.' It was a good way of explaining the principle.

I brought in Bertie Auld quite soon after I joined Hibs. I wanted him to keep playing and offered him the chance to play in a deep position on the left of midfield, but he was reluctant to continue playing, so I took him onto the staff, largely because I knew he had a football brain which would benefit the team as a whole. Later, I added John Lambie, who became Mr Partick Thistle later in his career. John has always publicly given me great credit for teaching him a lot, but in fact he was always a natural motivator, as he has shown over the years. And I cannot think where he learned all those curses . . .

All too soon, we had to put practice behind us and start the real thing. We began the 1971–72 season with the League Cup, and the opening match was against Motherwell at Fir Park. We won 3–0 and it was quite as comfortable as the scoreline suggests. We went on to top our section but a 2–0 defeat at Brockville could not be overcome at Easter Road and we went out of the League Cup at that stage.

Things were quite different in the League, where we began with a 2–0 victory over Hearts at Tynecastle – something which is always likely to endear you to the Hibs fans. We remained unbeaten until the end of September, and it was something of a honeymoon period for the team and myself.

Defeat by Celtic and Aberdeen brought us back down to earth. Jock Stein's team ran away with the League that year, but, for a time, Rangers, Aberdeen and ourselves all looked capable of mounting a challenge. We were undone by the odd daft result, notably a loss to East Fife. By the beginning of 1972, it was clear that we were going to finish quite high up the table, and on occasion we put together some startling results, beating Falkirk 6–0 and St Johnstone 7–1. Late in the season, we won five of the last six matches to finish fourth on level points with Rangers, though they had a better goal difference. Only champions Celtic and my old club Aberdeen finished ahead of us on points.

That left only the Scottish Cup, and from the start of the competition, it was clear that we were on a roll. We beat Partick away, then Airdrie at Easter Road to set up a quarter-final with Aberdeen. A 2–0 victory put us into the draw for the semi-final, and the SFA's wee wooden balls kept Celtic and Rangers apart, as they always seemed to do. We had to face the latter side, and in our first encounter we drew 0–0.

The replay was on a Monday night at Hampden Park, and in that match we saw John Brownlie at his best. I had begun to play Alex Edwards in an unusual position. Very few managers sussed that I was no longer playing him as an out-and-out winger. That was where he lined up, but he would soon move slightly inside from the wing to the gap where an old-fashioned inside-right might have operated. This baffled full-backs, who did not know whether to come with him or stay in their normal position. John Brownlie, with his pace, could go down the wing and exploit the space, but sometimes he and Edwards would exchange places, and in that game we destroyed Rangers down the right wing. By full time, we had beaten Rangers 2–0, and in my first season as manager, I had taken Hibs to a Scottish Cup final.

My experience at Aberdeen had taught me one thing above all – that winning trophies counted for everything at a football club, and for sides outside of the Old Firm, winning the Scottish Cup was a massively important achievement. The traditions of Celtic and Rangers are what make them the forces they are. Both clubs are used to winning, and, in any sphere of life, if you get into a habit, you tend to retain it. That is why they will always be dominant in Scottish football. You can complain about the way they reached their superior position because of their particular histories on either side of the religious divide, but there is no denying that they are used to winning and that that tradition keeps them at the top of Scottish football.

For a club like Hibs, which had won the Scottish Cup only once in its history, in 1902, just getting into the final was a truly wonderful feat. On 6 May 1972, I was delighted and proud to lead my team to Hampden Park to play Celtic in front of 106,000 people, and despite the eventual result, nothing can ever detract from the fact that we made it to the final in our first season together.

I knew before the match that we were in trouble. The players' faces said it all. Celtic and Hibs gathered in the same hotel for lunch, and while our boys were nervous and restless, the Celtic squad were buoyant. It was difficult to get our boys to relax, as they had never been in that situation before. There had been a lot of media attention in the days running up to the final, and despite my best efforts to deflect that from the squad, the hype still got to them. I could not help feeling misgivings, but I hid them well and delivered my usual team talk.

Before the match, I had told Alan Gordon that if Celtic got a corner or a free kick close to goal, he should get back and mark Billy McNeill. Alan could match the Celtic captain in the air. But, inexplicably, he was posted missing the very first time McNeill came forward, and big Billy scored from close range.

Alan redeemed himself with the equaliser, but the damage was done, and though we competed well for the rest of the half, they went ahead through a Dixie Deans header. In the 54th minute,

Deans scored again, and from then on Celtic were rampant. Wee Dixie got his hat-trick after 89 minutes, and Lou Macari got two late goals as we tried to get forward and make a game of it. To this day, I maintain we did not deserve to lose 6–1, and most neutral observers concluded the same.

We came back to Edinburgh to a warm reception but not the jamboree we would have experienced had we won. Before we left Hampden, I met some of the pressmen I knew well, and one of them asked, 'Where do you go from here, Eddie?' I remember growling one short sentence: 'We'll be back.' I meant that we would return to Hampden and win trophies, because that is what I genuinely felt at the time. Not even I could believe how soon that would come true.

Only recently, I saw a video of that team from the early 1970s. There was a tremendous balance to the side, as there was a mix of speed and power, skill and strength. I have to admit that I had forgotten just what a good team they were, and the quality of the football was quite sublime at times. The speed of the passing, the interlinking exchanges and the way the team moved up and down the field as a unit were wonderful to see again after all those years.

I believe the name of the video was *Turnbull's Tornadoes*, the nickname we were given quite early on and which was popularised by a song, which was even released as a single. It was written by the chairman's wife, Sheila Hart, who was a very talented musician and played the fiddle and other instruments.

How better to close this chapter of my life than with her words, which summed up what that team meant to so many.

'Turnbull's Tornadoes'

United we stand here, divided we fall
We play for each other, when we're on the ball.

TURNBULL'S TORNADOES

Our fans are the greatest, they cheer us each game,
We're Turnbull's Tornadoes, Hibernian's the name.

(Chorus)
Hibs, Hibs, Hibs for the Cup,
Our team's the greatest, they never give up.
Hibs, Hibs, the boys in the green,
The best brand of football the world's ever seen.

We're all for each other, each man plays for all,
We give our best football, to answer the call.
While we entertain you, to win is our aim,
We're Turnbull's Tornadoes, Hibernian's the name.

(Chorus)
Hibs, Hibs, Hibs for the Cup,
Our team's the greatest, they never give up.
Hibs, Hibs, the boys in the green,
The best brand of football the world's ever seen.

We're Turnbull's Tornadoes, yes that's who we are,
We play for the Hibees, we're known near and far.
Our fans are the greatest, they cheer us each game,
We're Turnbull's Tornadoes, Hibernian's the name.

(Chorus)
Hibs, Hibs, Hibs for the Cup,
Our team's the greatest, they never give up.
Hibs, Hibs, the boys in the green,
The best brand of football the world's ever seen.

14

Glory Days

If losing the Cup by such a margin had been the biggest
disappointment of my managerial career, the first seven months
of the next season were to prove a total contrast, bringing some of
the greatest success I would ever enjoy.

At the end of the season, I had told Joe Baker he had to leave
Easter Road. It was not easy to say goodbye to a man who had
been a star during his first period at Hibs and whom I had played
alongside, but at 32, he was not the player he had been when he
had famously become the first 'Scotsman' to play for England and
had moved to Italy. He was one of twelve players I let go – shades
of Aberdeen – as I set about rebuilding the side.

The season began with a tournament I didn't actually like all
that much – at first! Back then, the SFA were not prepared to allow
companies to sponsor existing tournaments, so the Drybrough
Cup was an invention of the brewers of that name; it rewarded the
top-scoring teams in the League with a tournament of their own.

The first competition took place in 1971, just days after I had
left Aberdeen. The top four from the First Division were seeded to
play the top four from the Second Division, and eventually my old
club Aberdeen and Celtic won through to the final on 7 August, all
the ties and semis having been played in a week.

I have to say I watched with mixed feelings as Aberdeen won

2–1, thanks to a penalty by Joe Harper and the winner from Davie Robb. 'My' Aberdeen had won a trophy, and that didn't help my mood at Hibs.

But a year later and after a full season with the emerging Tornadoes, it was Hibs' turn for some beer money. In the semi-final, we hammered Rangers, who had nine of the team which had won the European Cup-Winners' Cup only two months previously. We beat them 3–0 in front of a crowd of 27,000, with a goal from Pat Stanton and a double from Alan Gordon, and that gave us a final against Celtic.

I always used to say, 'Was there ever a bad Hibs v. Celtic match?' Both clubs have a culture of playing attacking football, and there was a traditional rivalry between the Edinburgh and Glasgow teams regarding which was the more entertaining side. Over the years, there have been many high-scoring encounters between Hibs and the club which, as is never forgotten in Leith, purloined our best players when they started up in 1888. There's a lot of long memories in Scottish football.

A trophy is a trophy and a final is a final, and there was also sponsor's money to be won. The memories of the Scottish Cup final defeat were fresh in our minds. There would be no repeat of that debacle – I would make sure of that. The crowd of 50,000 at Hampden Park did not know it, but they were about to get a treat.

From the start, we were brilliant. Nobody could have lived with us in that first half. I had left out Alex Edwards because I had remembered how he had been so quiet in the Scottish Cup final, but that meant plenty room for John Brownlie to get forward and Sloop was quite superb. Our defence was rock solid, Pat Stanton and Alex Cropley controlled the midfield, and Alan Gordon, Jimmy O'Rourke and Arthur Duncan ran riot up front. If I had been a cat, I would have been purring. To the total disbelief of the Celtic fans, and probably our own supporters too, we romped into a three-goal lead, with Alan Gordon scoring two and then pressuring big Billy McNeill into conceding an own goal.

There was a pitch invasion by Celtic fans, and it upset our rhythm. Big Billy then inspired their comeback. He scored their first, and Jimmy Johnstone bagged two excellent goals for a 3–3 scoreline at ninety minutes.

I came onto the pitch and sat the players down. I knew this was a key point in the team's progress. If Celtic, as everybody expected, strolled the game in extra time, it would be a big psychological blow to us. I told them to keep playing football, to keep passing and keep the ball on the ground, and they would get their reward. When Jimmy O'Rourke got our fourth goal, I could sense the day was ours. Arthur Duncan's wonderful late solo effort made sure the Cup came to us, and I had won my first trophy with Hibs.

Some people were quick to say it was 'only' the Drybrough Cup (actually, one of them was me!), but I knew we had started something which the fans would enjoy. The proof of that was the big crowd which came to applaud the cup-winners when we played West Bromwich Albion in a friendly the following Tuesday.

We made a fine start to the League, losing only to Aberdeen, Dundee and Rangers before Christmas and handing out some thumpings – as when we thrashed Ayr United 8–1. But it was cups at home and abroad which saw us at our best.

Throughout my time at Hibs, there was nothing quite like the atmosphere of the big European nights at Easter Road. The top foreign opposition always brought out a big crowd, and we had many memorable encounters. In 1972, because Celtic had won the League, we were put into the European Cup-Winners' Cup as losing finalists in the Scottish Cup. In the first round, we were drawn against Sporting Lisbon of Portugal, and the first leg was set for 13 September in Lisbon.

The manager of Sporting Lisbon was the selfsame Ronnie Allen who had been manager of Wolves in the USA in 1967. I reckoned that I owed him one for the defeat which he had inflicted on Aberdeen in the final of the President's Cup. I knew the Portuguese were a strong side and we would have to defend, but I felt that if we could get an away goal, then we had a very good chance of beating them at Easter Road. We defended well, but they scored two, while Arthur Duncan gave us a real chance with a fine goal. With away goals counting double, we needed only a single counter at Easter Road as long as they didn't score any.

I was still worried, because Sporting Lisbon had shown they were capable of scoring and had a great striker, a Brazilian called Héctor Yazalde, who would become the top scorer in Europe the following season. Sure enough, in the return leg in front of 26,000 people, it was the Brazilian who equalised late in a first half which we had dominated and during which Alan Gordon had headed a goal which had put us ahead on aggregate.

Now they only needed one goal to force extra time, but in the second half we were playing down the slope and that, coupled with the backing of our fans, gave us the edge. It is still one of the best 45 minutes I've ever seen from a team I managed. With Duncan and Edwards on the wings and Cropley and Stanton in midfield, we utterly outplayed the Portuguese, though they started the half well. But from the fifty-fifth minute, we enjoyed eight minutes of football from a dream. Alan Gordon set up Jimmy O'Rourke for our second, then Gordon got his own second as we swept them aside. In the 63rd minute, O'Rourke got his second, and in between their goalie made a couple of excellent saves. It was fabulous stuff. Jimmy got his hat-trick from a penalty after 80 minutes, and their centre-half, Manaca, was so befuddled by the end that he put through his own goal.

I have to say that Ronnie Allen and his team took their defeat very sportingly. At the dinner in the North British Hotel, I reminded Ronnie about the American final, and he said, 'Well, you certainly got your revenge tonight!'

The next round gave us a trip which nobody wanted, to Albania to play Besa Kavaje. I knew we would beat them over two legs, but I told the team to start the way they had left off against Lisbon. In the first leg at Easter Road, they went one better, Jimmy O'Rourke scoring a second successive hat-trick in Europe, with two from Arthur Duncan and one each from John Brownlie and Alex Cropley giving us a 7–1 victory.

Going to Albania was like taking a step back into the Middle Ages. The country was under the control of the supposedly Communist dictator Enver Hoxha, and it was easily the poorest nation in Europe. I will never forget arriving at the airfield in Albania, because it was located between mountains, and the pilot had to weave the plane around to get us down – frightening stuff.

The Albanians seemed scared of anything Western, and they searched every bag and case we had. As I had done when Aberdeen travelled to Yugoslavia, I insisted that we bring our own food. We did not fear being poisoned, but I can tell you that I would not like to have been forced to eat the local chow. It looked and smelled disgusting, but somehow they seemed to have plenty of dark chocolate, though that is no use for people to live on. Virtually every face we saw in Albania showed evidence of malnutrition. The signs of extreme poverty were everywhere, and even during the match, Besa could not escape their lowly status. Their shirts were supposed to be cherry red, but they had been washed so many times that they were a light pink shade, and the numbers had been put on with crayon or something. It was almost a relief to get a 1–1 draw and get out of the place.

Meantime, we had advanced to the Scottish League Cup final, with a 6–2 away thrashing of Airdrieonians being particularly memorable, if only because one of their 'fans' hurled a brick through our team bus window as we left Broomfield.

A 1–0 victory over Rangers in the semi-final led to the 'all green' final between ourselves and Celtic. It would give me a unique record

– the only manager to best Jock Stein at Hampden in the finals of three separate tournaments with two different teams. Given Stein's place in the history of Scottish football, that's not a bad record.

Our first goal that day was a beauty. I had preached to the players that they should be inventive even at free kicks; in a lovely move, Alex Edwards lobbed the ball to Pat Stanton, and we were 1–0 up.

I had spotted during the first half that there was a bit of a gap on the left side of Celtic's defence, and I sent Alex Edwards to fill the hole, which also allowed John Brownlie to get forward more often down the right wing. Edwards was a very clever player with a real football brain, and he gave Celtic no peace at all in the rest of the match.

Yet Celtic never lie down. Kenny Dalglish scored their goal and was outstanding throughout, but Jimmy O'Rourke scored what proved to be the winning goal with a terrific shot from 25 yards. There were about 12 minutes left when the match restarted, and they seemed to drag on into eternity, but the final whistle eventually put an end to the doubts. We had won the Scottish League Cup and had beaten one of the best sides in Europe to do so.

We deserved to win the Cup that day. We were the superior team, and Jock Stein himself admitted as much. The Celtic manager made a point of shaking the hand of every Hibs player, and told me the better team had won.

It was the most fantastic experience for the players. The club laid on a terrific reception back in Edinburgh, with a traditional open-topped bus tour of the inner city, along Princes Street and back to Easter Road. It was not over-the-top stuff. We had done something I had never done as a player – won a cup at Hampden Park. Now I knew what we had missed back in the '40s and '50s, and it was an amazing feeling to achieve a cup win as a manager.

The key to the success of that Tornadoes team was that we had players in important positions who could change a game in an instant. They were creative players who were not afraid to try something, and the likes of Edwards and Cropley could turn attack into defence with one pass. For any team to be successful, you have to have width, and I cannot understand why so many sides nowadays do not play with wingers. I used to say to the players, 'How do you open up a tin can?' and they soon learned that the answer was 'From the outside.' I would preach incessantly to them that they needed to get wide, as they would do the most damage from the wings and round the back, hitting the byline and crossing from there. That's what Edwards and Duncan, Cropley and Brownlie could do. They all played for each other, and midfield and forwards were not afraid to come back and help out the defence. But most of all, we scored goals. By Hogmanay of 1972, we had scored more than 100 goals in competitive matches since August.

We had also won two trophies but were shortly to win a prize beyond compare: footballing immortality, at least anywhere the fortunes of Hibs or Hearts are followed.

The most famous match I have ever been involved in, as far as Hibs fans are concerned anyway, took place a little more than three weeks after the League Cup final, on 1 January 1973, when we played Hearts at Tynecastle in the First Division.

Some time before the match, I called John Fraser into my room. I knew I could trust my former playing colleague implicitly. Indeed, for many years, I gave this faithful and loyal man an important task – he would take my detailed plans for every match and for every training programme to the club secretary to be typed up. He thus knew a lot of my secrets, but he never once revealed them. Those files, by the way, were lost in one of the redevelopments at Easter Road. I'm not boasting, but I think an important bit of the club's history, and maybe even Scottish football history, was lost with them.

I wanted something to give us an edge against Hearts, so I said to John that I wanted him to go and watch them a couple of times in preparation for the Ne'erday game. We were still in with a chance of the League title, and I knew that if we beat Hearts, that might set us up for a serious challenge in the spring. That was my main aim – it was always nice to beat Hearts, but that season we had bigger ambitions.

John went off to watch Hearts and came back to report that he had spotted a possible weakness in their game plan. Bobby Seith was manager at Tynecastle and he was experimenting with a new system, despite his players' misgivings. To John must go the credit for much of what transpired that Ne'erday. 'They only play with three up front and they don't play with a left-winger, boss,' said John, and I immediately grasped the possibilities. If John Brownlie did not have to worry about an outside-left, he could get forward and help Alex Edwards. We would blitz them down the right. The game plan was set.

It nearly all went wrong, because Hearts had a couple of early chances, which Jim Herriot saved. But soon we began to pass the ball mesmerically and were tearing Hearts apart. After Jimmy O'Rourke scored the opener, I knew we were going to do something memorable, and much of the attacking was indeed down the right wing.

It happens to every team: you have an off day, while your opponents are unstoppable. That was us that Ne'erday – a Panzer tank would not have stopped us. We were 3–0 up after twenty-seven minutes, and added two more by half-time. It may seem strange to say, but Hearts' goalkeeper, Kenny Garland, was actually playing quite well!

So what do you say to your team in the dressing-room at half-time when you are 5–0 up against your deadliest rivals? A myth has grown up, perhaps because I mentioned avoiding injuries, that I told our boys to go easy in the second half. But the point about any myth is that it is not true, and I can assure you that at half-time on 1 January 1973, I said nothing of the sort! I told the team to get back out onto that Tynecastle pitch and keep playing the same way, and added that above all they needed to keep their concentration. When you are five goals up, it is easy to be sidetracked. Effectively, I said 'give no quarter', and I meant every word; for I knew that if the positions were reversed, Hearts would do the same to us.

By the end of a totally one-sided match, Jimmy O'Rourke, Alan Gordon and Arthur Duncan had each scored two, and Alex Cropley added the other for a 7–0 victory which shocked Scottish football. And if it had not been for Kenny Garland, it could well have been more!

How good were we that day? In the programme notes for our next match, against East Fife, I wrote: 'It was as fine a display as I can recall in the past 25 years; delightful football played at a breathtaking pace, and the team I played in didn't produce anything like it.' Looking back, that may have been an exaggeration, but at the time, we knew we had done something very special, and the very fact that the game is still talked about 30-odd years later shows the impact it had.

Sadly, things did not go well for us after that astonishing high point of the season. John Brownlie broke a leg, we had other injuries and suspensions, and then we had to face the very strong Yugoslavians Hadjuk Split in the quarter-finals of the Cup-Winners' Cup.

In the first leg, at Easter Road, we were again in brilliant form and were leading 4–1 with just 13 minutes to go through a hat-trick from Alan Gordon and one from Arthur Duncan. They won a corner on the left at the Dunbar Road end, and, uncharacteristically, our defence missed tackles, allowing Hlevnjac to pull back a vital goal. At 4–1 we had a real chance of going through to the semis, but that late goal really worried me, as Hadjuk would only need to score twice in Split to qualify on the away-goals rule.

The Hadjuk stadium was a small and tidy ground with the terracing close to the pitch. I have never experienced a noise like it. Their fans created a non-stop cacophony, and our guys were definitely intimidated by it. Poor Jim Herriot didn't handle the atmosphere well, and I blamed him for all three goals. He missed two crosses which allowed Surjac and Hlevnjac to score, and then, with the goalkeeper posted missing at a cross, John Blackley sliced into his own goal. Though we had chances, we were unable to take advantage of them, and we were out 4–5 on aggregate, away goals counting double. I rarely used Jim Herriot again after that, and, with Jim McArthur signed from Cowdenbeath, Herriot moved on to St Mirren later that year.

Losing that quarter-final was a crushing disappointment, as I really felt we could have gone on and won the Cup-Winners' Cup; but such was the disappointment of the defeat in Split that we did not win a game after that for the rest of the season. Rangers put us out of the Scottish Cup before Celtic got their revenge for the League Cup match by winning 3–0 at Easter Road to clinch their eighth successive title, while we finished behind Rangers in third place, to qualify for Europe again.

I had been pleased to see McArthur, Tony Higgins, Des Bremner and others come into the team, so I only made one significant signing in the next few months.

We got Joe Harper thanks to a tip-off from an old friend, Joe Mercer, who at that time was managing Manchester City. He was visiting Easter Road and asked Tom Hart to send for me. I was delighted to see him and even more pleased when the conversation got around to Joey. 'He's not happy at Everton and Harry Catterick [their manager] might sell him.' Tom Hart immediately said, 'Do you want him?' and my mind went into overdrive. At Aberdeen, Joe had played alongside Jim Forrest, and they had formed a very good partnership. I thought he could do the same with Alan Gordon, and the deal was done within a few days. Sadly, although Joe got his share of goals, he never really hit it off with the Hibs fans. Football supporters are a law unto themselves with their likes and dislikes, and Joe was never taken to the hearts of the Easter Road support, eventually moving back to Aberdeen for more success.

Before all that, we completed a superb hat-trick of victories over Celtic in cup finals in July 1973. In the Drybrough Cup, we once again beat Rangers in the semi-finals, with Des Bremner and Tony Higgins scoring in a 2–1 win. That match went to extra time, and so did the final at Hampden a few days later.

Celtic dominated the first half, Dalglish hitting the crossbar, but we came good in the second half after I sent on Alex Cropley for the young Iain Munro, who was rather overawed by the occasion. In extra time, we were again the better side, and, in the last minute, Cropley and Tony Higgins combined to set up Alan Gordon for the winner.

We had another trophy, but I knew we had a tough season ahead if we were to match the feats of the big two from Glasgow. We were also to make our first foray into the UEFA Cup, as the old Inter-Cities Fairs Cup was now known.

In that tournament, we had a comfortable 3–1 aggregate victory over Iceland's IB Keflavik before we faced Leeds United in the second round. This was the Leeds of Billy Bremner, Trevor Cherry, Terry Yorath, Allan Clarke, Peter Lorimer and Joe Jordan. Yet, over 210 goalless minutes, we matched them, and we should have won.

Big Tony Higgins was one of those players who could win matches on his own if he was on song, and if he had been a bit more consistent, he would have been one of the best players in Scotland for many years. I will never forget the performance he gave down at Elland Road, where he virtually ran over the top of the Leeds defence. He was superb, and we deserved a result if only because of him. Tony always talked a good game and stuck up for himself, so it was no surprise to me that he later became the head of the Scottish Professional Footballers' Association, a job he has done well now for many years.

The return leg against Leeds was totally frustrating. We matched them and often outplayed them, and I still cannot believe that referee Herr Schiller of Austria disallowed a perfectly good goal from Alan Gordon after consulting with his linesman. After extra time, the tie went to penalties, and, as luck would have it, it was Pat Stanton who missed as everyone else scored. He sent substitute goalkeeper Glan Letheren the wrong way, but the ball rebounded off the post. It was a very cruel way to lose to the Englishmen.

In December 1973, I made the headlines for the wrong reasons, as I had told the referee of the Scottish League Cup quarter-final second leg, Alistair McKenzie, what I thought of him. Personally, I thought I was rather mild, since I didn't question his parentage, merely his competence. Mr McKenzie did not take kindly to my remarks and included them in his report to the SFA. I was duly summoned before the Referees' Committee a few days before Christmas. I got an unwelcome present: a fine of £20 and a warning as to my future conduct. I felt the sentence was a bit harsh, considering that in ten years as a manager, I had never been in trouble with the beaks before.

We had lost our chance to defend the League Cup when Rangers beat us over two legs, and we went out of the Scottish Cup to Dundee after a replay; but the most agonising loss was to Celtic on 23 February 1974. Our title challenge was solid up until then, but that day we lost 2–4 to Celtic at Easter Road, and at the end of the season we were second, just four points behind them. Another case of 'if only'.

The following season, 1974–75, saw us in the UEFA Cup again, and, in one of our finest-ever performances, we slaughtered Rosenborg of Norway by a score which remains the club's record in Europe, a massive 9–1, which followed a 3–2 victory for us over there, giving a 12–3 aggregate.

In the second round, we met one of the biggest clubs in the world, Italy's Juventus. It was then that we ran into a crazy fixture mess. We had already qualified for the Scottish League Cup final, so in quick succession we met Celtic in the League, Juventus, Celtic in the final and Juventus again. Our season would be made or broken in the space of two and a half weeks.

We did not make a good start. Celtic were rampant at that time and hammered us 5–0 in the League. Juventus – Dino Zoff, Roberto Bettega, Claudio Gentile and all – then came to Easter Road, and, on a night of incredible emotions, we came from behind to lead, only to lose two late goals.

Juventus started by defending in depth, as I had expected, but we were getting through and should have had a penalty when Morini checked Joe Harper. Instead, the Swiss referee gave an indirect free kick for obstruction. Two minutes before the interval, we took a real sucker-punch when Gentile scored. But we would not lie down. First Pat Stanton and then Alex Cropley scored – the crowd were in ecstasy at that point.

Yet I feared the Italian breakaways, and, sure enough, Juventus came back to equalise, with Jim McArthur at fault for Altafini's goal. As we continued to attack, Juventus twice broke clear in the last ten minutes to score through Cuccuredu and Altafini.

We had no chance in Turin and duly lost 4–0, which brought to an end a shattering period for us. For, on 26 October, we contested our second Scottish League Cup final in three years.

It was an amazing game of football, and gave quizmasters a question that will be asked for years: who scored a hat-trick in a cup final and still ended up on the losing side?

The man in question was Joe Harper. Some people said Joe was a bit chunky, but I told them that I had seen the great Ferenc Puskás playing for Real Madrid against Eintracht Frankfurt in that wondrous European Cup final at Hampden in 1960, and he and Joe could have swapped suits, as they were both 'chunky'.

That day at Hampden, I told the team to go out and attack from the start. Celtic were carving up defences for fun at the time, so I reasoned the only way to win was to score as much as we could. Unfortunately, it didn't quite work out that way, and after Jimmy Johnstone scored first, we were always in trouble. Dixie Deans scored the second, but when Joe got his first, I thought we had the glimmer of a chance. But Paul Wilson got a third, and from then on we were always chasing the game. The final score was 3–6; at least we had played our part in a hugely entertaining match.

But after that devastating series of losses, I realised that the squad needed to be strengthened in depth, and to do that we required money, which in turn meant selling players. One of the biggest losses was Alex Cropley. He was a terrific midfielder, who, like me, played for Scotland against non-cap countries and only received his commemorative cap recently. Though he was gifted and inventive, I never felt he was quite the same player after he broke his ankle in a tackle involving Alex Ferguson for Falkirk. It's the main reason why Fergie is not my favourite person in football. Cropley had been with us nearly seven years when I sold him to Arsenal for £150,000 in December 1974. The same day, I signed Ally McLeod from Southampton for £30,000. He was a steal at that price.

Later, I sold Alan Gordon to Dundee and transferred Iain Munro to Rangers, in return for Alex Scott and Graeme Fyfe. Alan was getting on, but Iain was a young player. Everyone at Easter Road could see he was a classy type, but he was one of those strong-minded individuals who sometimes need to be taught a lesson. We were playing Hearts at Tynecastle, and he was not having a good day. I substituted Iain, and as he was running up the tunnel, I followed him and said, 'That's the fastest you've run all day.' He was astonished at this remark and even more upset when I told him to report to Easter Road at 10 a.m. the following day. It was a Sunday, and he should have had a day off, but, sure enough, at the appointed moment he came walking in the door of the stadium only to be met by myself: 'Right, you can go home now.' His face was a picture, but he had been taught something about professionalism which he never forgot, and in time he came to appreciate my methods.

Largely because of Celtic's domination, the football authorities decided that the structure of the Scottish League needed to be altered to make it more competitive. The top ten clubs in the First

Division at the end of season 1974–75 would form the new Scottish Premier League. Funnily enough, that was the season Rangers broke Celtic's stranglehold on the League title, and, after Celtic's nine successive championships, Rangers took over at the top. Once again, we were in second place with forty-nine points, seven points behind Rangers.

I wondered how I would cope with the new ten-team league, in which the pressure to deliver results would be immense. It was bad enough in the old league, as my stomach had told me for some time; I had developed an ulcer, and the problem would not go away. Eventually, at the end of the season, I realised that I would have to go into hospital to get it sorted. Even though we were only a few weeks away from the wedding of my daughter, Valerie, to Alistair, I still thought it was justifiable to have the operation, as I felt I had plenty of time to recuperate. In those days, Hibs had a very fine doctor, Jimmy Ledingham, and he assured me that it was a straightforward operation and that I would be in and out in a few days. 'Don't worry, Eddie, you'll be out in plenty of time for the wedding, and you'll be able to enjoy it all the more,' he said.

At first, everything seemed to go swimmingly. I thought I was making a tremendous recovery, but one day Jimmy Ledingham came to see me in hospital. I was sitting talking to him, quite normally, when I noticed that Jimmy was staring intently at me. He got up and left, and the next thing I knew was that a trolley was beside the bed and I was being rushed down to the operating theatre. He had looked into my eyes and seen that I was jaundiced. I had caught a serious infection and was in immediate danger of a possibly fatal collapse.

If Jimmy Ledingham had not come down to see me that day, then I might not be here. It took me some time to recover, and unfortunately I missed my daughter's wedding. On the day of the wedding – 6 June 1975, at St Luke's Church, Edinburgh – I was lying in bed feeling very woozy when all of a sudden the doors of the ward opened and a vision in white entered. It was Valerie, who had come straight from the ceremony with Alistair to share their joy with me. I thought I was dreaming at first. She looked so beautiful and happy, I was just glad to have the opportunity to see her on her big day. I told Alistair to take good care of my girl, and he must have listened, as he and she have been married now for more than 30 years. It has been wonderful to watch their children, Graeme and Carolyn, growing up and becoming a credit to their parents.

My recovery was slow but sure, and in time I felt fitter than I had done for years. At the start of season 1975–76, we had a new league to look forward to and Europe – or should I say England – beckoned again.

For the second year running there would be a 'Battle of Britain' in the UEFA Cup, and this time our opponents would be the mighty Liverpool FC. Bill Shankly had shocked football by retiring the previous season, but Bob Paisley was a more than capable replacement.

At Easter Road, we started well and scored what proved to be the winning goal in the 20th minute, when Arthur Duncan ran down the wing and hit a low cross which Joe Harper smacked past Ray Clemence. We really rattled them with our pace, and their possession football began to fall apart. In the second half, Liverpool had a 'goal' chopped off for offside before we were awarded a penalty with ten minutes to go. Arthur Duncan was fouled, and John Brownlie stepped forward to place the ball on the spot. He had scored his last four penalties by thumping them home, and to this day I still do not know what made him try to be clever and place the ball by a keeper of Clemence's ability. The England international duly saved the kick, and that was to prove vital.

In the return leg, we went to Anfield with one aim in mind, to get an away goal, which meant attacking them. And we did so from the start.

No one in our defence was able to cope with John Toshack, who played out of his skin that night. After we had conceded a bad one to big John, Alex Edwards struck a beauty. At half-time, with Liverpool needing to score twice more, I felt we were in the driving seat, and the Kop was pretty silent. But Toshack got a second in the 54th minute, and Liverpool were right back in it. The clincher for them was a disaster for us. John Blackley should have booted the ball anywhere for safety, but instead he allowed Kevin Keegan to rob him, and Toshack's header from Keegan's cross slipped under Jim McArthur's arm. It was a terrible goal to lose, and Liverpool had beaten us 3–2 on aggregate.

It was Toshack's first hat-trick for Liverool, and all three goals came from his head. We had given a good account of ourselves, however, and the English media acknowledged as much. We were the only team to beat Liverpool in Europe that season. They would go on to win the tournament, as well as the English championship, before winning back-to-back European Cups, yet we had almost matched them, and it was only Toshack's brilliance that was the difference between us.

We did quite well in the new Premier League, finishing third behind Rangers and Celtic to qualify for the UEFA Cup again, but from the start I felt that the new format, with each team playing all the others four times per season, would not actually lead to any improvement in the overall standard of Scottish football. The fact that two teams out of the top ten would be relegated each season convinced me that managers would opt for a safety-first policy. That indeed proved to be the case, and very few managers ever did like the Premier League. When there are sixteen or eighteen clubs in a division, it allows you to try things, but in a ten-team league, there is very little room for error, and consequently managers are under pressure as soon as anything goes wrong. It was supposed to increase competitiveness, but all it did was ensure that the Old Firm got even richer, and, apart from a brief period in the 1980s when other teams managed to get a look-in, Celtic and Rangers have shared the League title between them ever since. And, to my mind, the quality of Scottish football has not improved, either.

That season, we suffered two more disasters, being put out of the Scottish Cup at the quarter-final stage by Motherwell in a tie that took three games to resolve, while by far our worst performance came in the League Cup against Montrose, who were in the league below us, the then new First Division.

We won the first leg at home 1–0, thanks to a Joe Harper penalty and scored early at Links Park through Arthur Duncan. That, though, seemed to spur Montrose on, and, with nothing to lose, they began to attack. Bobby Livingston made it 2–1 and Les Barr equalised. With two minutes left of extra time, Barr was deep in his own half and swung his boot for a mighty clearance. The wind caught the ball and it bounced up and over Jim McArthur. The distance of his 'shot' was later measured at 75 yards. What a way to lose a cup tie.

During the 1975–76 season, I received a 'promotion' when Tom Hart invited me to join the board of directors. At the time, it was reported that Hart had spoken of my moving upstairs to the post of general manager by the late 1970s, just as Willie Waddell had done at Rangers when Jock Wallace replaced him as manager. After that first board meeting, I was given the task of finding someone that I could work with, who, in the fullness of time, would take over as manager. Having not long recovered from the ulcer operation and its aftermath, I agreed that it was wise to look ahead to the day when I might want to take things easier.

It was not until 1979 that I plumped for a potential successor, when I brought former Hibs player Peter Cormack back to Easter Road from Bristol City with the intention of grooming him to take over from me. He had gained vast experience down south with Nottingham Forest and Liverpool, and I felt that with some tuition he could do the manager's job for Hibs. Peter had a dodgy knee, but it was not really a factor since I was not buying him first and foremost as a player – indeed he only played in 20-odd games – but as a future manager of the club. For various reasons, the main one being my departure, Peter's transition to manager did not come about, but it shows you how we were all trying to think ahead at the time.

I made mistakes in signing players over the years – all managers do. But I do not accept that the most controversial transfer in which I was involved during my career was an error. During the 1976–77 season, I took an avalanche of criticism for allowing Pat Stanton to leave Easter Road. Many people simply forgot, or chose not to remember, that Pat himself had asked for a transfer the previous year. He was unhappy about several things, and at the age of 32, he had a feeling, I think, that he wanted to try another club. He had been with Hibs since he was a teenager, so it was a real shock when he put in his request, which the board accepted in October 1975. That request was later withdrawn, but it alerted people to the fact that Pat would be happy to move. When the call came from Jock Stein early in the following season, I felt it would be the best thing all round for Pat to move on. Jock wanted a seasoned professional who could help him with the development of their young players at Parkhead, while the financial terms made it an attractive move for Pat. He and Jock spoke quite briefly and agreed the move, while I did what I thought was a very good piece of business.

We had sold players like Alex Cropley for good money, but in Pat's case, money was not an issue, as I had spotted a young player on Celtic's books who I thought would do a real job for us, so I persuaded Jock into a swap deal. Jackie McNamara was only 23 at the time, and I had followed his progress since he was 15. I felt he could be a mainstay of the team for years to come, especially after orthopaedic surgeon Bill McQuillan fixed his troublesome knee and I moved him from right-half into the defence.

I tried to point out to the fans that we were getting a good young player in return for a very good veteran. In the next match programme, I wrote:

I can appreciate that the waygoing of Pat Stanton was an unpleasant shock for the fans but the influx of new players in recent months indicates how I am trying to remould the team. Pat had not figured much in the side this season and though his efforts on behalf of Hibs have been tremendous in the past 13 years, no player can go on forever in the demanding midfield position.

Therefore, he was given the opportunity to sign for Celtic when Jock Stein asked whether a deal could be done. We have obtained a young go-ahead player who has a lot to give Hibs.

As things turned out, I was proven absolutely correct. After winning medals with Celtic, Pat unfortunately had to retire a couple of years later after being injured. Jackie McNamara played on until 1985 and became a favourite of the Hibs fans. His son, Jackie Jr, somehow slipped through Hibs' net and went on to captain Celtic and Scotland.

I had a difficult time from then on in trying to rebuild the side, as the Tornadoes continued to leave. A year or so later, Eric Schaedler came to see me and said he was no longer enjoying things. He had been one of the stalwarts but I had suspected for some time that he was not fully concentrating on the job. I asked him to keep quiet and did a deal with Dundee which brought Bobby Hutchinson to us. Poor Bobby was badly injured in a pre-season match up at Inverness and was rushed to hospital with some internal damage. He was never quite the same player again.

I did make some very successful signings, however. Des Bremner was a versatile player with a tremendous engine, whom we signed for virtually nothing from Deveronvale in the Highland League. I played him at right-back, right-half and centre-half. But he could be quite maddening at times, because he would often give away the ball – and just as often win it back again. I remember one game at Tannadice when he was filling in for John Brownlie, who had broken his leg. Dessie went charging up and down the right wing so much during the first half that at the interval, I told Alex Edwards to take the ball off him and give him a rest. But Dessie was having none of it and carried on regardless for the rest of the match. Eventually, he moved on to Aston Villa, where he won a European Cup-winner's medal and enjoyed a great career.

By season 1976–77, Ally McLeod had already proved to be one of my better signings. He was one of the cleverest players I ever managed. The fans often thought that he was being lazy, but in fact he was just using the brains in his head, rather than those in his feet, and would not waste his time chasing after balls that he knew he would not get. And he scored some terrific goals over the years.

Good young players on our books, such as Gordon Rose and local lad Willie Murray, gave me confidence that we could rebuild the team. One player I did not sign, even though he was a Hibs fan, was Gordon Strachan. It has been said I thought he was too wee, but the real reason we didn't sign him was simple – his father. Gordon had been scouted by us, and we were prepared to offer him terms, but his father seemed to think the deal wasn't good enough. We exchanged words, and that was the end of Gordon's chances of playing for Hibs. I had never tolerated parental interference, and I wasn't going to start then. Of course, Gordon went on to enjoy a magnificent career, but I was not to know that at the time.

For some reason, we suffered a loss of confidence in that 1976–77 season. We would often take the lead, but just could not kill off our opponents, and we notched up the barely believable total of eighteen League draws – in other words, half of our matches – ten of them at home. I remember saying to the players that season that an away draw was at least half a loaf, but a home draw was no loaf at all.

In the UEFA Cup, we met FC Sochaux of France in two of the most boring matches of my time at Hibs. A John Brownlie goal gave us a lead to take to France, and there we fought a dour rearguard action to gain a 0–0 draw.

Next up was Swedish club Östers Vaxjo, and with John Blackley and John Brownlie scoring, I felt we had done enough at home.

Around that time, we received the sad news that Davie Shaw had passed away. My old colleague from playing days and my predecessor as Aberdeen manager had been a great friend and colleague over many years, and I was deeply saddened by his death.

Whereas our defence had been so solid in France in the previous round, it collapsed in Sweden, and we were thumped 4–1, reaching a new nadir in our fortunes.

But the lowest point in that season came with our loss to First Division Arbroath in the Scottish Cup. Again, we were unable to finish off a side and drew with them at Gayfield, John Blackley scoring a rare goal. But they really surprised us at Easter Road in the replay. After we went ahead, they scored through Tommy Yule and John Fletcher, and, try as we might, we could not equalise. Not for the first or last time, a few fans called for my head on a platter that night, and things did not improve as we failed to make Europe for the first time since I had become manager. That Hearts were relegated at the end of the season was no compensation – not least because we would lose money as a result of missing the Edinburgh derby.

That was not the only reason I was worried about the following season. From about early 1977 on, things had started to become pretty difficult between Tom Hart and myself. We had been friends, but latterly he began to treat me as just another worker in his companies, there to do his bidding. It was sad, and I knew that if results did not improve I would be on my way out of Easter Road. Nor did I have any friends at court, as my fellow directors were too scared to say anything. When the chairman and manager are at loggerheads in a club, there is only ever one winner. He did back my judgement, however, and even paid out money when I thought it necessary.

Things got even worse when we crashed out of the League Cup at the first time of asking to Queen of the South from the First Division. And in the Scottish Cup, we lost to Partick after a replay. But my main concern was the League, because for the first three months, we hardly kicked a ball straight. We were well down the table and had lost nine out of fifteen matches by the end of November.

I worked the players harder than ever, and slowly but surely we turned things around, losing only one of our next fourteen matches. Celtic were dreadful that year, and when we hammered them 4–1 in April, we had all but qualified for Europe.

Early in the next season, I knew we needed fresh blood, and I had spotted a player whose personal history told me he could do a job for us. Ralph Callachan had played for Hearts and had moved to Newcastle for £90,000, but he hadn't settled there. Now, I had found out many years before that Ralph had been a Hibs fan as a boy, so I moved for him in August 1978. I drove down with Tommy Younger in his big car and picked up Ralph, then told him to get his boots on, as he was playing that afternoon! He was a likeable fellow who went on to play for eight years at Easter Road, but I never thought he really fulfilled his potential.

In the UEFA Cup first round, we were drawn against Norrköping of Sweden, and they gave us a real fright in the first leg, which we just managed to win 3–2. A superb defensive performance over there saw us come away with a 0–0 draw. In the second round, we drew the French team Strasbourg. Before the first leg, I went over to France to watch them play, and I was very impressed with the quality of their players. I knew we were in for a tough tie, and in the away leg, which was played first, most of our players had an off night.

As usual, I was watching the match from the stand, and sitting directly behind me was an Edinburgh man, Hamish Henderson. Tom Hart was sitting behind him, and it was one of those periods when the chairman and I were not seeing eye to eye.

Midway through the second half, Hart asked Hamish to pass on a message. He tapped me on the shoulder and said, 'Excuse me, Mr Turnbull, I don't quite know how to tell you this, but the chairman has asked me to say this to you . . . when are you going to get that **** off.' Hamish will tell you that I didn't bat an eyelid and replied instantly, 'Ask him which of our ***** would that be?'

I was frankly surprised that we only lost 2–0, but in the return leg our lads really raised their game and took the fight to Strasbourg. It was heartbreaking to win 1–0 yet fail to gain that second goal.

At various times in the season, I felt my job was at stake, but we rallied to finish fifth in the League – won by Celtic in the last match of the season, against Rangers – and, thankfully, we had a terrific run in the Scottish Cup, which included a memorable win over Hearts in the quarter-final. I had made George Stewart captain and he was both an outstanding leader and in scoring form that day. In the semi-final, we beat Aberdeen and, for the fourth time in my managerial career, my team was in the Scottish Cup final.

In the days leading up to the final, we were written off by every pundit, including some former Hibs players. But I used that to our advantage, telling the team that they could show everybody that they were nobody's whipping boys. Significantly, Rangers' manager, John Greig, went out of his way to say it would be a tough game, and he was not wrong, for the guts and determination Hibs showed turned the final into a marathon affair over three games.

In the final proper, their goalkeeper, Peter McCloy, made three great saves, but he also just about halved Colin Campbell in two inside the box. The referee, Brian McGinley, just waved play on. It was a blatant penalty, and Ally McLeod was in such fine form at that time that I'm sure he would have scored from the spot. They say that the breaks even themselves out over the course of a season or a cup run, but that one went against us, and I'm convinced it cost us the Scottish Cup.

The first replay was played in dreadful wet conditions, and our defence was superb in a match that went to extra time. There were no penalty shoot-outs in the Cup in those days, so a second replay took place the following Monday, 28 May.

Once again, I thought we had our hands on the Cup as we tore Rangers apart in the first half. Tony Higgins put us ahead after 16 minutes, but we just could not finish off the Glasgow team. Big Derek Johnstone's equaliser before half-time came off a rebound when Tommy McLean's 25-yarder took a slight deflection on its way to Jim McArthur, who couldn't hold it.

Johnstone had moved up front, and he scored his second after an hour, but still we did not give up. The penalty award which allowed us to equalise in the 78th minute was soft; McCloy's offence in the first match was much worse. Ally McLeod made no mistake, and we almost snatched it late on when Bobby Hutchinson, who I had sent on to replace Tony Higgins, grazed the outside of the post with a shot.

Jim McArthur saved a penalty from Alex Miller, but in the second half of extra time Davie Cooper swung in a cross and Arthur Duncan dived to try and head clear, only for the ball to end up in our net. We had lost the Scottish Cup by an own goal, and after 330 minutes of unceasing effort, we had nothing to show but losers' medals. I don't think Arthur ever forgave himself, but he was such a great player for Hibs over the years that no one held it against him.

To lose in such a fashion was truly awful, a devastating blow to everyone at the club. As subsequent events would show, the damage to the squad's confidence would last for the whole of the next season. That loss also cost us a place in Europe, as we had finished fifth in the League.

During the run-up to the following season, Tom Hart gave me a public vote of confidence. I knew then that it was only a matter of time before I went.

But I was in demand elsewhere. Earlier in my managerial career, I had been made a good offer to go to South Africa and coach a team there, and in 1979 I was invited to spend a month in Canada training their coaches, but I couldn't accept either offer. But when Scotland manager Jock Stein contacted me and asked for help, with the Under-21 side in particular, I accepted with alacrity. It was an honour to be part of the national coaching set-up and great to work with big Jock, and, to be fair, Tom Hart did not stand in my way. Once before I had been asked to consider managing Scotland – only it was the top job, and at that time I was at Aberdeen and simply couldn't combine the two posts, as the SFA wanted me to do.

I really enjoyed my Scotland duties, but I knew I was on borrowed time at Hibs. Yet just around the corner was another quite incredible adventure for myself and Hibs, one that I will never forget, as it involved an incredible player and a tragedy that William Shakespeare himself would have found difficult to chronicle.

15

Oh, by George – Bestie and his Part in my Downfall

In my far-from-humble opinion, there have been four footballers in my time on this planet who have been far and away above everyone else that played the game. In no particular order, they are: Johan Cruyff of Holland; Diego Maradona of Argentina; Pelé of Brazil; and George Best of Northern Ireland – and Hibs.

It still looks strange on the page, even now. George Best of Hibs. And if I had had my way, it never would have happened.

Let me put that remark in context. In May 1979, we had finished a season in which we had come very close to winning another major trophy and had narrowly missed out on a place in Europe. I had a sinking feeling that the following season was going to be quite difficult, because we really needed to replace some players, but Tom Hart did not see it that way, and there was no money forthcoming for serious investment in players during the close season.

As chairman, Hart had certainly put his own money into the club, but he was not the kind of man to throw away hard cash on a hopeless cause. That was why he had taken big money for the likes of Alex Cropley, who was sold to Arsenal, and Des Bremner, who went to Aston Villa. I think Hart realised even then that things were not going to go very smoothly in financial terms and wanted to ensure that there was some money in the bank.

In many ways, Hart treated Hibs like his building company and treated the staff of the football club in a similar fashion to the way he treated his employees in the building trade. He was not above demanding that people be shown the door. He also used Hibs as a way of promoting his other businesses, and it became something of a standing joke that Friday lunchtimes would see councillors and other cronies arrive at Easter Road for a spot of well-watered dining. It was one aspect of the chairman's activities that I did not particularly like, but he owned the club and could do what he wanted with it. The other directors did not argue with him, and he brought his son Alan onto the board and eventually made him vice-chairman. For good or ill, Tom Hart was Hibs.

We had our occasional run-ins, including one spectacular barney in the North British Hotel, but we were still friendly enough until things started to go wrong at the start of season 1979–80. Hart did not like our failures one bit, and, like so many other chairmen, he shied away from the problems, rather than working with the manager he had put in charge to find a solution. This man had been my friend, but now he saw me more as an underachieving employee.

It did not help that we went out of the League Cup in only the second round, beaten in both legs by Kilmarnock. The League started even more badly for us, with defeat away to Rangers and Aberdeen, and after a victory against Dundee, we went on possibly the worst run in the club's recent history, going 12 games without a victory.

I think it was during October that I first heard a rumour linking us with George Best. What had happened was that Stewart Brown of the *Evening News* had heard on the grapevine that George Best had returned from America, where he had been playing with the Fort Lauderdale Strikers, although Fulham still held his league registration. Brown told Hart that Best might be available, as he was unhappy with his playing arrangements at Fulham. Hart was intrigued, and from the outset he began to see that the arrival of George Best might just deflect some of the criticism that was coming his way as well as mine. I do not think he could face the prospect of sitting in the directors' box at Easter Road while we struggled to avoid relegation, and by the beginning of November, the drop was a real possibility for us. So, all of a sudden, the chairman pulled a rabbit from the hat in the shape of George Best.

I knew absolutely nothing about it. The deal was done behind my back, and contracts were signed guaranteeing George a particular sum of money at the time he turned out for the team. It went without saying that he had secured a promise from Hart that he would play in every game possible. The man who actually picked the team, i.e. myself, was not even consulted about this contract with George.

Looking back on it, perhaps I should have walked away from Easter Road at that point. It had been a principle of mine from the day I started at Queen's Park that I had to have control over team matters. The board at Aberdeen had given me this power, and Tom Hart himself had also promised me complete control when I went to Hibs. Now, more than eight years later, the understanding between us was broken. It was symptomatic of the deteriorating relationship between the chairman and myself at the time. He did not like the results and was not prepared to give me the time and money I needed to put things right. But he was prepared to spend a lot of cash on bringing George Best to Easter Road against my advice.

Now, I was a huge admirer of George in his prime, but I just could not see what he would bring to Hibs at that stage in his career. Everyone in football and quite a lot of people outside it knew about George's boozing, and at the age of 33, he was overweight, unfit and, frankly, not ready to play professional football at a high level.

I tried to reason with Tom Hart, to tell him that his money would be better spent elsewhere on the team and that that way maybe, just maybe, we could turn things around and survive in the Premier League. However, Hart just would not listen to me. He wanted a quick fix and the public off his back, when I knew that the only solution was genuine investment in solid players, and hard work on the part of every single person at Easter Road.

Yet I did not suffer any considerable anguish wondering what to do. I reasoned that the man with the money was calling the shots and the rest of the board were in his pocket, so I would be better off trying to work with the chairman and Georgie to see if there was any way of securing survival for Hibs. Best had worked many miracles on the field of play, and perhaps he could achieve just one more. But I very much doubted it.

We were firmly stuck at the bottom of the Premier League when Hart announced that he had signed George Best. There was a fee of around £50,000 involved, and though I was told many times by supposedly informed people that George was getting £2,000 per game, I never actually knew how much he was paid, and, frankly, I did not want to know. It was certainly much more than my salary, and many of the players were getting less than a tenth of that sum.

I knew that the huge imbalance in earnings was in itself certain to cause friction in the dressing-room eventually. Indeed, shortly after the signing the players asked for a meeting with Tom Hart and questioned him as to how much exactly George was getting. The chairman refused to tell them, but, after some argument with the players, Hart agreed to double the win bonus for the remaining League and cup games in the season. Unfortunately, he did not have to pay out all that much.

Before he arrived at Easter Road, Hart wanted me to check Best out down south, so we flew to London, and, in typical Hart style, there was a chauffeured limousine to take us to Ipswich, where George was playing in a testimonial.

That game, with its friendly atmosphere and no serious tackling, taught me nothing; but then, I already knew everything I needed to know about George. Tommy Docherty was the boss who was blamed for Best's premature departure from Manchester United, but all that the Doc had insisted on was that George turn up for training on time and relatively sober. My reasoning was simple: if George had not been bothered turning up for training in a city in which he lived, now that his home and family, not to mention his drinking chums, were in London, why would he bother coming along to a training session in another country? And if men like Matt Busby and Tommy Docherty could not control him, what chance did I have?

I advised Hart that he should not sign George, but the chairman was having none of it, and this was the start of the long falling out between him and myself. The supporters knew nothing about this, of course, and those who were around at the time will only recall their amazement when it was announced that the 'Fifth Beatle', as he had been known back in the 1960s, had signed for Hibs. I have to say I was pretty stunned myself, but not in a pleasant way.

Many people in and around the club knew that I was not happy with the situation, but I had to put a brave face on it. Best came along with his then wife, Angie, to Easter Road, and, of course, a media circus gathered. The signing had made front-page news across the UK, but it was just as quickly forgotten.

The first real chance I got to talk to George by myself was when we were playing a friendly against Leicester and we went for dinner afterwards. Like everyone else, I was, of course, charmed by this handsome and engaging man. That evening, however, I neither saw nor heard anything that made me change my mind; I just knew he was not going to be a good signing for us. His blue eyes had the look of a hard drinker about them, the yellowing skin around them a sure sign. I had seen plenty of faces like it in my career, and there was no mistaking the signs of someone who was on the skids.

The rest of the squad were generally delighted to meet George, and there was good banter among them. Ally McLeod wisecracked that George was only there to lace up his boots, while most of them just wanted to know whether all the stories about George and his various women were true. Later, when George bothered to actually grace the dressing-room with his presence, the lads were always trying to snaffle some of the very expensive fragrances which George kept in his kitbag. It was rumoured that one of the concoctions cost around £100 per bottle.

One of the first things the others noticed was the meticulous care George took with his feet. He would sit for ages after training and playing, making sure they were clean, dry and pampered with all sorts of medicinal powders. I recently told a Celtic-supporting friend that fact, and he was astonished because one of the Celtic squad had told him that Henrik Larsson was similarly obsessed with his feet – and he's not too bad a player either.

While a few of the Hibs lads were so incensed at his earnings that they could not disguise their ill feeling, most of the players did indeed take to George, and no wonder. He did not come across as a big-head, even if he occasionally dropped a name or two. 'Yeah, Miss World, lost her phone number,' that sort of thing.

He did seem, right from the start of his stay in Edinburgh, to have an almost magnetic attraction for women, just as he had always done. They did not quite fling themselves at him, but many were not slow in coming forward. There was a conveyor belt of women lining up to meet him, and a few of the unmarried young players were more than happy to tag along with George in the hope of latching on to one or two of his cast-offs. George himself would assist our lads in that department; he once called the home of a player late at night insisting that he should jump on a train and come through from Glasgow, as there was a spare young lady waiting for him.

I had hoped that George would try to control himself, but the drinking began right away. At training early in his stay at Easter

Road, it was quite obvious that George had been out the previous night for a session on the booze. His eyes were pink and yellow, and he reeked of alcohol. He was staying at the North British Hotel (a good choice by Hart, given that there were 50 pubs within a square mile of the place), and it soon became a Mecca for those who wanted to be able to say that they had been out drinking with George Best. And if you believed every story about the number of women who ended up back in his hotel room, you would have to conclude that a lot of Edinburgh ladies were keeping a wee secret from their boyfriend or husband. No doubt, some 26 or 27 years later, there are still some women in the city with a story to tell . . .

A whole mythology has grown up about how I tried to tame George Best, by either stopping him drinking or posting spies in various hostelries to report back to me that George had been out on the tiles. Let me assure you that there is not a single shred of truth in those claims. From the outset, I told Tom Hart that I wanted nothing to do with imposing discipline on Georgie, and in the five months that I was his manager, I did not do a single thing to curb his activities. Several times I was asked to do so, and on each occasion I refused. I knew that drink was his problem and that to try to stop him would be completely useless, because Best was to all intents and purposes an alcoholic. The only person who could stop George drinking was himself, and he showed absolutely no inclination to do so.

There were nights when he would simply disappear from his hotel, and pub managers would call me saying he was lying pissed in the corner. One well-known pub near the North British is the Jinglin' Geordie, then the haunt of many of the city's journalists, as it was literally across Fleshmarket Close from the back door of the *Scotsman* and *Evening News* offices. George was duly photographed in a heap alongside a table of empty glasses, and though some of the players said it had all been a set-up, I knew otherwise – the manager of the pub had called me to tell me of George's condition.

I said to him what I told everyone who warned me that George was out on the town and inebriated: 'Call Tom Hart, it's his problem.'

My main concern was not George's alcoholism but how I would fit him into the playing system which we were trying to operate at the time. Without the rigours of regular training sessions, it was difficult to see how George would learn the formations and the moves which are so vital to establishing a pattern of play. Almost from the start of his time with us, he had a lackadaisical attitude to training. Don't get me wrong, when he turned up, he was thoroughly professional, training as hard as anyone, and indeed he would often stay for sessions after the rest had finished. He would take goalkeeper Jim McArthur and one of the young players out to practise crossing and shooting, and often it was a pleasure just to sit and watch him training this way.

That was what was so maddening. Had he trained comprehensively and got himself fit, he would have been magnificent, even at the age of 33. But drink had him in its grasp, and there was no chance of getting a full 90 minutes out of him – my bet was 20, tops.

In practice matches, I decided to play him in a position where he could do the least harm to the rest of the team and from where he might even be able to create things. I gave him the number 10 shirt I had worn myself so long ago and directed him to play on the left of midfield, behind the strikers.

It was soon clear to me that certain players did not want to have anything to do with George on the pitch. I had seen this before with him. To anyone in football, it was obvious that he and Bobby Charlton didn't get on at Man United, just from the exasperated reactions of the older man. The only man who could exercise some kind of control over Best in his days at Old Trafford was Denis Law, and that was because George was physically scared of 'the Lawman'. Now I could see the same thing happening with my side. All the carefully nurtured team spirit I had tried to create was disintegrating before my eyes. We needed to play as a team if we were to have any chance of making a concerted effort to haul ourselves out of the relegation zone. Teamwork all but disappeared, however, when George arrived.

The chairman would not listen to my pleas and ignored my calls when Best started to miss training. It went against everything Hibs stood for that one man was given such special treatment, and the chairman's refusal to back his manager in that situation could mean only one thing. You didn't need a university education to deduce what was going to happen to me; by late 1979, I knew the sack was inevitable.

So what do you do in that situation? Walk away from the team you love and have people question your sanity because you refused to work with George Best? Eventually, I just decided to soldier on. I had my orders, and I obeyed them. On 24 November 1979, George Best made his debut for Hibs at Love Street, the home of St Mirren.

It was during that match that I got the final proof that Best was not the player he could or should have been. At one stage, he found himself in space on the edge of the box, and in days gone by, he would have done a lightning-fast shimmy and dispatched the ball into the net. This time, his legs seemed to be unable to follow what his brain was telling them. It's a well-known phrase in football that 'your legs have gone' – signifying that a veteran cannot keep up with the pace of the game. So it was with George Best – his legs were gone, and anybody with any nous about football could see it. Yet, in typical fashion, he scored late in the game to announce his arrival in Scottish football. Unfortunately, we were already two goals behind at that time, and a sort of pattern had been set for the rest of the season.

Great play had been made of the fact that the chairman was paying the huge salary to George out of his own pocket, but I know that it was not the case that Hart had to stump up for Best's wages. At that time, we were averaging an attendance of around 8,000 at Easter Road, but on the day when George made his home debut against Partick Thistle on 1 December, an astonishing crowd of 20,662 turned out. It was quite clear that most of them were there to be able to say to their children and grandchildren that they had seen George Best in the flesh, that they had witnessed his home debut match for Hibs. And who can blame them? I have to say I was excited myself to see what this living legend might do in the green and white of Hibs, though, in my case, I had serious doubts about his ability to do anything sensible.

The gates for his first two home matches were something like 20,000 more than had been anticipated. The extra sums raised were more than enough to pay George's fees for the season. It was the fans who financed George Best's stay at Easter Road, not Tom Hart.

We won that match 2–1, with a penalty from Ally McLeod and an own goal by Brian Whittaker. Could George's magic be working for us? Once again, in that game there were moments of genius from George, and, yes, sometimes he was a move ahead of his colleagues, but that only served to confirm my fears that Best was out of step with the rest of the team. And all the time, I had that deep-down feeling that you get when you know that something is going to go badly wrong.

Watching George was like being a witness to a car accident taking place in slow motion. And it was only a matter of time before the head-on smash occurred.

Meantime, Hibernian FC was heading out of the Premier League at a rate of knots. By the end of November, we had won just one match, and the writing was on the wall both for the club and for my continued occupation of the manager's office. The press were merciless, but they weren't telling me anything I didn't know. The chants of 'Turnbull must go' were only slightly abated by the George Best sideshow.

Either side of New Year, 1980, we saw the best of Best in Scotland. Against Rangers in late December on a frosty pitch, his natural balance gave him a huge advantage and he taunted the Rangers defence. At one point a beer can – those were the days before the ban on drink – was thrown at him as he moved to take a corner at the Dunbar Road end. George picked up the can and took a swig from it, to the delight of the entire crowd. Inspired by him, we won the game 2–1.

In early January, against Celtic at Easter Road, George was out on the left wing before cutting inside and hitting a ferocious shot which took Celtic goalkeeper Peter Latchford with it into the back of the net. Later, that effort would be named Goal of the Season by BBC Scotland.

We then beat Morton to give ourselves the ghost of a chance of survival, but in February 1980, the Best train hit the buffers, as I knew it would. George simply went absent from training sessions. I called Hart. 'Where's your man Best?' I demanded to know. The chairman did not have a clue. None of us did, until he was pictured in a newspaper leaving a pub or nightclub in London. But because he was Georgie, Hart just told me to get on with things. And then Best did something that not even Tom Hart could ignore.

We were due to play Ayr United on Sunday, 17 February in the Scottish Cup at Easter Road, but the night before the game, George got to drinking with the French rugby team, who had been staying at the North British. A waiter at the hotel was Tom Hart's personal snitch, and he called the chairman to say that George had been in a night-long session with the French players, who had played Scotland at Murrayfield that day and were no longer on duty. The French players were drowning their sorrows big style, as Andy Irvine had inspired a super late fight-back by the Scots, who snatched a 22–14 victory.

Those big French guys could put it away, and that was one drinking contest Best should have lost, but guess who was last man standing at the bar in the wee small hours? Hart called me from the hotel to ask me to come over and try to get George sorted, but I sent John Fraser and Stan Vincent. I was sticking to my guns that Hart was the man responsible for Best. 'He's your problem, you signed him' was the gist of my remarks, although they were rather more forcefully put.

George was completely comatose, and indeed when Hart first knocked on the door, Best did not respond, as he was out for the count. What seemed like all the black coffee in the hotel was poured into him, but still George couldn't budge. 'I'm pissed,' was all he could say.

The fans knew nothing of this, and when it was announced that Willie Murray would play instead of George, there was a chorus of booing. That was dreadful for young Willie to hear, and I was livid. I told the chairman exactly what had happened, and this time Hart reacted by sacking George. I was neither pleased nor displeased; by then, I had guessed that my own days were numbered. And I really didn't have anything against George personally. Sober, he was a lovely guy, soft-spoken and actually quite shy – perhaps he had started off needing alcohol to overcome that shyness. He and I would sit and blether about football for ages, and I was always struck by his genuine love of the game.

Now he was gone, or so I thought. A week after he was 'sacked', Tom Hart did his sums and saw what George's going would do to the gate. He relented, but it was another two weeks before George was fit enough to play again.

By that time, we were doomed. Relegation was virtually certain, and the only bright spot in the season was our Scottish Cup run, which, frankly, was keeping me in a job. After beating Ayr United without the assistance of Best, we toiled against Berwick Rangers, beating them 1–0 in a replay. That put us in the semi-final of the Scottish Cup, against Celtic, and surely now, on the big stage of

Hampden against a big-name club, we would see George really perform.

But I didn't really expect him to do so, because I had long since concluded that George was not capable of sustaining any kind of performance for more than a few minutes at a time. So it proved in a match in which we were utterly humiliated by the score of 5–0. George drifted out of the game for long periods, and all my predictions about his inability to blend with the rest of the team came true as he failed to find colleagues with pass after pass.

It was not just the scale of the defeat but the abject manner of it which brought about my demise as manager of Hibs. In a sense, George Best had put the final nail in my coffin.

To be truthful, unless we had actually won the Cup, I cannot see that I would have survived in the job. For some time before my dismissal, none of the other directors could look me in the eye, and I had been in football long enough to know what was coming.

Three days after the semi-final, on Tuesday, 15 April, I went into training but was summoned upstairs to the boardroom. I knew that could mean only one thing. It was all over in seconds, Hart thanking me for my services and me getting out the door as quickly as possible. I could have stayed and argued, but what would the point have been? I suppose I should have hung out for a better financial deal. I got no big pay-off – I was allowed to keep my Audi car. But I just wanted out of there. My sacking had been inevitable from the day George Best walked in the door, and now it had happened. But I sure as hell was not going to cry about it.

Club secretary Cecil Graham was deputed to deal with the press and he issued a statement: 'Hibs and Mr Turnbull have parted in amicable terms.' All I can say is 'Bollocks to that.' We 'parted company' because the chairman would not invest when I asked him to and then insisted on bringing in an alcoholic who disrupted our team and destroyed any chance I might have had of grinding out a survival plan.

Willie Ormond took over as manager, but it was a hopeless task. Hibs won only one of their seven League matches after I left and finished bottom by eight points.

For the first time in 49 years, Hibs were relegated, and I was out of a job at the age of 57.

But George Best was not paid off. He went back to Fort Lauderdale for the summer and played quite a lot of games. He actually looked fitter when he came back to Hibs for four First Division matches the following season. But it couldn't last, and after twenty-two games and just three goals, he got a better offer and signed for San Jose Earthquakes back in the USA.

He was made captain for his final match against Falkirk in October, before Tom Hart announced in typically grandiose style: 'The marriage between George Best and Hibernian football club is over.' What a pity the marriage had never been consummated in the first place.

All of these memories came flooding back to me when George finally lost his battle with the bottle in November 2005. It was an awful day, especially when reporters and camera crews came to call for my reminiscences. I was interviewed in the churchyard near my home, and I became quite emotional as I recalled the better side of Bestie, and the tragic nature of his life.

And, as always with George, there was a touch of melancholy humour around. Carol recalled, 'I got George's autograph, you know.'

'Aye,' I replied, 'and in return he got your man the sack!'

To this day, I still have nothing but admiration for George as a player in his teens and twenties. I just feel that it was unutterably sad that he allowed his extraordinary God-given talents to be diluted with alcohol to the point where they disappeared from view, and he became not George the gifted footballer but George the never-recovering alcoholic.

At his peak, he had everything. Pace, power, skill, strength in the air and in the tackle, and the ability to float over the lunges of lesser men trying to stop him. All of these and much more made Best the complete player, right up there with Cruyff, Maradona and Pelé. Indeed, if he had looked after himself like the great Brazilian did, then George might well have been ranked above even Pelé. His tragedy truly was that he could beat everybody bar himself.

Though he contributed to me losing my job, I feel no bitterness towards George Best. Like everybody else, I prefer to recall the moments of genius that lit up the footballing stage. Sadly, though, all too few of those glimpses of George's best came while he was wearing a Hibs jersey.

Best did come back to Easter Road with the Earthquakes for a friendly, and turned out for his great pal Jackie McNamara's testimonial in 1984, but I didn't go along to meet him. My only surprise was that he didn't come to see me. After all, by then I was running a pub. And do you know, I would have stood him a drink – but nothing with alcohol in it.

16

In the End is my Beginning

I had made my exit from Easter Road with as much dignity as possible, and my overwhelming feeling was one of disappointment that I had not been given the proper backing to do the job of staving off relegation. Tom Hart had left me high and dry, and he and his cronies had badly let me down, first of all by undermining me with the imposition of George Best on the side, and secondly by failing to recognise what I kept telling them, which was that Bestie was a liability who could get the team deeper into trouble.

When Hart had taken over at Hibs, he had promised me that he would rebuild 'the family' at Easter Road. Well, families are supposed to stick by each other through thick and thin, but it did not happen in my case. Hart had tried to model himself on Harry Swan but failed dismally to match the old chairman when the going got rough.

Now the club was relegated, and I was out of a job, for only the second time in my football career. It was to be the last time as well, because though I did not know it at the time, my active career was over. I am often asked why I walked away from the game at a relatively young age. The answer is twofold. First of all, nobody came looking for me with any kind of a serious offer; but mostly, I was totally fed up with football and didn't actually go looking for a job in the game. I'm sure I could have found something if I had wanted to, but the events of the final season at Easter Road had left their mark on me. The truth was that I was just demoralised by what had happened.

There is a good old Scots word which sums up exactly how I felt at the time: I was scunnered.

I had never had a testimonial from Hibs, despite a total of 26 years of service to the club, and I had no pension arrangements. To this day, the only pension I have is the state pension, and, as any OAP will tell you, it is never enough. Back in 1980, I needed to earn a living, so I contacted a friend in the brewery business, and I was able to train as a public-house manager and take over a pub, Mac's Bar, near to Easter Road. The lads who frequented the premises were always trying to get me to go to a Hibs game, but I never did take up the offer. We were close enough to hear the roars of the crowd on a Saturday afternoon, but during the years I ran the pub, I was never tempted to go back to Hibs.

My health had deteriorated and I had to have a hip replaced, to be followed by the other one a few years later. In between those operations, as I was nearing retirement, I felt pain in my back. I went to the doctor, who referred me to the Western General Hospital. There, I was given the devastating news that I had lung cancer. It was not totally unexpected, as I had been a heavy smoker as a young man, though I had given up while at Aberdeen.

I had stopped smoking because of my daughter. One day, Valerie came home from school and said that there had been a lesson that day about the dangers of smoking. She said, 'Mum, I'm not going to sit in the same room as you and Dad, because smoking is dangerous.' I gave up smoking right there and then. But it was too late. Obviously, it was completely shocking to hear that diagnosis, which can so often be a death sentence. But from the start, I was determined to beat the disease.

The surgeons told me that they had to operate, and I went under the knife expecting to come round with a small, neat scar. Instead,

I found myself missing half a lung and with a scar that stretched halfway round my body. I suspect that only the fact that I had kept myself very fit enabled me to deal with the cancer and the trauma of the operation, and I can remember the wonderful feeling when the surgeons told me that I was clear of the disease.

But it wasn't to be my last brush with the Big C. Just over six years ago, I was diagnosed with bowel cancer and once again went under the knife. And again, I beat the disease. Indeed I had an endoscopy during the time I was writing this book and received the news that I was still clear of cancer.

So, two bouts of cancer, an ulcer operation, two hip replacements and a heart attack – I've had my money's worth from the National Health Service. And I will not hear a word said against the NHS. All the doctors and nurses who have helped me over the years have been wonderful, and I know I would not be here without them.

After my stint running the pub, I was quite happy living in peaceful retirement. My only connection with football was when I met up with Lawrie Reilly for our regular golf matches, or when sportswriters would call me up for my views on a subject, which I usually declined to give. I did feel strongly that Hearts owner Wallace Mercer's planned 'merger' in 1990 – in reality, it was a takeover – between Hearts and Hibs would be the death of my old club, but I was ill at the time and couldn't take a full part in the 'Hands Off Hibs' campaign. I did speak out again in 1998 when Hibs were facing relegation, and my view was that the board, and not then manager Jim Duffy, were to blame for the crisis.

But by and large, I was happy to live quietly and not go running to the press with my opinions on everything, as some former managers do. I have to say that, with few exceptions, the modern crop of younger football writers does not impress me. They do not appear to have the knowledge of the game that their predecessors had. That is perhaps because they do not have the contact with managers and players that was common in my day, and the media today does not respect footballers and managers in the way that journalists did during my career.

I always had pretty good relations with the media; that aspect of football management has always been important and is probably even more so in these days when there are so many more newspapers, television channels and radio stations. I was never at my best on television. Gordon Smith, the former BBC correspondent in Edinburgh, tells the story of how he ran out of film because I couldn't stop cursing someone or other!

In my early days as a player and manager, there were plenty of good journalists whom you could trust with a private story, knowing they would not reveal it. I knew they needed background information to help them do their job properly, and, in return, a few of them would occasionally pass on tips about players and even jobs. As I have told you, I learned about the possibility of the Queen's Park and Aberdeen jobs from sportswriters. The likes of R.E. Kingsley and Willie Allison of the *Sunday Mail*; John Rafferty of *The Scotsman*; 'the Voice of Football', John 'Voicey' MacKenzie of the *Daily Express*; Tommy Gallacher of the *Dundee Courier*; Hugh Taylor and Alex Cameron of the *Daily Record*; the man with a finger in every pie, Jim Rodger; George Aitken, Harry Andrews and Gair Henderson; Stewart Brown of the *Edinburgh Evening News*; and Jimmy Forbes of the *Aberdeen Evening Express* all wrote well and accurately – and they could keep a confidence.

My rules for dealing with the press were simple: if they reported what I said accurately, then that was fine, and they were also entitled to criticise me. But if they misquoted me or got something wrong about me or the team, I let them know about it. Over the years, one or two of them were pinned to the wall to hear my verdict, but I can't remember actually punching any of them . . . unlike a few players I could name.

After more than two decades away from the game, I got back to following football almost by chance in the 2001–02 season. I had on occasion watched the Hibs players at training sessions under the previous manager, Alex McLeish, but I was still not tempted to go to a game. Then a match was being held at Selkirk to commemorate Bobby Johnstone, who hailed from that town, and I went down as a guest to watch the game between Hibs and Manchester City. The City side was made up largely of their youth team, and the coach was one of those who kept bawling instructions. I was standing near the dugout and gave him a piece of my mind, to the effect that he should shut up and let the boys play. Someone who heard my remarks was Rod Petrie, the chief executive of Hibs, and afterwards I was briefly introduced to him. Rod is a likeable and sincere man, and I took to him right away.

A few days later, an invitation arrived from Rod to join him at Easter Road for a match, and I've been going ever since. I'm sure I drive Rod mad at times, like on the occasion I took the mickey out of former Scotland manager Berti Vogts. I told him I knew all about German football because Hibs had put their champions out of the first European Cup. Rod has got used to me, and he has been a great friend; I particularly appreciated being named along with Lawrie Reilly and Pat Stanton as the first 'Club Champions', part of a very worthy initiative to help the fans recognise the great history of their club.

Now I enjoy meeting other former players and the club's guests in the hospitality suite, and, as you would expect, I am not slow in passing on a wee tip to the modern generation of players. The Hibs' Former Players' Association has been a terrific institution too, and I have enjoyed many nights with supporters clubs as far away as London and Belfast.

I have also been a guest at Aberdeen, and I always enjoy my visits to Pittodrie or to the charity golf matches organised by Ian Taylor. I was once asked to make the half-time prize draw when they were playing Hearts, and I half expected a chorus of jeers from the maroon section of the crowd. But, thankfully, they gave me respectful applause. Which is just as well, as I had my answer ready for them: seven upraised fingers to recall a certain scoreline!

There have been many games I have enjoyed, but there are times when I despair of Scottish football. Take the national side, for instance. On the night I was awarded my cap at Hampden, Switzerland beat us 3–1, and I could not help noticing how they seemed much more cohesive, almost like a club side, while Scotland's players did not seem to know their roles. There were a number of times when a gaggle of our players went chasing the ball instead of staying in their positions to deal with the Swiss. But Walter Smith is a very good coach, and I'm sure in time he will get these mostly young players working together as a team.

And we do have fine young talents, who must be allowed to express themselves. So often these days, you can see coaches screaming at their players to stick to the system, and if I could do anything about the rules of the modern game, then it would be to banish coaches and managers from the touch-line. By all means, leave an assistant to pass on messages, but in these days of mobile phones and walkie-talkies, there is no need for 'the boss' to be in the dugout. I would make them all sit in the stand, where they would get a better view in any case. The fact is that a manager or coach should not need to be beside the pitch. You have worked with the players all week, you have worked out the tactics, you have given them their final instructions; but once the whistle goes, it should be up to the players to do the job you have prepared them to do. Instead, in the modern game, you often see players looking to the dugout for instructions just a few minutes into the match – that's just daft.

You look at some of the managers, jumping up and down in the technical areas and screaming and shouting at their players. That can't be good for them or the men on the pitch – that's if they can even hear what he's saying! Obviously, there are times when you have to intervene, either because your tactics aren't correct (not that you ever admit that!) or because players are not following instructions, or you can see that one of them is having an off day and you need to make a substitution. In my time as a manager, I always had a telephone beside my seat in the stand, and if I wanted to make a change, I would just call down and instruct one of the assistant trainers or coaches. I think part of the problem is that managers and coaches might not feel safe in the stand nowadays, but that never bothered me.

Precisely because my generation did not have coaches, I am a great believer in coaching from a very young age. We learned football in the street and by watching or reading about senior players and professionals. I remember reading about Charlie Napier who was known as Happy Feet, and asking myself why he got that nickname. It was because he had superb ball control and could dribble his way through a defence. I resolved to try and develop the sort of skill Charlie had, and practised morning, noon and night, and though I never quite managed to match Happy Feet, at least I did learn how to control a ball.

Times have changed, and football has moved on with society as a whole. Youngsters and their parents quite rightly demand proper football facilities, and I envy those kids who get to play on proper pitches and wear proper strips and boots. Recently, I saw a team in the local park who were immaculately turned out, and I could not resist telling the people in charge that I was delighted to see that the boys were taking pride in their appearance. 'If you are dressed well, there's a pretty good chance you'll play well,' I said. And they did!

Decent facilities, good pitches, proper strips are all important, but it all falls down if there is not proper coaching. In that park near my home, there are a lot of young kids playing football regularly, and many of them know me and know that I used to be a manager. I despair when I hear them talking of positions like sweeper and wing-back and even 'holding midfield player'. I once asked a boy who said that to me what he was 'holding'. Funnily enough, he couldn't tell me.

At that age, boys and girls shouldn't be worrying about whether they are a sweeper or whatever. They should just be given the ball and taught to try to control it and use it skilfully, then enjoy a game rather than worry about positions or tactics. 'Learn to love the ball,' is what I say to them. 'Take it to bed with you at night.'

The SFA over the years has been the subject of some derision for insisting on so many people taking coaching courses down at Largs. I cannot understand that attitude. Those courses began back in the 1960s, and the two men who got them up and running were Roy Small, who was in the physical education department at Jordanhill College in Glasgow, and Davy Russell, who had been a professional footballer with Tranmere Rovers after playing with East Fife. They had a great partnership, and though I had my doubts at first, I enrolled when I was at Aberdeen and completed the course over two years. I must have done something right, because no sooner had I received my certificate than Roy approached me and asked if I would join them on future courses as a practical coach. I was delighted to do so, because I had become convinced that the SFA course was among the best, if not the best, in the world. Don't forget, I had been to West Germany on their coaching courses, thanks to one of their FA officials whom I had met, and I wasn't too impressed with it. I also knew that the best coach in England was a Scot, Tommy Docherty, and his methods were seen as revolutionary. But they were viewed as such simply because he was taking what he had learned from the game and adding his own dimension.

At first, neither Rangers nor Celtic would allow their players to attend the courses at Largs, which I thought was very short-sighted of them. The first player from the Old Firm to attend one of the courses was Davy Wilson of Rangers, who went on to be quite a successful manager at clubs like Dumbarton. A couple of years ago, I was at Ibrox Park for a match, and afterwards in the hospitality area I met Davy, and he reminded me that he had been the first Rangers player to go on the course, saying that he had been 'knocked out' by the quality of the instruction. Neither Jock Stein nor Scot Symon nor Willie Waddell had much faith in the SFA course, but I believe Bertie Auld was the first Celtic player to attend, and he too went on to a long and successful career as a coach and manager, starting out with me at Hibs.

The SFA courses are now recognised across Europe for their quality, but I do think that some modern coaches have been given their badges very cheaply. Quite recently, I approached a head coach in Scottish football and asked him how one of his junior coaching staff had been able to obtain his qualifications when it was obvious to everyone that he had not a clue about coaching football. That head coach just shrugged his shoulders. It is attitudes like his which encourage the slipshod coaching that is prevalent in our game today.

The evidence of my own eyes over these past few years is enough to tell me that the basic skills have been neglected. When you see supposedly professional footballers unable to trap the ball or make a straightforward pass, you know that something is wrong with the game in Scotland. Players also learn bad habits from an early age, and that makes it so much harder to stop them committing the same mistakes time and time again.

People say to me that I am too severe on youngsters who make these errors, but that is actually one of the major problems in our football: it seems that you cannot tell the young that they are wrong. Too often, kids are just left to their own devices or are coached by people who do not know what they're talking about. We need coaches who have been well trained themselves and know the game. Just as there are good and bad teachers of English or mathematics, so there are good coaches and bad coaches. Some are fine and know their job, and others are a waste of space and may even be damaging the national game.

The good coach is the person who is able to impart knowledge to his pupils and inspire them to want to play the game and enjoy it. Above all, that is what coaches must do – make the game enjoyable for kids.

Qualified coaches – and hopefully that should include former professional footballers, though they do not always make the best teachers – must be allowed to go into schools and instruct the kids and show them exactly what to do with a ball. These coaches have to be able to say, 'No, that is wrong, this is how you do it properly,' and then insist that the children get it right and are able to practise what they are taught. There is no point in mollycoddling our youth, because professional football is a hard game, and unless we have sufficient young people coming through with the correct skill levels, we will not survive as a footballing nation.

I have no doubt that the people who should be doing something about this basic lack of skill are not tough enough to do what they should be doing, which is to stop Scotland from falling even further behind our neighbours in Europe. Look at Norway, for instance. When I was managing Hibs, we beat Rosenborg 9–1, but no one draws them now and expects to win by that sort of margin. I keep reading about all these grand plans by the SFA and others to alter our sorry record on basic skills teaching, but I see precious little evidence of any great changes. The fact is that the Norwegians completely changed the way they coached footballers, from primary school upwards, and they are reaping the rewards. Why not us?

By all means, let's get coaches working in schools, but let us also concern ourselves even more with the transitional period during which youth players become young professionals. Any club coach will tell you that the real mystery in the Scottish game is what happens to the many promising youngsters who lose their way and do not make the grade. They do well as youth footballers, but in the breakthrough to the senior ranks it seems that plenty goes wrong, and, with few exceptions, they do not make the grade. I believe the key to solving that problem is also coaching, and the likes of Celtic's Shaun Maloney, Chris Burke of Rangers and several of the young Hibs players show that it can be done.

Many of the players that I managed and the coaching staff that I worked with have been kind enough over the years to compliment me on the quality of my work as a coach. Perhaps they did not know that I had never received any real coaching myself. In that sense, guys like Tommy Docherty and myself were pioneers. What I began to do with Queen's Park and then developed at Aberdeen and Hibs was to take the practical aspects of the game and break them down into moves, then get the players to practise these over and over. Then I would insist they try things as if they were playing in a match. If they were practising a dead-ball move, then they would do so as if they were in a match situation. You might think this was simple reasoning, but it was judged to be way ahead of its time.

It is possible to break football down into its component parts, refine these parts with practice, then put them back together – just like Henry Ford and his assembly line for the Model T. But that doesn't mean that players should all be in the same mould; you can train footballers to do the simple things well, but ultimately the creativity of individuals is what needs to be encouraged most.

We need better coaches, yes, and a better national coaching system, but most of all we need better football clubs. They are the bedrock on which Scottish football is founded, and while I understand the terrible financial problems which most clubs have faced in recent years, I am still concerned at the lack of ambition being shown by once proud clubs.

Today there are two teams which dominate Scottish football, year in and year out; but when I was a player, in any given season as many as four or five teams could challenge for the title. Hibs, Hearts, East Fife, Raith Rovers, Clyde, Partick Thistle, Aberdeen and both the Dundee teams all had a chance of winning the League. It is now more than 20 years since a club other than Celtic or Rangers won the League. Don't get me wrong, it is not the fault of the Old Firm that other clubs cannot get their acts together to mount a sensible challenge. Yes, Hearts did it in season 2005–06, but their challenge petered out, and no other club came close to catching Celtic. Rangers had a bad year, but they will be back, for winning is the tradition for both those clubs, and it is difficult to see any other club consistently challenging them in the future.

That is why I contend that the overall standard of Scottish football is considerably lower than it used to be. Outside of the Old Firm, apart from Hearts last season, the SPL has not proved able to produce genuine and sustained challenges by any clubs, while outside the SPL, crowds have evaporated over the years. Yes, society has changed, but not to the extent that football must necessarily be an afterthought, as it is now for so many people.

A large part of the problem is that football has forgotten how to be entertaining. The man in the street wants some entertainment for his money, and if his team wins then so much the better. People want to see goals, fans want attacking football, they want to see great saves, wingers running at defenders and the ball being used skilfully. We all remember great goals, but we also recall moments of individual talent, and that is sadly lacking from our game, for two reasons. One is that coaches want their players to play exactly according to their dictates; but more often than not it is because players no longer have the skills to do the dummy, shimmy, feint or jink which in itself can be a highlight of a game. As for passing, it seems to be a lost art, which is a great pity, because it is the best way to move the ball forward in a flowing manner that leaves opponents floundering.

Fluid, creative football is both entertaining and successful.

The fact that they try to play that way is the reason I have been greatly heartened by the progress that Hibs have made under Tony Mowbray's managership. The current crop of players are capable of playing some very good football indeed, and there could be better times ahead at Easter Road.

I maintain that Hibs' fortunes tend to be cyclical. After the First World War, Hibs had an excellent side, and many older fans used to say to me that it was the best team ever to wear the green. Old Jimmy McColl, a legend in the club, played in that team, as did Hugh Shaw. The side which won the League title three times between 1948 and 1953, and competed in the first European Cup, was the next peak; and then the team which I managed in the 1970s was also a fine and successful side.

So perhaps it is time for another Hibs team to hit a peak of performance, and from what I have seen of Tony Mowbray's youngsters, they look capable of emulating the great sides of Hibs' past. They need to stay together for a couple of years yet, but if they can do so, they can match any of the best teams in Hibs' history.

The traditions of Hibs are long-held and honourable, and I often feel that the modern players at Easter Road do not appreciate just what a great club they are playing for. There are a few local lads in the team as I write, and they seem to have an appreciation of what Hibernian Football Club means to the people of Leith, Edinburgh and the surrounding area. But some are simply unaware of Hibs' history and therefore do not appreciate it. Maybe reading this book will help them to learn what Hibs are about!

If Hibs and Scottish football in general are going to go forward, we have to look back and learn from the men who improved our game. Look at the great managers I had to contend with – Jock Stein, Willie Waddell and Jock Wallace, to name but three men who could have managed any club, anywhere and done so successfully.

I have recorded my various tussles with Jock Stein earlier in this book, and all I can say is that earning his respect was one of the greatest compliments I was ever given.

Willie Waddell was totally committed to the Rangers cause. He was a clever manager. I heard that before Rangers' success in the European Cup-Winners' Cup of 1972, he gave every one of his players a photograph of their opposite number to study so that they would know exactly who they were facing – a simple but very effective idea in the days before DVDs and video recorders.

My favourite story, which sums him up, is about a time when Rangers were playing Raith Rovers, and he was experimenting with a two-man midfield. It was not working and the players protested that Raith were doing better because they had three in midfield. The Deedle growled, 'Any two Rangers players are worth three of any other team.'

Yet I often got one over on him. We were drawn to play Rangers in a reserve cup tie at Aberdeen, and instead of the normal daytime match, I insisted that we play the game in midweek at night. As soon as the Deedle heard that, he came on the phone and asked me what I was playing at. I told him I was thinking of the Aberdeen fans, who were entitled to see good players even if they were reserves.

'But that will cost us money,' he complained, no doubt thinking of the hotel bills for an overnight stay in Aberdeen.

'But, Willie, you're always telling us that you're the biggest club in Scotland, so I'm sure you can afford it,' I replied. 'The game goes ahead at night.'

It was another example of not giving in to Old Firm intimidation, at which Waddell and Stein were past masters.

I had a particular liking for Jock Wallace. He was taken to Ibrox by Willie Waddell, who admired his coaching work at Tynecastle. They made a good pairing, as Jock was a tough man and the Deedle was never one for the rougher part of the job. A big, bluff former soldier, Jock was a motivator, who was always preaching the value of 'character' in his players. I suspect, though, that they did not thank him for one particular activity aimed at building stamina and 'character'.

Jock is often credited with the idea of taking players to Gullane Beach in East Lothian for pre-season toughening. Even climbing the huge sand dunes at Gullane slowly is a formidable task, but Jock had his players running up and down the dunes until the point of exhaustion and beyond. I was always amazed when this Gullane training routine was hailed as revolutionary – more than a decade before, I had been doing the same with the Hibs players I had trained. But I didn't really mind, because Jock always showed me respect, and he was quick to acknowledge that I was the man who gave him his coaching certificate on the SFA course at Largs.

Those courses were hard work, but at night we had some fun in the local pub. I remember Jock and former Hearts coach John Cumming one night when we had gone for a jar. The barman never had to collect the glasses: the guys would throw them to John, and he would head them down for big Jock, who would catch them. They were a hard pair, I can tell you.

Bill Shankly was as big a character, as his legend says. Several years after he gave me a hard time for Aberdeen's 'offside' tactics in the 1970 Scottish Cup final, when I was with Hibs, we played Liverpool, and Shanks invited me to his golf club – and over a drink he was still arguing that we had played an offside trap!

Bill's brother, Bob, was a good friend of mine. He had a long career in the game as a player and a manager, and we were in touch frequently. Friendship didn't stop him being a tough man to deal with. While I was at Aberdeen and he was managing Hibs, I once begged him to let me sign a player, but even though the man wasn't playing for the first team, Bob wouldn't let him go to a rival club.

Matt Busby was a wonderful player and manager, and having played for Hibs, he had a lot of respect for Harry Swan and Willie McCartney. We played Manchester United a lot in those days. After every game, there was a banquet, and he was the life and soul of the party. Yet he could be utterly ruthless as a manager, and I came to know that a hard edge is necessary if you are going to do the job right.

One of my oldest friends in football is Tommy Docherty. The Doc was as sharp as a tack and had that great Glasgow humour and wit. We met on Scotland duty and have stayed friends over many years. Indeed, he was in Edinburgh while I was writing this book and he gave a typically hilarious speech at a tribute dinner for Lawrie Reilly at Easter Road.

Back in the '60s, he was ahead of his time because, like me, he wasn't afraid to learn new coaching and training methods and try new tactics. I have to say he used to kid the Chelsea players rotten, but he had them eating out of his hand. Later, we went on a coaching course in West Germany together, but, frankly, the Scottish course was much better, and we didn't learn too much except that German beer is very good. He too could be tough, as he showed when dealing with the wayward George Best.

And what of the greatest players I've encountered in my career? Throughout this book, I have mentioned the many excellent footballers I trained and managed. Joe Baker, Martin Buchan, Robert Clark, Joe Harper, Henning Boel, John Brownlie, Alex Edwards, Alex Cropley, Pat Stanton, Jackie McNamara – too many to name, and so many who are now legends.

There were others I admired but never managed. I liked Jim Baxter a lot. Slim Jim was a Hibs supporter when he was a laddie, and his dad used to take him to Easter Road. But Hibs could not match the lure or the money of Rangers, and so he took his great talent to Ibrox. You can have all the defensive or midfield systems in the world, but when you have a Baxter against you, there is no chance of the system winning. Natural talent will always win out, and Jim had it in abundance. He also had a bit of swagger, an arrogance almost, that let you know that he was the boss on the pitch. When he played keepie-uppie at Wembley against England, he became the idol of Scotland, and despite all his well-publicised problems with alcohol and ill health in later life, he stayed popular with the Scottish fans, which I think says a lot about the way we view football.

When I was manager at Hibs, the player I most feared was Kenny Dalglish of Celtic. He had it all, and you could never relax when he was on the ball. Later on, when I was helping out Jock Stein when he managed Scotland, Jock told me that Kenny had a secret fuel – fish and chips! We were in the team hotel late at night when Kenny wanted to go out. This was very suprising, because Kenny was a model professional who never gave any trouble. 'It's OK,' said Jock, who was always strict about players observing curfews, 'he's just popping out for a fish supper.' And the next day, he played a blinder. So there you have it, the secret of Kenny Dalglish's success: just like Alf Tupper, the Tough of the Track in the old *Victor* comic, Kenny was kept going by fish and chips.

Those are just two of the great players I liked to watch, but if you were to ask me who collectively were the best, well, I suspect you will guess the reply. Smith, Johnstone, Reilly, Turnbull, Ormond – we few, we happy few, we band of brothers. To play with them was a privilege beyond compare, and while I am secure in the knowledge that my managerial career left its own legacy, to be remembered as one of the Famous Five is the greatest honour of all.

If you look at what the best managers and players in our history have in common, you will see that they had skill, determination and dedication, but they also did things in their own fashion. Nobody can or should imitate any other person in football slavishly; but you should learn from the best before going on to do things your way.

And ultimately, as I look back on my life, that is my conclusion about myself. In the words of that old Sinatra song, 'I did it my way,' and I make absolutely no apologies for that.

But no man can achieve things on his own, especially in football.

I often say that the loneliest job in the world is that of a football manager, and when I think back to the many, many days and nights during which I sat working out every detail of my plans for Queen's Park, Aberdeen and Hibs, I remember the feeling of isolation.

Yet for more than 83 years, I have not been alone. I had my family and the larger community at Carronshore, my Navy family, my Queen's Park, Aberdeen and, above all, my Hibs families.

And beside me for most of those 83 years has been my wife, Carol. I know I have not been the easiest person in the world to live with at times, and there were many periods when she did not see me for days on end because I was so involved in football, but she has always been there for me, as have my daughter, Valerie, and her family.

I do not have the words to record my love and appreciation for them, but I do want to thank my family for everything they have done for me and everything they mean to me.

When I think back on the many, many happy memories of my life, my various families have been the key to the success I enjoyed, and I like to think I gave them a little of me in return.

In finishing this record of what I hope you'll agree has been an interesting life, I can only conclude one thing: I've had a ball.

And if I'm allowed a few more years yet, I thoroughly intend to carry on having a ball!